THE PROMISE OF WORLD PEACE

A Letter by the Universal House of Justice
to the Peoples of the World

30th Anniversary Special Edition

The Bahá'í Chair for World Peace
University of Maryland, College Park

In 1985, the Universal House of Justice addressed a message to the peoples of the world inviting them to consider that a new social order can be fostered by humanity's consciousness of its own oneness. This message was presented to world leaders and countless others during the United Nations International Year of Peace.

THE PROMISE OF WORLD PEACE
A Letter by the Universal House of Justice to the Peoples of the World

30th Anniversary Special Edition

Prepared for publication by the Bahá'í Chair for World Peace at the
University of Maryland, College Park

© Copyright 2015 University of Maryland.

ISBN-13: 978-0-9899170-9-4
ISBN-10: 0989917096

Suggested bibliographic citation for this publication:
    Universal House of Justice. *The Promise of World Peace: A Letter
    by the Universal House of Justice to the Peoples of the World*.
    30th Anniversary Special Edition. College Park, MD: The
    Bahá'í Chair for World Peace, University of Maryland, 2015.

For more information on the Universal House of Justice, please visit:
universalhouseofjustice.bahai.org

For more information on the Bahá'í Chair for World Peace, please
visit: bahaichair.umd.edu

Publication production and editing by Nadim van de Fliert,
University of Maryland

Book interior and cover designed by Lori E. Allan, LoriEvelyn.com

CONTENTS

FOREWORD

The state of the world is unpredictable and volatile. Growing dissention, violence, and disunity are disrupting and reshaping the world order of the post-Cold War era. Manifold conflicts, rising inequality, economic insecurity, discrimination and violence against women, tensions and divisions caused by religious conflicts, a growing culture of hate, the scourge of prejudice and racism, environmental degradation, lack of universal education, and failure to teach a concept of world citizenship – these are among the complex challenges facing the global community. At the heart of these conflicts are outdated patterns of thought and behavior, obsolete social structures and institutions incapable of addressing the needs of an ever-changing world.

The Promise of World Peace, a statement written by the Universal House of Justice*, the International Council of the Bahá'í Faith, provides a framework defining the obstacles to peace in terms of profound challenges confronted by humanity. It offers perspectives on which thoughts have to be harmonized in relation to these challenges, which in turn provide the means by which people of goodwill can devise practical solutions to the barriers to peace. The statement advocates an approach to peacemaking as far more than simply the elimination of war or the prohibition of its weapons and methods; it asserts that peace stems from an inner state, one that is supported by values and a spiritual framework to shape its architecture. It also examines the prospects for peace beyond the purely political terms in which the subject is frequently discussed and explores the role that social actors and structures play in removing obstacles and creating paths to cooperation. The document's perspective supports a unique process in the exploration of peace that calls attention to the value of establishing agreement both on principle and unity in action, as a

---

*For more information visit: universalhouseofjustice.bahai.org

prelude to concentrating on the solutions to the social disorders confronting humanity.

In celebration of the significant contribution that this document, first published in 1985, has made toward reconceptualization of the profound challenges toward peace, the perspectives it has offered, and the endeavors of exploration and discourse which, in the intervening 30 years, it has inspired, the Bahá'í Chair for World Peace, in collaboration with the Bahá'í International Community at the United Nations, organized a conference on the theme Global Transformations: Context and Analytics for a Durable Peace. Scholars from throughout the world were invited to advance intellectual discourse on challenging issues that pose barriers to a durable peace and to offer and explore pertinent solutions.

We are pleased to offer this new edition of The Promise of World Peace to a new generation of readers in the hopes that its study will generate research and scholarly publications on the concepts it has proposed. This special volume is published in ten languages: Arabic, Chinese, English, French, Hindi, Persian, Portuguese, Russian, Spanish, and Swahili, as a reflection of the Statement's universal relevance to the pursuit of worldwide peace within an emerging global civilization.

Knowledge is a powerful source for the enhancement of human consciousness and the spread of solutions to remove any social problem. History has repeatedly proven the courage and tenacity of human capacity in overcoming insurmountable impediments and dilemmas. We are hopeful that through hard work and bold scholarship our efforts will forge a pathway leading to the happiness, prosperity, and advancement of humanity.

— The Bahá'í Chair for World Peace

The Promise of World Peace

English

October 1985

To the Peoples of the World:

The Great Peace towards which people of good will throughout the centuries have inclined their hearts, of which seers and poets for countless generations have expressed their vision, and for which from age to age the sacred scriptures of mankind have constantly held the promise, is now at long last within the reach of the nations. For the first time in history it is possible for everyone to view the entire planet, with all its myriad diversified peoples, in one perspective. World peace is not only possible but inevitable. It is the next stage in the evolution of this planet—in the words of one great thinker, "the planetization of mankind."

Whether peace is to be reached only after unimaginable horrors precipitated by humanity's stubborn clinging to old patterns of behaviour, or is to be embraced now by an act of consultative will, is the choice before all who inhabit the earth. At this critical juncture when the intractable problems confronting nations have been fused into one common concern for the whole world, failure to stem the tide of conflict and disorder would be unconscionably irresponsible.

Among the favourable signs are the steadily growing strength of the steps towards world order taken initially near the beginning of this century in the creation of the League of Nations, succeeded by the more broadly based United Nations Organization; the achievement since the Second World War of independence by the majority of all the nations on earth, indicating the completion of the process of nation building, and the involvement of these fledgling nations with older ones in matters of mutual concern; the consequent vast increase in co-operation among hitherto isolated and antagonistic peoples and groups in international undertakings in the scientific, educational, legal, economic and cultural fields; the rise in recent decades of an unprecedented number of international humanitarian organizations; the spread of women's and youth movements calling for an end to war; and the spontaneous spawning of widening networks of ordinary people seeking understanding through personal communication.

The scientific and technological advances occurring in this unusually blessed century portend a great surge forward in the social evolution of the planet, and indicate the means by which the practical problems of humanity may be solved. They provide, indeed, the very means for the administration of the complex life of a united world. Yet barriers persist. Doubts, misconceptions, prejudices, suspicions and narrow self-interest beset nations and peoples in their relations one to another.

It is out of a deep sense of spiritual and moral duty that we are impelled at this opportune moment to invite your attention to the penetrating insights first communicated to the rulers of mankind more than a century ago by Bahá'u'lláh, Founder of the Bahá'í Faith, of which we are the Trustees.

"The winds of despair," Bahá'u'lláh wrote, "are, alas, blowing from every direction, and the strife that divides and afflicts the human race is daily increasing. The signs of impending convulsions and chaos can now be discerned, inasmuch as the prevailing order appears to be lamentably defective." This prophetic judgement has been amply confirmed by the common experience of humanity. Flaws in the prevailing order are conspicuous in the inability of sovereign states organized as United Nations to exorcize the spectre of war, the threatened collapse of the international economic order, the spread of anarchy and terrorism, and the intense suffering which these and other afflictions are causing to increasing millions. Indeed, so much have aggression and conflict come to characterize our social, economic and religious systems, that many have succumbed to the view that such behaviour is intrinsic to human nature and therefore ineradicable.

With the entrenchment of this view, a paralyzing contradiction has developed in human affairs. On the one hand, people of all nations proclaim not only their readiness but their longing for peace and harmony, for an end to the harrowing apprehensions tormenting their daily lives. On the other, uncritical assent is given to the proposition that human beings are incorrigibly selfish and aggressive and thus incapable of erecting a social system at once progressive and peaceful, dynamic and harmonious, a system giving free play to individual creativity and initiative but based on co-operation and reciprocity.

As the need for peace becomes more urgent, this fundamental contradiction, which hinders its realization, demands a reassessment of the assumptions upon which the commonly held view of mankind's historical predicament is based. Dispassionately examined, the evidence reveals that such conduct, far from expressing man's true self, represents a distortion of the human spirit. Satisfaction on this point will enable all people to set in motion constructive social forces which, because they are consistent with human nature, will encourage harmony and co-operation instead of war and conflict.

To choose such a course is not to deny humanity's past but to understand it. The Bahá'í Faith regards the current world confusion and calamitous condition in human affairs as a natural phase in an organic process leading ultimately and irresistibly to the unification of the human race in a single social order whose boundaries are those of the planet. The human race, as a distinct, organic unit, has passed through evolutionary stages analogous to the stages of infancy and childhood in the lives of its individual members, and is now in the culminating period of its turbulent adolescence approaching its long-awaited coming of age.

A candid acknowledgement that prejudice, war and exploitation have been the expression of immature stages in a vast historical process and that the human race is today experiencing the unavoidable tumult which marks its collective coming of age is not a reason for despair but a prerequisite to undertaking the stupendous enterprise of building a peaceful world. That such an enterprise is possible, that the necessary constructive forces do exist, that unifying social structures can be erected, is the theme we urge you to examine.

Whatever suffering and turmoil the years immediately ahead may hold, however dark the immediate circumstances, the Bahá'í community believes that humanity can confront this supreme trial with confidence in its ultimate outcome. Far from signalizing the end of civilization, the convulsive changes towards which humanity is being ever more rapidly impelled will serve to release the "potentialities inherent in the station of man" and reveal "the full measure of his destiny on earth, the innate excellence of his reality."

I

The endowments which distinguish the human race from all other forms of life are summed up in what is known as the human spirit; the mind is its essential quality. These endowments have enabled humanity to build civilizations and to prosper materially. But such accomplishments alone have never satisfied the human spirit, whose mysterious nature inclines it towards transcendence, a reaching towards an invisible realm, towards the ultimate reality, that unknowable essence of essences called God. The religions brought to mankind by a succession of spiritual luminaries have been the primary link between humanity and that ultimate reality, and have galvanized and refined mankind's capacity to achieve spiritual success together with social progress.

No serious attempt to set human affairs aright, to achieve world peace, can ignore religion. Man's perception and practice of it are largely the stuff of history. An eminent historian described religion as a "faculty of human nature." That the perversion of this faculty has contributed to much of the confusion in society and the conflicts in and between individuals can hardly be denied. But neither can any fair-minded observer discount the preponderating influence exerted by religion on the vital expressions of civilization. Furthermore, its indispensability to social order has repeatedly been demonstrated by its direct effect on laws and morality.

Writing of religion as a social force, Bahá'u'lláh said: "Religion is the greatest of all means for the establishment of order in the world and for the peaceful contentment of all that dwell therein." Referring to the eclipse or corruption of religion, he wrote: "Should the lamp of religion be obscured, chaos and confusion will ensue, and the lights of fairness, of justice, of tranquillity and peace cease to shine." In an enumeration of such consequences the Bahá'í writings point out that the "perversion of human nature, the degradation of human conduct, the corruption and dissolution of human institutions, reveal themselves, under such circumstances, in their worst and most revolting aspects. Human character is debased, confidence is shaken, the nerves of discipline are relaxed, the voice of human conscience is stilled, the sense of decency and shame is obscured, conceptions of duty, of solidarity, of reciprocity and loyalty are distorted, and the very feeling of peacefulness, of joy and of hope is gradually extinguished."

If, therefore, humanity has come to a point of paralyzing conflict it must look to itself, to its own negligence, to the siren voices to which it has listened, for the source of the misunderstandings and confusion perpetrated in the name of religion. Those who have held blindly and selfishly to their particular orthodoxies, who have imposed on their votaries erroneous and conflicting interpretations of the pronouncements of the Prophets of God, bear heavy responsibility for this confusion—a confusion compounded by the artificial barriers erected between faith and reason, science and religion. For from a fair-minded examination of the actual utterances of the Founders of the great religions, and of the social milieus in which they were obliged to carry out their missions, there is nothing to support the contentions and prejudices deranging the religious communities of mankind and therefore all human affairs.

The teaching that we should treat others as we ourselves would wish to be treated, an ethic variously repeated in all the great religions, lends force to this latter observation in two particular respects: it sums up the moral attitude, the peace-inducing aspect, extending through these religions irrespective of their place or time of origin; it also signifies an aspect of unity which is their essential virtue, a virtue mankind in its disjointed view of history has failed to appreciate.

Had humanity seen the Educators of its collective childhood in their true character, as agents of one civilizing process, it would no doubt have reaped incalculably greater benefits from the cumulative effects of their successive missions. This, alas, it failed to do.

The resurgence of fanatical religious fervour occurring in many lands cannot be regarded as more than a dying convulsion. The very nature of the violent and disruptive phenomena associated with it testifies to the spiritual bankruptcy it represents. Indeed, one of the strangest and saddest features of the current outbreak of religious fanaticism is the extent to which, in each case, it is undermining not only the spiritual values which are conducive to the unity of mankind but also those unique moral victories won by the particular religion it purports to serve.

However vital a force religion has been in the history of mankind, and however dramatic the current resurgence of militant religious fanaticism, religion and religious institutions have, for many decades, been viewed by increasing numbers of people as irrelevant to the major concerns of the modern world. In its place they have turned either to the hedonistic pursuit of material satisfactions or to the following of man-made ideologies designed to rescue society from the evident evils under which it groans. All too many of these ideologies, alas, instead of embracing the concept of the oneness of mankind and promoting the increase of concord among different peoples, have tended to deify the state, to subordinate the rest of mankind to one nation, race or class, to attempt to suppress all discussion and interchange of ideas, or to callously abandon starving millions to the operations of a market system that all too clearly is aggravating the plight of the majority of mankind, while enabling small sections to live in a condition of affluence scarcely dreamed of by our forebears.

How tragic is the record of the substitute faiths that the worldly-wise of our age have created. In the massive disillusionment of entire populations who have been taught to worship at their altars can be read history's irreversible verdict on their value. The fruits these doctrines have produced, after decades of an increasingly unrestrained exercise of power by those who owe their ascendancy in human affairs to them, are the social and economic ills that blight every region of our world in the closing years of the twentieth century. Underlying all these outward afflictions is the spiritual damage reflected in the apathy that has gripped the mass of the peoples of all nations and by the extinction of hope in the hearts of deprived and anguished millions.

The time has come when those who preach the dogmas of materialism, whether of the east or the west, whether of capitalism or socialism, must give account of the moral stewardship they have presumed to exercise. Where is the "new world" promised by these ideologies? Where is the international peace to whose ideals they proclaim their devotion? Where are the breakthroughs into new realms of cultural achievement produced by the aggrandizement of this race, of that nation or of a particular class? Why is the vast majority of the world's peoples sinking ever deeper into hunger and wretchedness when wealth on a scale undreamed of by the Pharaohs, the Caesars, or even the imperialist powers of the nineteenth century is at the disposal of the present arbiters of human affairs?

Most particularly, it is in the glorification of material pursuits, at once the progenitor and common feature of all such ideologies, that we find the roots which nourish the falsehood that human beings are incorrigibly selfish and aggressive. It is here that the ground must be cleared for the building of a new world fit for our descendants.

That materialistic ideals have, in the light of experience, failed to satisfy the needs of mankind calls for an honest acknowledgement that a fresh effort must now be made to find the solutions to the agonizing problems of the planet. The intolerable conditions pervading society bespeak a common failure of all, a circumstance which tends to incite rather than relieve the entrenchment on every side. Clearly, a common remedial effort is urgently required. It is primarily a matter of attitude. Will humanity continue in its waywardness, holding to outworn concepts and unworkable assumptions? Or will its leaders, regardless of ideology, step forth and, with a resolute will, consult together in a united search for appropriate solutions?

Those who care for the future of the human race may well ponder this advice. "If long-cherished ideals and time-honoured institutions, if certain social assumptions and religious formulae have ceased to promote the welfare of the generality of mankind, if they no longer minister to the needs of a continually evolving humanity, let them be swept away and relegated to the limbo of obsolescent and forgotten doctrines. Why should these, in a world subject to the immutable law of change and decay, be exempt from the deterioration that must needs overtake every human institution? For legal standards, political and economic theories are solely designed to safeguard the interests of humanity as a whole, and not humanity to be crucified for the preservation of the integrity of any particular law or doctrine."

II

Banning nuclear weapons, prohibiting the use of poison gases, or outlawing germ warfare will not remove the root causes of war. However important such practical measures obviously are as elements of the peace process, they are in themselves too superficial to exert enduring influence. Peoples are ingenious enough to invent yet other forms of warfare, and to use food, raw materials, finance, industrial power, ideology, and terrorism to subvert one another in an endless quest for supremacy and dominion. Nor can the present massive dislocation in the affairs of humanity be resolved through the settlement of specific conflicts or disagreements among nations. A genuine universal framework must be adopted.

Certainly, there is no lack of recognition by national leaders of the world-wide character of the problem, which is self-evident in the mounting issues that confront them daily. And there are the accumulating studies and solutions proposed by many concerned and enlightened groups as well as by agencies of the United Nations, to remove any possibility of ignorance as to the challenging requirements to be met. There is, however, a paralysis of will; and it is this that must be carefully examined and resolutely dealt with. This paralysis is rooted, as we have stated, in a deep-seated conviction of the inevitable quarrelsomeness of mankind, which has led to the reluctance to entertain the possibility of subordinating national self-interest to the requirements of world order, and in an unwillingness to face courageously the far-reaching implications of establishing a united world authority. It is also traceable to the incapacity of largely ignorant and subjugated masses to articulate their desire for a new order in which they can live in peace, harmony and prosperity with all humanity.

The tentative steps towards world order, especially since World War II, give hopeful signs. The increasing tendency of groups of nations to formalize relationships which enable them to co-operate in matters of mutual interest suggests that eventually all nations could overcome this paralysis. The Association of South East Asian Nations, the Caribbean Community and Common Market, the Central American Common Market, the Council for Mutual Economic Assistance, the European Communities, the League of Arab States, the Organization of African Unity, the Organization of American States, the South Pacific Forum—all the joint endeavours represented by such organizations prepare the path to world order.

The increasing attention being focused on some of the most deep-rooted problems of the planet is yet another hopeful sign. Despite the obvious shortcomings of the United Nations, the more than two score declarations and conventions adopted by that organization, even where governments have not been enthusiastic in their commitment, have given ordinary people a sense of a new lease on life. The Universal Declaration of Human Rights, the Convention on the Prevention and Punishment of the Crime of Genocide, and the similar measures concerned with eliminating all forms of discrimination based on race, sex or religious belief; upholding the rights of the child; protecting all persons against being subjected to torture; eradicating hunger and malnutrition; using scientific and technological progress in the interest of peace and the benefit of mankind—all such measures, if courageously enforced and expanded, will advance the day when the spectre of war will have lost its power to dominate international relations. There is no need to stress the significance of the issues addressed by these declarations and conventions. However, a few such issues, because of their immediate relevance to establishing world peace, deserve additional comment.

Racism, one of the most baneful and persistent evils, is a major barrier to peace. Its practice perpetrates too outrageous a violation of the dignity of human beings to be countenanced under any pretext. Racism retards the unfoldment of the boundless potentialities of its victims, corrupts its perpetrators, and blights human progress. Recognition of the oneness of mankind, implemented by appropriate legal measures, must be universally upheld if this problem is to be overcome.

The inordinate disparity between rich and poor, a source of acute suffering, keeps the world in a state of instability, virtually on the brink of war. Few societies have dealt effectively with this situation. The solution calls for the combined application of spiritual, moral and practical approaches. A fresh look at the problem is required, entailing consultation with experts from a wide spectrum of disciplines, devoid of economic and ideological polemics, and involving the people directly affected in the decisions that must urgently be made. It is an issue that is bound up not only with the necessity for eliminating extremes of wealth and poverty but also with those spiritual verities the understanding of which can produce a new universal attitude. Fostering such an attitude is itself a major part of the solution.

Unbridled nationalism, as distinguished from a sane and legitimate patriotism, must give way to a wider loyalty, to the love of humanity as a whole. Bahá'u'lláh's statement is: "The earth is but one country, and mankind its citizens." The concept of world citizenship is a direct result of the contraction of the world into a single neighbourhood through scientific advances and of the indisputable interdependence of nations. Love of all the world's peoples does not exclude love of one's country. The advantage of the part in a world society is best served by promoting the advantage of the whole. Current international activities in various fields which nurture mutual affection and a sense of solidarity among peoples need greatly to be increased.

Religious strife, throughout history, has been the cause of innumerable wars and conflicts, a major blight to progress, and is increasingly abhorrent to the people of all faiths and no faith. Followers of all religions must be willing to face the basic questions which this strife raises, and to arrive at clear answers. How are the differences between them to be resolved, both in theory and in practice? The challenge facing the religious leaders of mankind is to contemplate, with hearts filled with the spirit of compassion and a desire for truth, the plight of humanity, and to ask themselves whether they cannot, in humility before their Almighty Creator, submerge their theological differences in a great spirit of mutual forbearance that will enable them to work together for the advancement of human understanding and peace.

The emancipation of women, the achievement of full equality between the sexes, is one of the most important, though less acknowledged prerequisites of peace. The denial of such equality perpetrates an injustice against one half of the world's population and promotes in men harmful attitudes and habits that are carried from the family to the workplace, to political life, and ultimately to international relations. There are no grounds, moral, practical, or biological, upon which such denial can be justified. Only as women are welcomed into full partnership in all fields of human endeavour will the moral and psychological climate be created in which international peace can emerge.

The cause of universal education, which has already enlisted in its service an army of dedicated people from every faith and nation, deserves the utmost support that the governments of the world can lend it. For ignorance is indisputably the principal reason for the decline and fall of peoples and the perpetuation of prejudice. No nation can achieve success unless education is accorded all its citizens. Lack of resources limits the ability of many nations to fulfil this necessity, imposing a certain ordering of priorities. The decision-making agencies involved would do well to consider giving first priority to the education of women and girls, since it is through educated mothers that the benefits of knowledge can be most effectively and rapidly diffused throughout society. In keeping with the requirements of the times, consideration should also be given to teaching the concept of world citizenship as part of the standard education of every child.

A fundamental lack of communication between peoples seriously undermines efforts towards world peace. Adopting an international auxiliary language would go far to resolve this problem and necessitates the most urgent attention.

Two points bear emphasizing in all these issues. One is that the abolition of war is not simply a matter of signing treaties and protocols; it is a complex task requiring a new level of commitment to resolving issues not customarily associated with the pursuit of peace. Based on political agreements alone, the idea of collective security is a chimera. The other point is that the primary challenge in dealing with issues of peace is to raise the context to the level of principle, as distinct from pure pragmatism. For, in essence, peace stems from an inner state supported by a spiritual or moral attitude, and it is chiefly in evoking this attitude that the possibility of enduring solutions can be found.

There are spiritual principles, or what some call human values, by which solutions can be found for every social problem. Any well-intentioned group can in a general sense devise practical solutions to its problems, but good intentions and practical knowledge are usually not enough. The essential merit of spiritual principle is that it not only presents a perspective which harmonizes with that which is immanent in human nature, it also induces an attitude, a dynamic, a will, an aspiration, which facilitate the discovery and implementation of practical measures. Leaders of governments and all in authority would be well served in their efforts to solve problems if they would first seek to identify the principles involved and then be guided by them.

III

The primary question to be resolved is how the present world, with its entrenched pattern of conflict, can change to a world in which harmony and co-operation will prevail.

World order can be founded only on an unshakable consciousness of the oneness of mankind, a spiritual truth which all the human sciences confirm. Anthropology, physiology, psychology, recognize only one human species, albeit infinitely varied in the secondary aspects of life. Recognition of this truth requires abandonment of prejudice — prejudice of every kind — race, class, colour, creed, nation, sex, degree of material civilization, everything which enables people to consider themselves superior to others.

Acceptance of the oneness of mankind is the first fundamental prerequisite for reorganization and administration of the world as one country, the home of humankind. Universal acceptance of this spiritual principle is essential to any successful attempt to establish world peace. It should therefore be universally proclaimed, taught in schools, and constantly asserted in every nation as preparation for the organic change in the structure of society which it implies.

In the Bahá'í view, recognition of the oneness of mankind "calls for no less than the reconstruction and the demilitarization of the whole civilized world — a world organically unified in all the essential aspects of its life, its political machinery, its spiritual aspiration, its trade and finance, its script and language, and yet infinite in the diversity of the national characteristics of its federated units."

Elaborating the implications of this pivotal principle, Shoghi Effendi, the Guardian of the Bahá'í Faith, commented in 1931 that: "Far from aiming at the subversion of the existing foundations of society, it seeks to broaden its basis, to remold its institutions in a manner consonant with the needs of an ever-changing world. It can conflict with no legitimate allegiances, nor can it undermine essential loyalties. Its purpose is neither to stifle the flame of a sane and intelligent patriotism in men's hearts, nor to abolish the system of national autonomy so essential if the evils of excessive centralization are to be avoided. It does not ignore, nor does it attempt to suppress, the diversity of ethnical origins, of climate, of history, of language and tradition, of thought and habit, that differentiate the peoples and nations of the world. It calls for a wider loyalty, for a larger aspiration than any that has animated the human race. It insists upon the subordination of national impulses and interests to the imperative claims of a unified world. It repudiates excessive centralization on one hand, and disclaims all attempts at uniformity on the other. Its watchword is unity in diversity."

The achievement of such ends requires several stages in the adjustment of national political attitudes, which now verge on anarchy in the absence of clearly defined laws or universally accepted and enforceable principles regulating the relationships between nations. The League of Nations, the United Nations, and the many organizations and agreements produced by them have unquestionably been helpful in attenuating some of the negative effects of international conflicts, but they have shown themselves incapable of preventing war. Indeed, there have been scores of wars since the end of the Second World War; many are yet raging.

The predominant aspects of this problem had already emerged in the nineteenth century when Bahá'u'lláh first advanced his proposals for the establishment of world peace. The principle of collective security was propounded by him in statements addressed to the rulers of the world. Shoghi Effendi commented on his meaning: "What else could these weighty words signify," he wrote, "if they did not point to the inevitable curtailment of unfettered national sovereignty as an indispensable preliminary to the formation of the future Commonwealth of all the nations of the world? Some form of a world super-state must needs be evolved, in whose favour all the nations of the world will have willingly ceded every claim to make war, certain rights to impose taxation and all rights to maintain armaments, except for purposes of maintaining internal order within their respective dominions. Such a state will have to include within its orbit an international executive adequate to enforce supreme and unchallengeable authority on every recalcitrant member of the commonwealth; a world parliament whose members shall be elected by the people in their respective countries and whose election shall be confirmed by their respective governments; and a supreme tribunal whose judgement will have a binding effect even in such cases where the parties concerned did not voluntarily agree to submit their case to its consideration.

"...A world community in which all economic barriers will have been permanently demolished and the interdependence of Capital and Labour definitely recognized; in which the clamour of religious fanaticism and strife will have been forever stilled; in which the flame of racial animosity will have been finally extinguished; in which a single code of international law—the product of the considered judgement of the world's federated representatives—shall have as its sanction the instant and coercive intervention of the combined forces of the federated units; and finally a world community in which the fury of a capricious and militant nationalism will have been transmuted into an abiding consciousness of world citizenship—such indeed, appears, in its broadest outline, the Order anticipated by Bahá'u'lláh, an Order that shall come to be regarded as the fairest fruit of a slowly maturing age."

The implementation of these far-reaching measures was indicated by Bahá'u'lláh: "The time must come when the imperative necessity for the holding of a vast, an all-embracing assemblage of men will be universally realized. The rulers and kings of the earth must needs attend it, and, participating in its deliberations, must consider such ways and means as will lay the foundations of the world's Great Peace amongst men."

The courage, the resolution, the pure motive, the selfless love of one people for another—all the spiritual and moral qualities required for effecting this momentous step towards peace are focused on the will to act. And it is towards arousing the necessary volition that earnest consideration must be given to the reality of man, namely, his thought. To understand the relevance of this potent reality is also to appreciate the social necessity of actualizing its unique value through candid, dispassionate and cordial consultation, and of acting upon the results of this process. Bahá'u'lláh insistently drew attention to the virtues and indispensability of consultation for ordering human affairs. He said: "Consultation bestows greater awareness and transmutes conjecture into certitude. It is a shining light which, in a dark world, leads the way and guides. For everything there is and will continue to be a station of perfection and maturity. The maturity of the gift of understanding is made manifest through consultation." The very attempt to achieve peace through the consultative action he proposed can release such a salutary spirit among the peoples of the earth that no power could resist the final, triumphal outcome.

Concerning the proceedings for this world gathering, 'Abdu'l-Bahá, the son of Bahá'u'lláh and authorized interpreter of his teachings, offered these insights: "They must make the Cause of Peace the object of general consultation, and seek by every means in their power to establish a Union of the nations of the world. They must conclude a binding treaty and establish a covenant, the provisions of which shall be sound, inviolable and definite. They must proclaim it to all the world and obtain for it the sanction of all the human race. This supreme and noble undertaking — the real source of the peace and well-being of all the world — should be regarded as sacred by all that dwell on earth. All the forces of humanity must be mobilized to ensure the stability and permanence of this Most Great Covenant. In this all-embracing Pact the limits and frontiers of each and every nation should be clearly fixed, the principles underlying the relations of governments towards one another definitely laid down, and all international agreements and obligations ascertained. In like manner, the size of the armaments of every government should be strictly limited, for if the preparations for war and the military forces of any nation should be allowed to increase, they will arouse the suspicion of others. The fundamental principle underlying this solemn Pact should be so fixed that if any government later violate any one of its provisions, all the governments on earth should arise to reduce it to utter submission, nay the human race as a whole should resolve, with every power at its disposal, to destroy that government. Should this greatest of all remedies be applied to the sick body of the world, it will assuredly recover from its ills and will remain eternally safe and secure."

The holding of this mighty convocation is long overdue.

With all the ardour of our hearts, we appeal to the leaders of all nations to seize this opportune moment and take irreversible steps to convoke this world meeting. All the forces of history impel the human race towards this act which will mark for all time the dawn of its long-awaited maturity.

Will not the United Nations, with the full support of its membership, rise to the high purposes of such a crowning event?

Let men and women, youth and children everywhere recognize the eternal merit of this imperative action for all peoples and lift up their voices in willing assent. Indeed, let it be this generation that inaugurates this glorious stage in the evolution of social life on the planet.

IV

The source of the optimism we feel is a vision transcending the cessation of war and the creation of agencies of international co-operation. Permanent peace among nations is an essential stage, but not, Bahá'u'lláh asserts, the ultimate goal of the social development of humanity. Beyond the initial armistice forced upon the world by the fear of nuclear holocaust, beyond the political peace reluctantly entered into by suspicious rival nations, beyond pragmatic arrangements for security and coexistence, beyond even the many experiments in co-operation which these steps will make possible lies the crowning goal: the unification of all the peoples of the world in one universal family.

Disunity is a danger that the nations and peoples of the earth can no longer endure; the consequences are too terrible to contemplate, too obvious to require any demonstration. "The well-being of mankind," Bahá'u'lláh wrote more than a century ago, "its peace and security, are unattainable unless and until its unity is firmly established." In observing that "mankind is groaning, is dying to be led to unity, and to terminate its age-long martyrdom," Shoghi Effendi further commented that: "Unification of the whole of mankind is the hall-mark of the stage which human society is now approaching. Unity of family, of tribe, of city-state, and nation have been successively attempted and fully established. World unity is the goal towards which a harassed humanity is striving. Nation-building has come to an end. The anarchy inherent in state sovereignty is moving towards a climax. A world, growing to maturity, must abandon this fetish, recognize the oneness and wholeness of human relationships, and establish once for all the machinery that can best incarnate this fundamental principle of its life."

All contemporary forces of change validate this view. The proofs can be discerned in the many examples already cited of the favourable signs towards world peace in current international movements and developments. The army of men and women, drawn from virtually every culture, race and nation on earth, who serve the multifarious agencies of the United Nations, represent a planetary "civil service" whose impressive accomplishments are indicative of the degree of co-operation that can be attained even under discouraging conditions. An urge towards unity, like a spiritual springtime, struggles to express itself through countless international congresses that bring together people from a vast array of disciplines. It motivates appeals for international projects involving children and youth. Indeed, it is the real source of the remarkable movement towards ecumenism by which members of historically antagonistic religions and sects seem irresistibly drawn towards one another. Together with the opposing tendency to warfare and self-aggrandizement against which it ceaselessly struggles, the drive towards world unity is one of the dominant, pervasive features of life on the planet during the closing years of the twentieth century.

The experience of the Bahá'í community may be seen as an example of this enlarging unity. It is a community of some three to four million people drawn from many nations, cultures, classes and creeds, engaged in a wide range of activities serving the spiritual, social and economic needs of the peoples of many lands. It is a single social organism, representative of the diversity of the human family, conducting its affairs through a system of commonly accepted consultative principles, and cherishing equally all the great outpourings of divine guidance in human history. Its existence is yet another convincing proof of the practicality of its Founder's vision of a united world, another evidence that humanity can live as one global society, equal to whatever challenges its coming of age may entail. If the Bahá'í experience can contribute in whatever measure to reinforcing hope in the unity of the human race, we are happy to offer it as a model for study.

In contemplating the supreme importance of the task now challenging the entire world, we bow our heads in humility before the awesome majesty of the divine Creator, who out of His infinite love has created all humanity from the same stock; exalted the gem-like reality of man; honoured it with intellect and wisdom, nobility and immortality; and conferred upon man the "unique distinction and capacity to know Him and to love Him," a capacity that "must needs be regarded as the generating impulse and the primary purpose underlying the whole of creation."

We hold firmly the conviction that all human beings have been created "to carry forward an ever-advancing civilization"; that "to act like the beasts of the field is unworthy of man"; that the virtues that befit human dignity are trustworthiness, forbearance, mercy, compassion and loving kindness towards all peoples. We reaffirm the belief that the "potentialities inherent in the station of man, the full measure of his destiny on earth, the innate excellence of his reality, must all be manifested in this promised Day of God." These are the motivations for our unshakable faith that unity and peace are the attainable goal towards which humanity is striving.

At this writing, the expectant voices of Bahá'ís can be heard despite the persecution they still endure in the land in which their Faith was born. By their example of steadfast hope, they bear witness to the belief that the imminent realization of this age-old dream of peace is now, by virtue of the transforming effects of Bahá'u'lláh's revelation, invested with the force of divine authority. Thus we convey to you not only a vision in words: we summon the power of deeds of faith and sacrifice; we convey the anxious plea of our co-religionists everywhere for peace and unity. We join with all who are the victims of aggression, all who yearn for an end to conflict and contention, all whose devotion to principles of peace and world order promotes the ennobling purposes for which humanity was called into being by an all-loving Creator.

In the earnestness of our desire to impart to you the fervour of our hope and the depth of our confidence, we cite the emphatic promise of Bahá'u'lláh: "These fruitless strifes, these ruinous wars shall pass away, and the 'Most Great Peace' shall come."

THE UNIVERSAL HOUSE OF JUSTICE

The Promise of World Peace

Arabic

تشرين الأول (أكتوبر) 1985

إلى شعوب العالم:

إنَّ السّلام العظيم الذي اتَّجهت نحوه قلوب الخَيِّرين من البشر عبر القرون، وتَغَنَّى به ذوو البص‑يرة والشّعراء في رؤاهم جيلاً بعد جيل، ووعدت به الكتب المقدّسة للبشر على الدّوام عصراً بعد عصر، إنَّ هذا السّلام العظيم هو الآن وبعد طول وقت في متناول أيدي أمم الأرض وشعوبها. فلأوّل مرّة في التّاريخ أصبح في إمكان كلّ إنسان أن يتطلّع بمنظار واحد إلى هذا الكوكب الأرضيّ بأسره بكلّ ما يحتوي من شعوب متعدِّدة مختلفة الألوان والأجناس. والسّلام العالميّ ليس ممكناً وحسب، بل إنّه أمر لا بدّ أن يتحقّق، والدّخول فيه يمثّل المرحلة التّالية من مراحل التّطوّر التي مرَّ بها هذا الكوكب الأرضيّ، وهي المرحلة التي يصفها أحد عظماء المفكّرين بأنها مرحلة "كَوكَبَة الجنس البشريّ".

إنَّ الخيار الذي يواجه سكّان الأرض أجمع هو خيار بين الوصول إلى السّلام بعد تجارب لا يمكن تخيُّلها من الرُّعب والهَلَع نتيجة تشبُّث البشريّة العنيد بأنماطٍ من السّلوك تَقادَم عليها على أن ثمة ملامح إيجابيّة تدعو إلى التّفاؤل، ومنها التّزايد المُطرِّد في نفوذ تلك الخطوات الحثيثة من أجل إحلال النّظام في العالم، وهي الخطوات التي بُوشِر باتِّخاذها مبدئيّاً في بداية هذا القرن عبر إنشاء عُصْبَة الأمم، ومن بعدها هيئة الأمم المتّحدة ذات القاعدة الأكثر اتِّساعاً.

ومن الملامح الإيجابيّة أيضاً أنَّ أغلبيّة الأمم في العالم قد حقَّقت استقلالها في فترة ما بعد الحرب العالميّة الثّانية، مِمَّا يشير إلى اكتمال المرحلة التّاريخيّة لبناء الدّول، وأنَّ الدّول اليافعة شاركت قريناتها الأقدم عهداً في مواجهة المسائل التي تهمّ كلّ الأطراف. ثم هناك ما تَبعَ ذلك من ازدياد ضخم في مجالات التّعاون بين شعوب ومجموعات، كانت من قَبْلُ منعزلةً متخاصمة، عبر مشاريع عالميّة في ميادين العلوم والتّربية والقانون والاقتصاد والثّقافة. يُضاف إلى كلّ هذا قيام هيئات إنسانيّة عالميّة في العقود القريبة الماضية بأعدادٍ لم يسبق لها مثيل، وانتشار الحركات النّسائيّة وحركات الشّباب الدّاعية إلى إنهاء الحروب، ثم الامتداد العَفوي المتوسِّع

لشبكات مُتنوّعة من النّشاطات التي يقوم بها أُناس عاديّون لخلق التّفاهم عبر الاتصال الشّخصيّ والفرديّ.

إنّ ما تحقّق من إنجازات علميّة وتقنيّة في هذا القرن الذي أُسبغَت عليه النّعَم والهبات بصورةٍ غير عاديّة، يَعدُنا بطَفْرَة تَقَدُّميّة عُظْمَى في مضمار التّطوّر الاجتماعـيّ لهذا الكوكب الأرضيّ، ويدلّ على الوسائل الكفيلة بحلّ المُشكلات الواقعيّة التي تُعاني منها الإنسانيّة. وتُوفّر هذه الإنجازاتُ بالفعل الوسائلَ الحقيقيّة التي يمكن بها إدارةُ الحياة المُعقّدة في عالمٍ مُوَحَّد. إلاّ أنّ الحواجز لا تزال قائمة. فالأمم والشّعوب، في علاقاتها بعضها مع بعض، تكتنفها الشّكوك، وانعدام التّفهّم، والتّعصّب، وفقدان الثّقة، والمصالح الذّاتيّة الضّيّقة.

ففي هذه البُرهة المناسبة يَجدُر بنا نحن أُمناءَ بَيْتِ العَدْلِ الأَعْظَم، مدفوعين بمَا يُملِيه علينا شعورُنا العميق بالتزاماتنا الأدبيّة وواجباتنا الرّوحيّة، أنْ نُلفِت أنظار العالم إلى البَيَانات النّيّرة النّافذة التي وجّهها لأوّل مرّة بهاءالله مؤسِّس الدّين البهائي إلى حُكّام البشر قبل نَيّف وقرن من الزمان.

فقد كتب بهاءالله "إنّ رياح اليأس تهبّ من كلّ الجهات، ويستشري الانقلاب والاختلاف بين البشر يوماً بعد يوم، وتبدو علامات الهَرْج والمَرْج ظاهرة، فأسباب النّظام العالميّ الرّاهن باتت الآن غير ملائمة". وتؤكّد التّجاربُ المشتركة التي مَرّت بها البشريّة هذا الحُكْم الذي حَمَلَ النّبوءَة بما سَيَحْدُث. فالعيوب التي يشكو منها النّظام العالميّ القائم تبدو جليّةً واضحة المعالم في عَجْز الدُّوَل المنتمية إلى الأمم المتّحدة – وهي دول ذات سيادة – عن طرْد شَبَح الحرب، وفي ما يُهدِّد العالم من انهيار نظامه الاقتصاديّ، وفي انتشار موجة الإرهاب والفَوْضَى، وفي المعاناة القاسية التي تجلبها هذه وغيرها من المِحَن لملايين متزايدة من البشر. وحقيقة الأمر، أنّ الكثير من الصّراع والعدوان أصبح من خصائص أنظمتنا الاجتماعيّة والاقتصاديّة والدّينيّة، وبلغ حدّاً قاد العديد من النّاس إلى الاستسلام للرّأي القائل بأنّ الإنسان فُطِرَ بطبيعته على سلوك طريق الشّرّ وبالتّالي فلا سبيل إلى إزالة ما فُطِرَ عليه.

ويتأصّل هذا الرَّأي في النُّفوس والتَّمسُّك به، نتج تَنَاقُضٌ وَلَّد حالةً من الشّلل أصابت شؤون البشر؛ فمن جهة لا تعلن شعوب كلّ الدّول عن استعدادها للسّلام والوئام فحسب، بل وعن تشوُّقها إليهما لإنهاء حالة الفَزَع الرّهيبة التي أحالت حياتها اليوميّة إلى عذاب. ومن جهة أخرى نجد أنّ هناك تسليماً لا جدل فيه بالافتراض القائل إنَّ الإنسان أنانيٌّ، مُحبٌّ للعدوان ولا سبيل إلى إصلاحه، وبناءً عليه فإنه عاجزٌ عن إقامة نظامٍ اجتماعيٍّ مسالمٍ وتقدُّميٍّ، مُتحرِّك ومنسجم في آن معاً، يُتيح أقصى الفُرَص لتحقيق الإبداع والمبادرة لدى الفرد، ويكون في ذات الوقت نظاماً قائماً على التّعاون وتبادل المنافع.

وبازدياد الحاجة المُلِحَّة لإحلال السّلام، بات هذا التّناقض الأساسيّ الذي يُعيق تحقيق السّلام يُطالبنا بإعادة تقييم الافتراضات التي بُنِيَ على أساسها الرَّأيُ السّائد حول هذا المَأزِق الذي واجه الإنسان عبر التّاريخ. فإذا ما أخضَعَت المسألة لبَحْثٍ مُجرَّد عن العاطفة تَكَشَّف لنا البرهان والدّليل على أنّ ذلك السّلوك بعيد كلّ البُعْد عن كونه تعبيراً عن حقيقة الذّات البشريّة، وأنّه يُمثِّل صورة مُشوَّهة للنّفس الإنسانيّة. وعندما تَتِمُّ لدينا القناعة حول هذه النّقطة، يصبح في استطاعة جميع النّاس تحريكُ قُوىً اجتماعيّة بَنَّاءةً تُشجِّع الانسجام والتّعاون عِوَضاً عن الحرب والتّصارع، لأنّها قوى منسجمة مع الطّبيعة الإنسانيّة.

إنَّ اختيار مثل هذا النَّهْج لا يعني تجاهلاً لماضي الإنسانيّة بل تفهُّماً له. والدّين البهائيّ ينظر إلى الاضطرابات الرّاهنة في العالم، والظّروف المُفجِعة التي تَمُرُّ بها الشّؤونُ الإنسانيّة على أنّها مرحلة طبيعيّة من مراحل التّطوُّر العُضْويّ التي تقود في نهاية الأمر، بصورةٍ حَتميّة، إلى وحدة الجنس البشريّ ضمن نظامٍ اجتماعيٍّ واحد، حدودُه هي حدود هذا الكوكب الأرضيّ. فقد مرَّ الجنس البشريّ، كوحدة عضويّة مُتميِّزة، بمراحل من التّطور تُشبِه المراحل التي تُصاحب عادةً عهد الطّفولة والحداثة في حياة الأفراد. وها هو يمرّ الآن في الحِقبة الختاميّة للمرحلة العاصفة من سنوات المراهقة، ويقترب من سنّ الرُّشْد التي طال انتظار بلوغها.

إنَّ الإقرار صراحةً بأنَّ التّعصّب والحرب والاستغلال لا تُمثِّل سِوَى مراحل انعدام النُّضج في المَجْرَى الواسع لأحداث التّاريخ، وبأنَّ الجنس البشريّ

يمرّ اليوم باضطرابات حَتْميّة تُسجِّل بلوغ الإنسانيّة سِنّ الرُّشْد الجماعيّ – إنَّ مثل هذا الإقرار يجب ألاّ يكون سبباً لليأس، بل حافزاً لأنْ نأخذ على عواتقنا المهمّة الهائلة، مهمّة بناء عالم يعيش في سلام. والموضوع الذي نحثُّكم على درسه وتَقَصِّيه هو أنَّ هذه المهمة مُمْكنةُ التَّحقيق، وأنَّ القوى البَنَّاءة اللازمة مُتوفّرة، وأنَّ البُنْيات الاجتماعيّة المُوحَّدة يمكن تشييدها.

ومهما حملت السّنوات المقبلة في الأجَل القريب من معاناة واضطراب، ومهما كانت الظّروف المباشرة حالكة الظّلام، فإنّ الجامعة البهائيّة تؤمن بأنَّ في استطاعة الإنسانيّة مواجهة هذه التّجربة الخارقة بثقةٍ ويقينٍ من النّتائج في نهاية الأمر. فالتّغييرات العنيفة التي تندفع نحوها الإنسانيّة بسِرعة متزايدة لا تشير أبداً إلى نهاية الحضارة الإنسانيّة، وإنّما من شأنها أن تُطلِق "القُدُرات الكامنة في مقام الإنسان"، وتُظْهِر "سُمُوَّ ما قُدِّر له على هذه الأرض" وتَكْشِف عن "ما فُطِرَ عليه من نفَيس الجوهر".

<h1 style="text-align:center">1</h1>

إنَّ النِّعَم التي اختصَّ بها الإنسان مُمَيِّزةً إيّاه عن كلّ نوع آخر من المخلوقات يمكن تلخيصها في ما يُعرف بالنّفس البشريّة، والعَقْلُ هو الخاصيّة الأساسيّة لهذه النّفس. ولقد مَكَّنَتْ هذه النِّعَم الإنسان من بناء الحضارات، وبلوغ الرّفاهيّة والازدهار الماديّ، ولكنّ النّفس البشريّة ما كانت لتكتفي بهذه الإنجازات وَحْدَها. فهذه النّفس بحُكم طبيعتها الخفيّة تَوَّاقةٌ إلى السّموّ والعلاء، تتطلّع نحو رحاب غير مرئيّة، نحو الحقيقة الأسمى، نحو هذا الجوهر الذي لا يمكن إدراك سِرِّه، جوهر الجواهر الذي هو الله سُبْحانه وتَعَالى. فالأديان التي نُزِّلَت لهداية الجنس البشريّ بواسطة شموس مُشْرِقةٍ تَعاقَبَتْ على الظّهور كانت بمثابة حَلْقة الوَصْل الرّئيسيّة بين الإنسان وتلْكَ الحقيقة الأسمى. وقد شَحَذت هذه الأديان قدرة الإنسان وهَذّبتها لِيُتَاحَ له تحقيق الإنجازات الرّوحيّة والتّقدّم الاجتماعيّ في آنٍ معاً.

وليس في إمكان أيّة محاولة جدِّية تهدف إلى إصلاح شؤون البشر، وتسعى إلى إحلال السّلام العالميّ، أن تتجاهل الدّين. فلقد حاك التّاريخ إلى حدٍّ بعيد نسيجَ ردائه من مفهوم الإنسان للأديان وممارسته لها. وقد وصف أحد المؤرّخين البارزين الدّين بأنّه "إحدى قدرات الطّبيعة الإنسانيّة"، ومما

يَصعُب إنكاره هو أنَّ إفساد هذه القدرة قد أسهم في خَلْق كثير من البلبلة والاضطراب في المجتمع الإنسانيّ، وزَرَعَ الصّراع والخصام بين أفراد البشر وفي نفوسهم. كما أنّه ليس في إمكان أيِّ شاهد مُنصِف أن ينتقص من الأثر البالغ للدّين في المظاهر الحضاريّة الحيويّة، يُضاف إلى ذلك، أنَّ الأثر المباشِر للدّين في مجالات التّشريع والأخلاق قد برهن تِباعاً على أنّه عاملٌ لا يمكن الاستغناء عنه في إقرار النّظام في المجتمع الإنسانيّ.

فقد كتب بهاءالله عن الدّين كعامل اجتماعيّ فعّال قائلاً: "إنّه السّبب الأعظم لنَظم العالم واطمئنان من في الإمكان". وأشار إلى أفول شمس الدّين أو فساده بقوله: "فلو احتجب سِراج الدّين لتطرّق الهرج والمرج وامتنع نَيِّر العدل والإنصاف عن الإشراق وشمسُ الأمن والاطمئنان عن الإنوار". والآثار البهائيّة تُقرِّر في تَعْدادها وحَصرها للنتائج المُترتِّبة على مثل هذا الفساد بأنَّ "انحراف الطّبيعة الإنسانيّة، وانحطاط السّلوك الإنسانيّ، وفساد النُّظُم الإنسانيّة وانهيارها، تَظْهر كلّها في مثل هذه الظّروف على أبشع صورة وأكثرها مَدْعاةً للاشمئزاز. ففي مثل هذه الأحوال ينحطّ الخُلُق الإنسانيّ، وتتزعزع الثّقة، ويتراخى الانتظام، ويَخْرَس الضّمير، ويغيب الخجل والحياء، وتندثر الحشمة والأدب. وتعوجّ مفاهيم الواجب والتّكاتف والوفاء والإخلاص وتَخْمُد تدريجيّاً مشاعر الأمل والرّجاء، والفرح والسّرور، والأمن والسّلام".

إذن، فإذا كانت الإنسانيّة قد وصلت إلى هذا المنعطف من الصّراع الذي أصابها بحالة من الشّلل، فإنّه بات لِزاماً عليها أن تثوب إلى رشدها، وتنظر إلى إهمالها، وتُفكِّر في أمر تلك الأصوات الغَاوية التي أصْغَتْ إليها، لكي تكتشف مصدر البلبلة واختلاف المفاهيم التي تُروّج باسم الدّين. فأولئك الذين تمسّكوا لمآرب شخصيّة تمسُّكاً أعمى بحَرْفيّة ما عندهم من آراء خاصة مُتزمِّتَة، وفرضوا على أتباعهم تفسيرات خاطئة متناقضة لأقوال أنبياء الله ورسله – إنَّ أولئك يتحمّلون ثِقْل مسؤوليّة خلق هذه البلبلة التي ازدادت حِدَّةً وتعقيداً بِما طرأ عليها من حواجز زائفة اختُلِقت لتَفْصِلَ بين الإيمان والعقل، وبين العلم والدّين. وإذا راجعنا بكلّ تجرُّد وإنصاف ما قاله حقّاً مؤسِّسو الأديان العظيمة، وتَفَحَّصْنا الأوساط التي اضطُرّوا إلى تنفيذ أعباء رسالاتهم فيها، فلن نجد هناك شيئاً يمكن أن تَسْتَنِد إليه النّزاعاتُ والتّعصّباتُ التي خَلَقت البلبلة والتّشويش في الجامعات الدّينيّة في العالم الإنسانيّ وبالتّالي في كافّة الشّؤون الإنسانيّة.

فالمبدأ الذي يفرض علينا أن نُعاملَ الآخرين، كما نُحِبّ أن يُعاملَنا الآخرون، مبدأٌ خُلُقيّ تكرّر بمختلف الصّور في الأديان العظيمة جميعاً، وهو يؤكّد لنا صحّة الملاحظة السّابقة في ناحيتَيْن مُعيّنتَيْن: الأولى، أنّه يُلخّص اتّجاهاً خُلُقيّاً يختصّ بالنّاحية التي تؤدّي إلى إحلال السّلام، ويمتدّ بأصوله عبر هذه الأديان بغضّ النّظر عن أماكن قيامها أو أوقات ظهورها، والثّانية، أنّه يشير إلى ناحية أخرى هي ناحية الوحدة والاتّحاد التي تُمثّل الخاصيّة الجوهريّة للأديان، هذه الخاصيّة التي أخْفَقَ البشر في إدراك حقيقتها نتيجة نَظْرَتهم المُشوّهة إلى التّاريخ.

فلو كانت الإنسانيّة قد أدركت حقيقة أولئك الذين تولّوا تربيتها في عهود طفولتها الجماعيّة كمُنفّذين لمسير حضارةٍ واحدة، لجَنَتْ دون شكّ من الآثار الخَيِّرة، التي اجتمعت نتيجة تَعاقُب تلك الرّسالات، محصولاً أكبر من المنافع التي لا تُحْصَى ولا تُعَدّ. ولكن الإنسانيّة فَشِلَت، ويا للأسف، في أن تفعل ذلك.

إنّ عودة ظهور الحَميّة الدّينيّة المُتطرِّفة في العديد من الأقطار لا تعدو أن تكون تشنّجاتِ الرّمَقِ الأخير. فالماهيّة الحقيقيّة لظاهرة العنف والتّمزّق المتّصلة بهذه الحميّة الدّينيّة تشهد على الإفلاس الرّوحيّ الذي تُمثّله هذه الظّاهرة. والواقع أنّ من أغرب الملامح الواضحة وأكثرها مدعاةً للأسف في تفشّي الحركات الرّاهنة من حركات التّعصّب الدّينيّ هي مدى ما تقوم به كلٌّ واحدة منها ليس فقط في تقويض القِيَم الرّوحيّة التي تسعى إلى تحقيق وحدة الجنس البشريّ، بل وتلك الإنجازات الخُلُقيّة الفريدة التي حقّقها كلّ دين من هذه الأديان التي تدّعي تلك الحركات أنّها قائمة لخدمة مصالحها.

ورَغمَ ما كان للدّين من قوّة حيويّة في تاريخ الإنسانيّة، ورغم ما كان لظهور الحميّة الدّينيّة أو حركات التّعصّب المتّصفة بالعنف من آثار تُثير النّفوس، فقد اعتبر عددٌ متزايدٌ من البشر، حِقَباً طويلةً من الزّمن، أنّ الأديان ومؤسّساتها عديمة الفائدة ولا محلّ لها في الاهتمامات الرّئيسيّة للعالم الحديث. وبدلاً من الاتّجاه نحو الدّين اتّجه البشر إمّا نحو لَذّةِ إشباع أطماعهم الماديّة، أو نحو اعتناق مذاهب عقائديّة صنعَها الإنسان بُغْيَةَ إنقاذِ المجتمع الإنسانيّ من الشّرور الظّاهرة التي يَنُؤ بحَمْلِها. ولكنّ المؤسف أنّ مذاهب عقائديّة متعدِّدة اتّجهت نحو تأليه الدّولة، ونحو إخضاع سائر البشر لسَطْوَةِ أمّةٍ

واحدة من الأُمَم، أو عِرْق من الأعراق، أو طَبَقَةٍ من الطّبقات، بَدَلَ أن تَتَبَنَّى مبدأ وحدة الجنس البشريِّ، وبَدَلَ أن تعمل على تنمية روح التّآخي والوئام بين مختلف النّاس. وباتت تسعى إلى خَنْق كلّ حوار ومَنْع أي تَبَادُل للرّأيِ أو الفكر، وذهبت إلى التّخلِّي دون شفقة عن الملايين من الذين يموتون جوعاً تاركةً إيّاهم تحت رحمة نظام سوق المعاملات التّجاريّة الذي يزيد بوضوح من حدّة المحنة التي يعيشها معظم البشر، بينما أفسحت المجال لقطاعاتٍ قليلة من النّاس لأن تتمتّع بتَرَفٍ وثراءٍ قلَّما تصوَّرهما أسلافنا في أحلامهم.

فكم هو فاجعٌ سِجلُّ تلك المذاهب والعقائد البديلة التي وضعها أولو الحكمة الدُّنيويّة من أهل عصرنا. ففي خِضَمِّ خَيْبةِ الأمل الهائلة لدى مجموعات إنسانيّة بأسرها، لُقِّنت الأماثيل لتتعبَّد عند محاريب تلك المذاهب، نَستقرئ عِبرَة التّاريخ وحُكْمَه الفاصل على قِيَم تلك العقائد وفوائدها. إنَّ المحصول الذي جَنَيْناه من تلك العقائد والمذاهب هو الآفات الاجتماعيّة والاقتصاديّة التي نُكِبت بها كلّ مناطق عالمنا في هذه السّنوات الختاميّة من القرن العشرين، وذلك بعد انقضاء عقودٍ طويلة من استغلالٍ متزايد للنّفوذ والسّلطة على يد أولئك الذين يَدينون بما حقَّقوه من سُؤدَدٍ وصعود في مجالات النّشاطات الإنسانيّة إلى تلك العقائد والمذاهب. وترتكز هذه الآفات الظّاهريّة على ذلك العَطَب الرّوحيّ الذي تعكسه نَزْعَة اللاَّمُبالاة المستَحْوذةُ على نفوس جماهير البشر في كلّ الأمم، ويعكسه خمود جَذْوَة الأمل في أفئدة الملايين مِمَّنْ يُقاسون اللَّوعَة والحرمان.

لقد آنَ الأوانُ كي يُسأل الذين دَعَوا النّاس إلى اعتناق العقائد الماديّة، سواءً كانوا من أهل الشّرق أو الغرب، أو كان انتماؤهم إلى المذهب الرّأسماليّ أو الاشتراكيّ – آنَ الأوان ليُسأل هؤلاء ويُحاسَبوا على القيادة الخُلُقيّة التي أخذوها على عواتقهم. فأَينَ "العالم الجديد" الذي وعَدَت به تلك العقائد؟ وأين السّلام العالميّ الذي يُعلنون عن تكريس جهودهم لخدمة مبادئه؟ وأين الآفاق الجديدة في مجالات الإنجازات الثّقافيّة التي قامت على تعظيم ذلك العِرق، أو هذه الدّولة، أو تلك الطّبقة الخاصّة؟ وما السّبب في أنَّ الغالبيّة العُظْمَى من أهل العالم تتنزلق أكثر فأكثر في غياهب المجاعة والبؤس في وقتٍ باتت في متناول يد أولئك الذين يتحكمون في شؤون البشر ثرواتٌ بَلَغَت حدًّا لم يكن لِيَحْلُم بها الفراعنة، ولا القياصرة، ولا حتى القوى الاستعماريّة في القرن التّاسع عشر؟

إنّ تمجيد المآرب الماديّة – وهو تمجيد يُمثِّل الأصول الفكريّة
والخصائص المشتركة لكلّ تلك المذاهب – إنَّ هذا التّمجيد على الأخصّ
هو الذي نجد فيه الجذور التي تُغذّي الرّأي الباطل الذي يدَّعي بأنَّ الإنسان
أنانيٌّ وعدوانيٌّ ولا سبيل إلى إصلاحه. وهذه النّقطة بالذات هي التي يجب
جلاؤها إذا ما أردنا بناء عالم جديد يكون لائقاً بأولادنا وأحفادنا.

فالقول بأنَّ القِيَم الماديّة قد فشلت في تلبية حاجات البشريّة كما
أثبتت التّجاربُ التي مَرَّت بنا، يفرض علينا أنْ نعترف بصدق وأمانة أنَّه
أصبح لِزاماً الآن بَذْلُ جَهْدٍ جديد لإيجاد الحلول للمشكلات المُضْنِية التي
يُعانيها الكوكب الأرضيّ. فالظّروف التي تحيط بالمجتمع الإنسانيّ، وهي
ظروف لا تُطاق، هي الدّليل على أنَّ فشَلنا كان فشلاً جماعيّاً بدون استثناء،
وهذه الحالة إنّما تُذْكي نَعْرَة التّزمُّت والإصرار لدى كلّ الأطراف بَدَلَ أن
تُزيلها. فمن الواضح إذَن أنَّ هناك حاجة مُلِحَّة إلى مجهود مشترك لإصلاح
الأمور وشفاء العِلَل. فالمسألة أساساً مسألةُ اتّخاذ مَوْقف. وهنا يَتَبَادَر إلى
الأذهان السّؤال التّالي: هل تستمرّ الإنسانيّة في ضلالها مُتمسِّكة بالأفكار
البالية والافتراضات العقيمة؟ أم يَعْمِد قادتها متّحدين، بِغَضِّ النّظر عن
العقائد، إلى التّشاوُر فيما بينهم بعزيمةٍ ثابتة بحثاً عن الحلول المناسبة؟

ويجدُر بأولئك الذين يهمّهم مستقبل الجنس البشريّ أن يُنعِموا النّظر
بالنّصيحة التّالية: "إذا كانت المُثُل التي طال الاعتزاز بها، والمؤسَّسات التي
طال احترامُها عبر الزّمن، وإذا كانت بعض الفروض الاجتماعيّة والقواعد
الدّينيّة قد قَصَّرت في تنمية سعادة الإنسان ورفاهيته بوجهٍ عامّ، وباتت عاجزةً
عن سدّ احتياجات إنسانيّة دائمة التّطوّر، فَلتندثِرْ وتَغِبْ في عالم النّسيان
مع تلك العقائد المُهْمَلة البالية. ولماذا تُستثنَى من الاندثار الذي لا بدّ أن
يُصيب كلّ مؤسّسة إنسانيّة في عالم يَخْضَع لقانون ثابت من التّغيير والفَنَاء.
إنّ القواعد القانونيّة والنّظريّات السّياسيّة والاقتصاديّة وُضِعت أصلاً من أجل
المحافظة على مصالح الإنسانيّة ككلّ، وليس لكي تُصلَّب الإنسانيّة بقصد
الإبقاء على سلامة أي قانون أو مبدأ أو المحافظة عليه".

2

إنَّ حَظرَ الأسلحة النَّوويّة، وتحريم استعمال الغازات السّامّة، ومنع حرب الجراثيم، إنَّ كلَّ ذلك لن يُزيل الأسباب الجَذريّة لاندلاع الحروب. ورغم وضوح أهميّة هذه الإجراءات العمليّة كعناصر لمسيرة السّلام، فهي في حدّ ذاتها سَطحيّة بحيث أنّها لن تكون ذات أثر دائم. فالبشر يتمتّعون بالبراعة لدرجةِ أنَّه باستطاعتهم إن أرادوا خَلق وسائل أخرى لشنّ الحروب. فبإمكانهم استخدام الأغذية، أو الموادّ الخام، أو المال، أو القوّة الصناعيّة، أو المذاهب العقائديّة، أو الإرهاب، أسلحةً يَطغَى بها الواحد منهم على الآخر في صراعٍ لا نهاية له طَمَعاً في السّيطرة والسّلطان. كما أنَّه من غير الممكن إصلاح الخَلَل الهائل في الشّؤون الإنسانيّة الرّاهنة عن طريق تسوية الصّراعات الخاصّة والخلافات المُعيّنة القائمة بين الدّول. لقد أصبح من الواجب إيجاد إطارٍ عالميّ حقيقي واعتمادُه لإصلاح الخلل.

ومن المؤكّد أنّ قادة العالم يُدرِكون أنّ المشكلة في طبيعتها عالميّةُ النّطاق، وهي واضحة المعالم في جملة القضايا المُتراكِمة التي يُواجهونها يوماً بعد يوم. وهناك أيضاً الأبحاث والحلول المطروحة التي تتكدّس أمامهم من قِبَل العديد من المجموعات الواعية المُهتمّة بهذه القضايا ومن وكالات الأمم المتّحدة، ممّا لا يَدَع لأحدٍ منهم مجالاً لعدم الإلمام بالمَطالب التي تتحدّاهم والتي لا بُدّ من مجابهتها. إلاّ أنّ هناك حالةً من شلل الإرادة. وهذه الحالة هي بيت القصيد والمسألة التي يجب بحثها بعناية ومعالجتها بكلّ عزم وإصرار. فحالة الشّلل هذه تَجد جذورها – كما سبق أن ذكرنا – في ذلك الاعتقاد الرّاسخ بأن البشر جُبلوا على التّصارع فيما بينهم وأنَّ هذه نَزعَةٌ لا يمكن تلافيها. ولقد ترتّب على هذا الاعتقاد تردُّدٌ في إعارة أيّ التفاتٍ إلى إمكانيّة إخضاع المصالح الوطنيّة الخاصة لمُتطلّبات النّظام العالميّ، وترتّب عليه أيضاً نَوعٌ من انعدام الرّغبة في اتّخاذ مَوقفٍ شُجاع يقضي بقبول النّتائج البعيدة المدى النّاجمة عن تأسيس سلطةٍ عالميّةٍ مُوحّدة. وفي الإمكان أيضاً تلمُّس حالة الشّلل هذه في أنّ جماهير غفيرة من البشر لا تزال إلى حدّ بعيد، رازحةً تحت وَطأة الجهل والاستعباد، وعاجزةً عن الإفصاح عن رغباتها في المطالبة بنظامٍ جديد يَضمَن لها العيش مع البشر كافّة في سلامٍ ووئامٍ ورخاء.

إنَّ الخطوات التّجريبيّة التي اتُّخِذت في سبيل تحقيق النّظام العالميّ، وخاصةَ تلك التي تمَّ اعتمادها منذ الحرب العالميّة الثّانية تُوحي بدلائل تبشّر بالأمل. فتزايُدُ الاتّجاه لدى مجموعات الأمم نحو إقامة علاقات تُمكّنها من التّعاوُن فيمَا بينها في القضايا ذات المصالح المشتركة يُشير إلى أنَّ الأمم كلّها باستطاعتها التّغلّب على حالة الشّلل هذه في نهاية المطاف. فرابطة دول جنوب شرق آسيا، وجامعة دول البحر الكاريبي وسوقها المشتركة، والسّوق المشتركة لدول أمريكا الوُسْطَى، والمجلس الاقتصاديّ للتّعاون المشترك، ومجموعة الدّول الأوروبيّة، وجامعة الدّول العربيّة، ومُنظّمة الوحدة الإفريقيّة، ومنظّمة دول القارّة الأمريكيّة، ومُنْتَدَى دول الباسيفيك الجنوبيّ – إنَّ كل هذه التّنظيمات وكلّ جهودها المشتركة تُمهّد السّبيل أمام قيام نظام عالميّ.

ومن العلامات الأخرى التي تُبشّر بالأمل، ازديادٌ ملحوظٌ في تركيز الاهتمام على عددٍ من أشدّ المشكلات تأصّلاً في هذا الكوكب الأرضيّ. ورغم تقصير هيئة الأمم المتحدة في بعض المجالات، فإنّها قد تَبَنَّت ما يزيد على أربعين بياناً وميثاقاً، وحتى في الحالات التي لم تكن فيها الحكومات مُتحمِّسة في التزاماتها تِجاه هذه البيانات والمواثيق، تولّد لدى العاديّين من البشر شعورٌ جديد بالحياة. إنَّ الإعلان العام لحُقوق الإنسان، وميثاق منع جرائم الإبادة العنصريّة وقانون الجزاء المتعلّق بهذا الميثاق، إضافةً إلى الإجراءات المماثلة المتعلقة بالقضاء على كل أنواع التّفرقة العرقيّة أو الجنسيّة أو الدّينيّة، والدّفاع عن حقوق الطّفولة، وحماية كلّ فرد من التّعرُّض للتّعذيب، ومحاولة القضاء على المجاعة وعلى سوء التّغذية، والعمل على استخدام التّقدم العلميّ والتّقنيّ لصالح السّلام ولفائدة الإنسان – إنَّ كلّ هذه الإجراءات، في حالة تنفيذها وتوسيع نطاقها بشجاعة لا بدّ أن تُعجِّل مجيء ذلك اليوم الذي يفقد فيه شَبَحُ الحرب نفوذَه في السّيطرة على العلاقات الدّوليّة. ولا حاجة هنا للتّأكيد على أهميّة القضايا التي تُعالجها هذه البياناتُ والمواثيق، ولكنْ نظراً إلى أنَّ لبعض هذه القضايا علاقةً وثيقة بموضوع السّلام في العالم، فإنّها تستحقُّ تعليقاً إضافيّاً.

فالتّفْرقة العُنْصُريّة هي أحد أشدّ الشّرور ضرراً وأذىً وأكثرها استشراءً، وهي عائقٌ رئيسيّ في طريق السّلام. والعمل بمبادئ هذه التّفرقة هو انتهاكٌ فاضح لكرامة الإنسان، ولا يمكن القبول به بأي عُذْرٍ من الأعذار. إنَّ التّفرقة

العنصريّة تُعيق نُمُوَّ الإمكانات اللامحدودة عند أولئك الذين يرزحون تحت نيرِها، كما أنّها تُفسِد أولئك الذين يُمَارسونها، وتُعطِّل تقدّم الإنسان ورُقِيّه، وإذا ما أريد القضاء على هذه المشكلة، فمن الواجب الاعترافُ بمبدأ وحدة الجنس البشريّ وتنفيذُ هذا المبدأ باتّخاذ الإجراءات القانونيّة المناسبة وبتطبيقه على نطاقٍ عالميّ.

أمَّا الفوارق الشّاسعة بين الأغنياء والفقراء، وهي مصدرٌ من مصادر المُعاناة الحادَّة، فتَضع العالم على شَفَا هاويةِ الحرب والصّراع وتَدَعُه رهنًا للاضطراب وعَدَم الاستقرار . وقليلةٌ هي المجتمعاتُ التي تمكّنت من معالجة هذه الحالة معالجةً فعّالة. ولذلك فإنَّ الحلَّ يتطلَّب تنفيذ جُمْلةٍ من الاتّجاهات العمليّة والرّوحيّة والخُلُقِيّة. والمطلوب هو أن ننظر إلى هذه المشكلة نَظْرَةً جديدةً تَستدعي إجراء التّشاوُر بين مجموعةٍ مُوسَّعة من أهل الاختصاص في العديد من المجالات العلميّة المُتنوّعة، على أن تتمَّ المُشاورات مُجرَّدةً عن المُجادلات العقائديّة والاقتصاديّة، ويشترك فيها أولئك الذين سوف يتحمَّلون مُباشرةً أثر القرارات التي يجب اتّخاذها بصورة ملحّة. إنَّ القضيّة لا ترتبط فقط بضرورة إزالة الهُوّة السّحيقة بين الفَقْر المُدْقِع والغِنَى الفاحش، ولكنّها ترتبط أيضاً بتلك القِيَم الرّوحيّة الحقّة التي يُمْكنها، إذا تمّ إدراكها واستيعابها، خَلْقُ اتّجاهٍ عالميّ جديد يكون في حدّ ذاته جُزءاً رئيسيّاً من الحلّ المطلوب.

إنَّ الوطنيّة المتطرِّفة، وهي شعور يَخْتَلِف عن ذلك الشّعور المشروع المتّزن المُتمثِّل في محبّة الإنسان لوطنه، لا بدّ أن يُستعاضَ عنها بولاءٍ أوْسَع، بمحبّة العالم الإنسانيّ ككلّ. يقول بهاءالله "إنَّ الأرض وطنٌ واحدٌ والبشرُ سكّانه". إنَّ فكرة المُواطِنيّة العالميّة جاءت كنتيجة مباشرة لتقلُّص العالم وتحوُّله إلى بيئة واحدة يَتَجاوَرُ فيها الجميع، بفضل تقدُّم العلم واعتماد الأمم بعضها على بعض اعتماداً لا مجال لإنكاره. فالمحبّة الشّاملة لأهل العالم لا تَسْتثني محبّة الإنسان لوطنه. فخير وسيلة لخدمة مصلحة الجزء في مجتمع عالميّ هي خدمة مصلحة المجموع. وهناك حاجةٌ قُصْوَى لزيادة النّشاطات الدّوليّة الرّاهنة في الميادين المختلفة، وهي نشاطاتٌ تُنمّي تَبادُل المحبّة والوئام وتخلق مشاعر التّضامُن بين الشّعوب.

كانت النّزاعات الدّينيّة عبر التّاريخ سبباً للعديد من الحروب والصّراعات، وآفةً من أعظم الآفات التي أعاقت التّقدّم والتّطوّر . ولقد

أصبحت هذه النّزاعات بغيضةً على نحو متزايد بالنّسبة لأتباع كلّ الأديان وكذلك بالنّسبة لمن لا يَدينون بدين. وإنَّ على أتباع الأديان كلّها أن يُواجهوا الأسئلة الأساسيّة التي تُثيرها هذه المُنازَعات، وأن يَجدوا لها أجوبةً واضحةً. فمثلاً، كيف يمكن لهم إزالة الخلافات القائمة بينهم من الوجهتَيْن النّظريّة والعمليّة على السّواء؟ إنَّ التّحدّي الذي يُواجِه قادة الأديان في العالم يَحملهم على أن يتمعَّنوا في مِحْنة الإنسانيّة بقلوبٍ تمتلئ حَناناً، وبرغبةٍ في توخّي الحقيقة، وأن يسألوا أَنفسهم، مُتذلّلين أمام الخالق العَليّ القَدير، ما إذا كان بإمكانهم دَفْنُ خلافاتهم الفِقهيّة بروح عالية من التَّسامُح ليستطيعوا العمل معاً في سبيل إحلال السّلام وتعزيز التَّفاهم الإنسانيّ.

إنَّ قضيّة تحرير المرأة، أي تحقيق المُساواة الكاملة بين الجنسَيْن، هي مطلبٌ مُهمٌّ من مُتطلبات السّلام، رغم أنَّ الاعتراف بحقيقة ذلك لا يزال على نطاقٍ ضيّق. إنَّ إنكار مثل هذه المساواة يُنزِل الظّلم بنصف سكّان العالم، ويُنمِّي في الرّجل اتّجاهات وعادات مؤذية تنتقل من محيط العائلة إلى محيط العمل، إلى محيط الحياة السّياسيّة، وفي نهاية الأمر إلى ميدان العلاقات الدّوليّة. فليس هناك أي أساسٍ خُلُقيّ أو عمليّ أو بيولوجيّ يمكن أن يبرّر مثل هذا الإنكار، ولن يستقرّ المناخ الخلقيّ والنّفسيّ الذي سوف يتسنّى للسّلام العالميّ النُّموّ فيه، إلاّ عندما تَدْخُل المرأة بكلّ تَرحاب إلى سائر ميادين النّشاط الإنسانيّ كشريكةٍ كاملةٍ للرّجل.

وقضيّة التّعليم الشّامل للجميع تستحقّ هي الأخرى أقصى ما يمكن من دعمٍ ومعونةٍ من قِبَل حكومات العالم أجمع. فقد اعتنق هذه القضيّة وانخرط في سِلك خدمتها رَعيلٌ من الأشخاص المخلصين يَنْتَمُون إلى كلّ دين وإلى كلّ وطن. وممَّا لا جدل فيه. أنَّ الجهل هو السّبب الرّئيسيّ في انهيار الشّعوب وسقوطها وفي تغذية التّعصّبات وبَقائها. فلا نجاح لأيّةِ أُمّةٍ دون أن يكون العلم من حقِّ كلّ مُواطِنٍ فيها، ولكنّ انعدام الموارد والمصادر يحدّ من قدرة العديد من الأمَم على سدّ هذه الحاجة، فيَفْرِض عليها عندئذ ترتيباً خاصّاً تَعتمِده في وضع جَدْولٍ للأولَويّات. والهيئَات صاحبةُ القرار في هذا الشّأن تُحْسِن عملاً إنْ هي أَخَذَت بعين الاعتبار إعطاءَ الأولويّة في التّعليم للنّساء والبنات، لأنَّ المعرفة تنتشر عن طريق الأُمّ المتعلِّمة بمُنْتَهى السّرعة والفعّاليّة، فتعمّ الفائدة المجتمع بأسره. وتمشيّاً مع مُقتضيات العصر

يجب أن نهتمّ بتعليم فكرة المُواطنيّة العالميّة كجزء من البرنامج التّربويّ الأساسيّ لكلّ طِفل.

إنَّ انعدام سُبُل الاتّصال بين الشّعوب في الأساس يُضْعِف الجهود المبذولة في سبيل إحلال السّلام العالميّ ويُهدِّدها. فاعتماد لُغَة إضافيّة كلغة عالميّة سيُسْهِم إسهاماً واسعاً في حلّ هذه المشاكل ويَستأهِل اهتماماً عاجلاً.

وفي سَرْدِنا لهذه القضايا كلّها نُقطَتان تَستدعِيان التّكرار والتّأكيد. النّقطة الأولى هي أنَّ إنهاء الحروب والقضاء عليها ليس مُجرّد إبرام مُعاهدات، أو توقيع اتّفاقيّات. إنَّ المَهمّة معقّدة تتطلّب مُستوىً جديداً من الالتزام بحلّ قضايا لا يُرْبَط عادةً بينها وبين موضوع البحث عن السّلام. ففكرة الأمن الجماعي أو الأمن المشترك تُصبح أضغاثَ أحلام إذا كان أساسُها الوحيد الاتّفاقات السّياسيّة. أمّا النّقطة الثّانيّة فهي أنَّ التّحدّي الأساسي الذي يُواجه العاملين في قضايا السّلام هو وجوب السُمُوّ بإطار التّعامُل إلى مستوى التّقيّد والمُثُل بشكلٍ يَتمَيّز عن أسُلوب الإذعان للأمر الواقع. ذلك أنَّ السّلام في جوهره يَنْبُع من حالةٍ تتبلور داخل الإنسان يَدْعَمها موقفٌ خُلُقيّ وروحيّ. وخَلْقُ مثل هذا الموقف الخُلُقيّ والرّوحيّ هو بصورة أساسيّة ما سوف يُمكّننا من العثور على الحلول النّهائيّة.

وهناك مبادئ روحيّة يَصِفُها البعض بأنها قِيَمٌ إنسانيّة يمكن عن طريقها إيجاد الحلول لكلّ مشكلة اجتماعيّة. وعلى وجه العموم، فإنَّ أيّة مجموعة بشريّة صادقةِ النّوايا تستطيع وضع الحلول العمليّة لمشكلاتها. ولكنَّ توفُّر النّوايا الصّادقة والخبرة العمليّة ليست كافيةً في غالب الأحيان. فالمِيزة الرّئيسيّة لأي مبدأ روحي تتمثّل في أنّه يُساعدنا ليس فقط على خلق نظرةٍ إلى الأمور تَنسجِم مع ما في قَرارة الطّبيعة الإنسانيّة، بل إنّه يُولّد أيضاً مَوْقفاً، وطاقةً مُحَرِّكةً، وإرادةً، وطُموحاً – وكلّ ذلك يُسهِّل اكتشاف الحلول العمليّة وطُرُق تنفيذها. ولا ريب في أنَّ قادة الحكومات وجميع من بِيَدهم مقاليد السُّلطة سيدعمون جهودهم في سبيل حلّ المشكلات إذا سَعَوا في بادئ الأمر إلى تحديد المبادئ وتعيينها، ومن ثمّ الاهتداء بهَدْيِها.

3

إنَّ المسألة الأولـى التي يجب حلّها هي كيفيّة تغيير العالم المُعاصر، بكلّ ما فيه من أنماط الصّراعات المتأصّلة وجَعْلُه عالماً يَسُوده التّعاوُن والانسجام.

فالنّظام العالميّ لا يمكن تثبيته إلاّ على أساس الوعي وعياً راسخاً لا يتزعزع بوحدة الجنس البشريّ، هذه الوحدة التي هي حقيقةٌ روحيّة تؤكّدها العلوم الإنسانيّة بأسرها. إنَّ علم الإنسان، وعلم وظائف الأعضاء، وعلم النّفس – هذه العلوم كلّها تعترف بانتماء الإنسان إلى أصلٍ واحد، رغم أنَّ المظاهر الثّانويّة لحياته تختلف وتتنوّع بصورة لا حصر لها ولا عدّ. ويتطلّب إدراك هذه الحقيقة التّخلّي عن التّعصّبات بكلّ أنواعها عِرقيّة كانت أو طبقيّة، أو دينيّة، أو وطنيّة، أو متّصلة باللّون أو بالجنس أو بمستوى الرُّقيّ الماديّ. وبمعنًى آخر تَرْك كلّ ما قد يُوحي إلى فئة من البشر بأنّها أفضل شأناً أو أسمى مرتبةً من سواها.

إنَّ القبول بمبدأ وحدة الجنس البشريّ هو أول مطلبٍ أساسيّ يجب توفُّره في عمليّة إعادة تنظيم العالم وإدارته كوطن واحد لأبناء البشر أجمع. والقبول بهذا المبدأ الرّوحيّ قبولاً عالميّ النّطاق ضروريٌّ بالنّسبة لأيّة محاولة ناجحة لإقامة صَرْح السّلام العالميّ. وبناءً على ذلك يجب إعلانه في كلّ أنحاء العالم، وجعله مادّةً تُدرَّس في المدارس، كما ينبغي المثابرة على تأكيده وإثباته في كلّ دولة تمهيداً لإحداث ما ينطوي عليه من تحوُّل عضوي في بُنْيَة المجتمع.

والاعتراف بمبدأ وحدة العالم الإنسانيّ يَستلزِم، من وجهة النّظر البهائيّة، "أَقلَ ما يمكن إعادة بناء العالم المُتمدِّن بأسره ونَزع سلاحه، ليصبح عالماً متّحداً اتّحاداً عضويّاً في كلّ نواحي حياته الأساسيّة، فيتوحّد جهازُه السّياسيّ، وتتوحّد مطامحه الرّوحيّة، وتتوحّد فيه عوالم التّجارة والمال، ويتوحّد في اللّغة والخطّ، على أن يبقى في ذات الوقت عالماً لا حدود فيه لتنوُّع الخصائص الوطنيّة والقوميّة التي يُمثِّلها أعضاء هذا الاتّحاد".

لقد أَسْهَب شوقي أفندي، وليُّ أمر الدِّين البهائي، في شرح الآثار المترتِّبة على تنفيذ هذا المبدأ الأساسيّ، عندما عَلَّق على هذا الموضوع عام 1931 بقوله: "بعيداً عن أيّة محاولة لتقويض الأُسُس الرّاهنة التي يقوم عليها المجتمع الإنسانيّ، يسعى مبدأ الوحدة هذا إلى توسيع قواعد ذلك المجتمع، وإعادة صياغة شكل مؤسّساته على نحو يَتَناسَق مع احتياجات عالمٍ دائمِ التّطوّر. ولن يتعارض هذا المبدأ مع أيّ ولاءٍ من الولاءات المشروعة، كما أنه لن ينتقص من حقٍّ أي ولاءٍ ضروريٍّ الوجود. فهو لا يستهدف إطفاءَ شُعْلَة المحبّة المتّزنة للوطن في قلوب بني البشر، ولا يسعى إلى إزالة الحكم الذّاتيّ الوطنيّ، الذي هو ضرورةٌ ملحّة إذا ما أُريدَ تجنُّب الشّرور والمَخاطر النّاجمة عن الحكم المركزيّ المُبالَغ فيه. ولن يتجاهل هذا المبدأ أو يسعى إلى طَمْس تلك الميّزات المتّصلة بالعِرق، والمناخ، والتّاريخ، واللّغة والتّقاليد، أو المتعلِّقة بالفكر والعادات، فهذه الفوارق تُميّز شعوب العالم ودُوَلَه بعضها عن بعض. إنّه يدعو إلى إقامة ولاءٍ أوسع، واعتناق مطامح أسمى، تَفوق كلَّ ما سَبَقَ وحَرَّك مشاعر الجنس البشريّ في الماضي. ويؤكِّد هذا المبدأ إخضاعَ المشاعر والمصالح الوطنيّة للمتطلّبات الملحّة في عالم مُوحّد، رافضاً المركزيّة الزائدة عن الحدّ من جهة، ومُستنكِراً من جهة أخرى أيّة محاولة من شأنها القضاء على التّنوّع والتّعدّد. فالشِّعار الذي يَرْفعه هو: "الوحدة والاتّحاد في التّنوّع والتّعدّد".

وانجازُ مثلُ هذه الأهداف يستلزم توفُّر عِدَّة مراحل عند تعديل المواقف والاتّجاهات الوطنيّة والسّياسيّة، هذه الاتّجاهات والمواقف التي باتت الآن تَميل نحو الفوضى في غياب قواعد قانونيّة مُحدَّدة أو مبادئ قابلة للتّنفيذ والتّطبيق على مستوى عالميّ ومن شأنها أن تُنظِّم العلاقات بين الدّول. وممّا لا ريب فيه أنّ عصبة الأمم، ثم هيئة الأمم المتّحدة، بالإضافة إلى العديد من التّنظيمات والاتّفاقيّات التي انبثقت عن هاتين الهيئتين العالميّتين قد ساعدت دون شكّ على تخفيف حدّة بعض الآثار السّلبيّة للنزاعات الدّوليّة، ولكنها أيضاً برهنت على أنّها تعجز عن منع الحروب والصّراعات، فالواقع أنّ عشرات الحروب قد نَشِبَت منذ انتهاء الحرب العالميّة الثّانية، وأنّ العديد منها لا يزال مُسْتَعِرَ الأُوار.

لقد كانت الوجوه البارزة لهذه المشكلة ظاهرةً للعَيان في القرن التّاسع عشر عندما أَصْدَر بهاءالله مقترحاته الأولى بصدد تأسيس السّلام العالميّ.

وعرض بهاءالله مبدأ الأمن الجماعي أو الأمن المشترك في بياناتٍ وجّهها إلى قادة العالم وحُكّامه. وقد كتب شوقي أفندي مُعلِّقاً على مَغْزَى ما صرَّح به بهاءالله بقوله: "إنَّ المغزى الذي يكمن في هذه الكلمات الخطيرة هو أنَّها تشير إلى أنَّ كَبْحَ جماح المشاعر المتعلقة بالسّيادة الوطنيّة المتطرّفة أمْرٌ لا مناص منه كإجراءٍ أوَّلي لا يمكن الاستغناء عنه في تأسيس رابطة الشّعوب المتّحدة التي ستَنْتَمي إليها مُستقبلاً كلّ دول العالم. فلا بُدّ من حدوث تطورٍ يقودُ إلى قيام شَكْلٍ من أشكال الحكومة العالميّة تخضع لها عن طيبِ خاطرٍ كلّ دول العالم، فتتنازل لصالحها عن كلّ حقٍّ في شنّ الحروب، وعن حقوقٍ مُعيّنة في فرض الضّرائب، وعن كلّ حقّ أيضاً يسمح لها بالتّسلّح، إلاّ ما كان منه يَكفي لأغراض المحافظة على الأمن الدّاخلي ضمن الحدود المَعنيّة لكلّ دولة. ويدور في فلَك هذه الحكومة العالميّة قوّةٌ تنفيذيّة دوليّة قادرة على فرض سلطتها العليا التي لا يمكن تحدِّيها من قِبَل أيّ مُعارضٍ من أعضاء رابطة شعوب الاتّحاد. يُضاف إلى ذلك إقامة بَرلمان عالميّ يَنتخب أعضاءَه كلّ شعب ضمن حدود بلاده، ويَحْظَى انتخابُهم بموافقة حكوماتهم الخاصّة، وكذلك تأسيسُ محكمة عُليا يكون لقراراتها صفَة الإلزام حتى في القضايا التي لم تكن الأطراف المَعنيّة راغبةً في طرحها أمام تلك المحكمة.

"... إنّها جامعةٌ عالميّة تزول فيها إلى غير رجعة كلّ الحواجز الاقتصاديّة ويقوم فيها اعتراف قاطع بأنَّ رأس المال واليد العاملة شريكان لاغنَى للواحد منهما عن الآخر، جامعةٌ يتلاشى فيه نهائيّاً ضجيج التّعصّبات والمُنازعات الدّينيّة، جامعةٌ تنطفئ فيها إلى الأبد نار البغضاء العرقيّة، جامعةٌ تَسُودها شِرْعَةٌ قانونيّة دوليّة واحدة تكون تعبيراً عن الرّأي الحصيف الذي يَصِل إليه بعنايةٍ مُمثّلو ذلك الاتّحاد، ويجري تنفيذ أحكامها بالتّدخُّل الفوريّ من قِبَل مجموع القوات الخاضعة لكلّ دولة من دول الاتّحاد. وأخيراً إنَّها جامعةٌ عالميّة يتحوّل فيها التّعصّب الوطني المتقلِّب الأهواء، العنيف الاتّجاهات، إلى إدراكٍ راسخ لمعنى المواطنيّة العالميّة – تلك هي حقّاً الخطوط العريضة لصورة النّظامِ الذي رَسَمَه مُسبقاً بهاءالله، وهو نظامٌ سوف يُنْظَر إليه على أنَّه أينع ثمرةٍ من ثمرات عصرٍ يكتمِل نُضْجُه ببطءٍ."

وقد أشار بهاءالله إلى تنفيذ مثل هذه الإجراءات البعيدة المدى بقوله: "سيأتي الوقت الذي يدرك فيه العموم الحاجة المِلحَّة التي تدعو إلى عقدِ اجتماعٍ واسع يشمل البشر جميعاً. وعلى ملوك الأرض وحُكّامها أن

يحضروه، وأن يشتركوا في مُداولاته، ويَدْرُسوا الوسائل والطُرق التي يمكن بها إرساء قواعد السّلام العظيم بين البشر".

إنَّ الشّجاعة والعزيمة، وصفاء النيّة، والمحبّة المُنزّهة عن المآرب الشّخصيّة بين شعبٍ وآخر، وكلّ الفضائل الرّوحيّة والخُلُقيّة التي يستلزمها تنفيذ هذه الخطوة الخطيرة نحو السّلام ترتكز على فِعْل الإرادة. ففي اتّجاهنا لخَلْق الإرادة الضروريّة علينا أن نأخذ بعين الاعتبار صادقين حقيقة الإنسان، أي فِكْرَه. فإذا تمكّنا من إدراك علاقة هذه الحقيقة النّافذة بالنّسبة لهذا الموضوع نتمكّن أيضاً من تقدير الضرورة الاجتماعيّة لترجمة فضائل هذه الحقيقة الفريدة إلى الواقع عن طريق المَشورة الودّيّة الصّادقة الرّزينة، ومن ثمّ العمل بمُقْتضَيات نتائج هذه المشورة. وقد لَفَتَ بهاءالله الأنظار مشدّداً على منافع المشورة في تنظيم الشّؤون الإنسانيّة وعلى أنّه لا يمكن الاستغناء عنها فقال: "تُسْبِغ المشورة وعياً أكبر وتُحيل الحَدْسَ إلى يقين. إنّها سراجٌ مُنير في ظلام العالم يُضيء السّبيل ويَهدي إلى الرّشاد. إنّ لكلّ شيء درجةً من الكمال والنّضوج تستمرّ وتَدُوم، ونضوج نعمة الإدراك يظهر جليّاً بواسطة المشورة". وبالمِثْل فإنّ محاولة تحقيق السّلام عن طريق المشورة بالذات كما اقترحها بهاءالله سوف تُساعد على نشر روح خَيِّرة بين أهل العالم لا يمكن لأيّة قوّة مُناهَضةٌ نتائجها النّافذة في نهاية الأمر.

أمّا فيما يختصُّ بالإجراءات المتعلّقة بذلك الاجتماع العالميّ فقد عَرَضَ عبد البهاء، ابن بهاءالله والذي خوّله والِدُه صَلاحيّة بيان تعاليمه، هذه العبارات المتّسمة بنَفاذ البصيرة: "عليهم أن يطرحوا أمر السّلام على بِساط المشورة العامّة، وأن يسعوا بكلّ وسيلة مُتاحة لهم إلى تأسيس اتّحادٍ يجمع دول العالم. وعليهم توقيعُ مُعاهدة مُلزِمة للجميع، ووَضْعُ ميثاق بنوده مُحدّدة، سليمة، وحصينة. وعليهم أن يُعلِنوا ذلك على العالم أجمع وأن يُحرِزوا موافقة الجنس البشريّ بأسره عليه. فهذه المهمّة العُلْيَا النّبيلة ‬- وهي المصدر الحقيقي للرفاهية والسّلام بالنّسبة للعالم كلّه ‬- يجب أن يُنظَرَ إليها جميع سكان الأرض على أنّها مهمّةٌ مقدّسة، كما ينبغي تسخير كلّ قوى البشريّة لضمان هذا الميثاق الأعظم ولاستقراره ودوامه. ويُعيّن هذا الاتّفاقُ الشّاملُ بتمام الوضوح حدودَ كلّ دولة من الدّول وتُخومها، ويَنُصّ نهائيّاً على المبادئ التي تقوم عليها علاقات الحكومات بعضها ببعض. ويُوثّق أيضاً المُعاهدات والواجبات الدّوليّة كلّها. وبالأسلوب ذاته يُحدّد بكلّ دِقّة وصَرامة

حَجْمَ تسلُّح كلّ حكومة، لأنَّ السّماح لأيّة دولة بزيادة جيوشها واستعداداتها للحرب، يثير شكوك الآخرين. والمبدأ الأساسي لهذا الاتّفاق الرّصين يجب أن يكون محدَّداً بحيث إذا أقدمت أيّ حكومة فيما بَعْدُ على انتهاك أي بندٍ من بنوده، هَبَّت في وجهها كلّ حكومات الأرض وفرضت عليها الخضوع التّامَّ، لا بل إنَّ الجنس البشريّ كلّه يجب أن يعقد العزم، بكلّ ما أُوتِي من قوّة، على دَحْر تلك الحكومة. فإذا ما اعْتُمِدَ هذا الدّواء الأعظم لعلاج جسم العالم المريض، فلا بدَّ أن يبرأ من أسقامه ويبقى إلى الأبد سليماً، مطمئناً، مُعافىً".

إنَّ انعقاد هذا الاجتماع العظيم قد طال انتظاره.

إنَّنا بكلّ ما يعتلج في قلوبنا من صادق المشاعر نُهيب بقادة كلّ الدّول أن يغتنموا الفرصة المؤاتية لاتّخاذ خطوات لا رجوع عنها من أجل دعوة هذا الاجتماع العالميّ إلى الانعقاد. وجميع قوى التّاريخ تَحُثّ الجنس البشريّ على تحقيق هذا العمل الذي سوف يُسجِّل على مدى الزّمان انبثاق الفجر الذي طال ترقُّبه، فَجْرِ بلوغ الإنسانيّة نُضْجِها.

فَهَل تَنْهَضُ الأمم المتحدة، بالدّعم المُطْلَق من كلّ أعضائها، وترتفع إلى مستوى هذه الأهداف السّامية لتحقيق هذا الحدث المُتَوِّج لكلّ الأحداث؟

فَلْيُدرِك الرّجال والنّساء والشّباب والأطفال، في كلّ مكان، ما سيُضْفيه هذا الحدث الضّروري على جميع الشّعوب من تَشْريف وإعزاز دائمَيْن. ولْيَرفَعوا أصواتهم بالموافقة والحَفْز على التّنفيذ. ولْيَكُنْ هذا الجيل، فعلاً، أول من يفتتح هذه المرحلة المَجيدة من مراحل تطوّر حياة المجتمع الإنسانيّ على ظهر هذا الكوكب الأرضي.

4

إنَّ التّفاؤل الذي يُخالِجنا مصدره رؤيا تَرتَسِم أمامنا، وَتَتَخطَّى فيما تَحْمِله من بشائر، نهايَة الحروب وقيامَ التّعاون الدّولي عبر الهيئات والوكالات التي تُشكَّل لهذا الغرض. فما السّلام الدّائم بين الدّول إلاّ مرحلةً من المراحل اللاّزمة الوجود، ولكنَّ هذا السّلام ليس بالضرورة، كما يؤكِّد بهاءالله، الهدف

النِّهائيّ في التَّطوّر الاجتماعيّ للإنسان. إنَّها رؤيا تتخطَّى هُدْنَةً أوَّليَّةً تُفْرَض على العالم خَوْفاً من وقوع مَجْزرة نَوَويَّة، وتتخطَّى سلاماً سياسيّاً تَدْخُله الدّول المُتنافِسة والمُتناحِرة وهي مُرْغَمة، وتتخطَّى ترتيباً لتسوية الأمور يكون إذعاناً للأمر الواقع بغْيَةَ إحلال الأمن والتَّعايُش المشترك، وتتخطَّى أيضاً تجارب كثيرةً في مجالات التَّعاوُن الدّوليّ تُمهِّد لها الخطوات السّابقة جميعها وتجعلها مُمكِنةً. إنَّها حقّاً رؤيا تتخطَّى ذلك كلّه لتكشف لنا عن تاج الأهداف جميعاً، ألاَ وهو اتِّحاد شعوب العالم كلّها في أُسرَةٍ عالميّةٍ واحدة.

لقد بات الاختلاف وانعدام الاتِّحاد خطراً داهماً لم يَعُدْ لدول العالم وشعوبه طاقةٌ على تحمُّله، والنَّتائجُ المترتِّبة على ذلك مُريعةٌ لدرجةٍ لا يمكن تصوُّرها، وجليَّةٌ إلى حدٍّ لا تَحتاج معه إلى دليل أو برهان. فقد كتب بهاءالله قبل نيِّف وقرن من الزَّمان قائلاً: "لا يمكن تحقيق إصلاح العالم واستتباب أمنه واطمئنانه إلاّ بعد ترسيخ دعائم الاتِّحاد والاتِّفاق". وفي الملاحظة التي أبداها شوقي أفندي بأنَّ "البشريّة تَئنُّ متلهِّفةً إلى تحقيق الاتِّحاد وإنهاء استشهادها الذي امتدّ عبر العُصور". يَعُود فيُعلِّق قائلاً: "إنَّ اتِّحاد الجنس البشريّ كلّه يُمثِّل الإشارة المُميِّزة للمرحلة التي يقترب منها المجتمع الإنسانيّ الآن. فاتِّحاد العائلة، واتِّحاد القبيلة، واتِّحاد "المدينة – الدّولة"، ثم قيام "الأُمَّة – الدّولة" كانت مُحاولات تَتَابَعَت وكُتِب لها كاملُ النَّجاح. أمَّا اتِّحاد العالم بدوله وشعوبه فهو الهدف الذي تسعى إلى تحقيقه بشريّةٌ مُعذَّبة. لقد انقضى عهد بناء الأُمَم وتشييد الدّول. والفَوْضَى الكامنة في النَّظريّة القائلة بسيادة الدّولة تتَّجه الآن إلى ذِرْوتها، فعالَمٌ يَنْمُو نحو النّضوج، عليه أن يتخلَّى عن التَّشبُّث بهذا الزَّيْف، ويعترف بوحدة العلاقات الإنسانيّة وشُمولِها، ويؤسِّس نهائيّاً الجهاز الذي يمكن أن يُجسِّد على خير وجه هذا المبدأ الأساسي في حياته".

إنَّ كلّ القوى المُعاصرة للتَّطور والتَّغيير تُثْبِت صحّة هذا الرّأي. ويمكن تلَمُّس الأدلَّة والبراهين في العديد من الأمثلة التي سبق أن سُقْناها لتلك العَلامات المُبشِّرة بالسّلام العالميّ في مجال الأحداث الدّوليّة والحركات العالميّة الرّاهنة. فهناك جَحافِل الرّجال والنّساء المُنْتَمين إلى كلّ الثَّقافات والأعراق والدّول في العالم، العامِلين في الوكالات الكثيرة والمُتنوِّعة من وكالات الأمم المتّحدة، وهم يُمثِّلون "جهازَ خِدْمَةٍ مَدَنيّة" يُغطِّي أرجاء هذا الكوكب الأرضي، وإنجازاتهم الرّائعة تَدُلّ على مدى التَّعاوُن الذي يمكن أن

نُحقّقه حتى ولو كانت الظّروف غير مُشجّعة. إنَّ النّفوس تَحِنُّ إلى الاتّحاد، وكأنّ رَبيعَ الرّوح قد أهلَّ، وهذا الحنينُ يُجاهِد ليتجسّد في مؤتمرات دوليّة كثيرة يَلتقي فيها أشخاصٌ من أصحاب الاختصاص في ميادين مختلفة من النّشاطات الإنسانيّة، وفي توجيه النّداءات لصالح المشاريع العالميّة المتعلقة بالطّفولة والشّباب. والحقيقة أنَّ هذا الحنين هو أصل حركات التّوحيد الدّينيّة، هذه الحركات الرّائعة التي صار فيها أتباع الأديان والمذاهب المُتخاصمة تاريخيّاً وكأنّهم مشدودون بعضهم إلى بعض بصورةٍ لا مجال إلى مقاومتها. فإلى جانب الاتّجاه المناقض في مَيْل الدّول إلى شنّ الحروب وتوسيع نطاق نفوذها وسُؤْدَدها، وهو اتّجاهٌ تُقَاومه دون كَلَل وبلا هَوادَة مسيرةُ الإنسان نحو الاتّحاد، تَبْقَى مسيرةُ الاتّحاد هذه من أبرز مَعالم الحياة فوق هذا الكوكب الأرضيّ سَيْطَرَةً وشُمولاً في السّنوات الختاميّة للقرن العشرين.

إنَّ التّجربة التي تُمثّلها الجامعةُ البهائيّة يمكن اعتبارها نَموذجاً لمثل هذا الاتّحاد المُتوسّع. وتَضُمُ الجامعة البهائيّة ثلاثة أو أربعة ملايين تقريباً من البشر يَنْتَمون أصلاً إلى العديد من الدّول والثّقافات والطّبقات والمذاهب، ويشتركون في سلسلة واسعة من النّشاطات مُسْهِمين في سدّ الحاجات الرّوحيّة والاجتماعيّة والاقتصاديّة لشعوب بلادٍ كثيرة. فهي وحدةٌ عُضويّة اجتماعيّة تُمثِّل تنوّع العائلة البشريّة، وتُدير شؤونها ضمن نظام من مبادئ المَشُورة مقبولٍ بصورة عامّة، وتعتزّ بالفَيْض العظيم كلّه من الهداية الإلهيّة في التّاريخ الإنسانيّ دون أيّ تمييز بين دين وآخر. وقيامُ مثل هذه الجامعة دليلٌ آخر مُقْنع على صِدْق رؤيا مُؤسّسها بالنّسبة لوحدة العالم، وبرهانٌ إضافي على أنَّ الإنسانيّة تستطيع العيش ضمن إطار مُجتمع عالميّ واحد لديه الكَفاءَةُ لمواجهة جميع التّحدِّيات في مرحلة النُّضْج والرَّشَاد. فإذا كان للتجربة البهائيّة أي حظٍّ في الإسهام بشَحْذ الآمال المتعلّقة بوحدة الجنس البشريّ، فإنّنا نكون سعداءَ بأن نعرضها نَموذجاً للدّرس والبحث.

وحينَ نتأمّل الأهميّة القُصْوَى للمهمّة التي تتحدّى العالم بأسره، فإنّنا نَحني رؤوسنا بتواضع أمام جَلال البارئ سُبْحَانه وتَعَالَى، الذي خلق بفضل محبّته اللّامُتناهية البَشَرَ جميعاً من طينة واحدة، ومَيّز جوهر الإنسان مُفضّلاً إيّاه على المخلوقات كافة، وشرّفه مُزيّناً إيّاه بالعَقْل، والحِكْمَة، والعِزّة، والخُلود، وأسبغ عليه "المِيزة الفريدة والموهبة العظيمة لِيَبْلُغَ محبّة الخالق

ومَعرِفَتَه"، هذه الموهبة التي "يجب أن تُعَدَّ بمثابة القوّة الخلّاقة والغَرَض الأصيل لوجود الخليقة".

نحن نؤمن إيماناً راسخاً بأنَّ البشر جميعاً خُلِقوا لكي "يَحْمِلوا حضارةً دائمةَ التَّقَدُّم" وبأنَّه "ليس من شِيَم الإنسان أن يسلك مسلك وحوش الغاب"، وبأنَّ الفضائل التي تَليق بكرامة الإنسان هي الأمانةُ، والتَّسامُحُ، والرَّحمةُ، والرَّأفةُ، والألْفةُ مع البشر أجمعين. ونَعود فنؤكِّد إيماننا بأن "القُدُرات الكامنة في مقام الإنسان، وسموّ ما قُدِّر له على هذه الأرض، وما فُطِرَ عليه من نفيس الجَوْهَر، لسوف تَظْهَر جميعها في هذا اليوم الذي وَعَدَ به الرَّحمن". وهذه الاعتبارات هي التي تُحرِّك فينا مشاعر إيمانٍ ثابتٍ لا يتزعزع بأنَّ الاتّحاد والسّلام هُمَا الهَدَفُ الذي يمكن تحقيقه ويسعى نحوه بَنو البشر.

ففي هذه اللحظة التي نَخُطّ فيها هذه الكلمات تَتَرامى إلينا أصوات البهائيّين المليئةُ بالآمال رغم ما لا يزال يتعرَّض له هؤلاء من اضطهادٍ في مَهْد دينهم. فالمَثَل الذي يضربه هؤلاء للثَّبات المُفْعَم بالأمل يجعلهم شهوداً على صحَّة الاعتقاد بأنَّ قُرْبَ تحقيق حُلْمِ السّلام، الذي راوَدَ البشريةَ لمُدَّة طويلة من الزَّمان، أصبح اليوم مشمولاً بعناية الله سُلْطَةً ونفوذاً، وذلك بفضل ما لرسالة بهاءالله من أثرٍ خلّاق يبعث على التَّغيير. وهكذا نَنْقُل إليكم هُنَا ليس فقط رؤيا تُجسِّدها الكلمات، بل نَستحضر أيضاً ما لِفِعل الإيمان والتَّضحية من نفوذ وقوّة. كما نَنْقُل إليكم ما يُحِسّ به إخوانُنا في الدّين في كلّ مكان من مشاعر الرّجاء تلهُّفاً لقيام الاتّحاد والسّلام. وها نحن ننضمّ إلى كلّ ضحايا العدوان، وكلّ الذين يحِنّون إلى زوال التَّطاحُن والصّراع، وكلّ الذين يُسْهِم إخلاصُهم لمبادئ السّلام والنّظام العالميّ في تعزيز تلك الأهداف المُشرِّفة التي من أجلها بُعِثَت الإنسانيّة إلى الوجود فضلاً من لَدُن الخالق الرَّؤوف الوَدُود.

إنَّ رغبتنا المُخْلِصة في أن ننقل إليكم ما يُساورنا من فَوْرَة الأمل وعُمْق الثِّقة، تَحْدونا إلى الاستشهاد بهذا الوَعْد الأكيد لبهاءالله: "لسوف تَزُول هذه النّزاعات العديمة الجَدْوَى، وتَنْقَضِي هذه الحروب المُدمِّرة، فالسّلام العظيم لا بُدَّ أنْ يَأْتي".

بَيْتُ العَدْلِ الأعْظَم

45

The Promise of World Peace

Chinese

1985年10月

致全世界人民：

　　大和平为世世代代的善良百姓所向往，为从古至今的圣贤和诗人所预言，为各个时代的经书圣典所许诺，如今，终于有望为各国人民实现了！有史以来第一次，人类所有的人能够从同一个客观角度观看到地球及居住其上的各式各样的人群。世界和平不仅是可能的，更是不可避免的。它是这个星球演进的下一个阶段，用一位伟大思想家的话来说，就是"人类的全球化"。

　　是在人类顽冥不化地死抱住陈规陋习不放，以致造成不可想象的灾难之后再亡羊补牢呢？还是现在就痛下决心，通过协商共议实现和平？这是地球上全体人类必须做出的抉择。当前，各国所面临的棘手问题已汇聚成整个世界共同关注的焦点，值此紧要关头，若不遏止住冲突与动乱的浪潮，将是违背良知和不负责任的。

　　种种好的迹象显示，人类正以越来越坚定有力的步伐向世界体制迈进。这个进程由20世纪初国际联盟的创建开始，继之以基础更为广泛的联合国组织的成立；第二次世界大战以后，世界大多数国家纷纷获得独立，表明国家创立的过程已告完成，新兴的国家已能与历史悠久的国家一起商讨和解决共同关心的事务；许多以往相互隔离与敌对的人民和团体，如今却在科学、教育、法律、经济和文化等领域展开越来越多的国际性合作；近几十年来成立的国际人道主义组织如雨后春笋，数目空前；妇女及青年的反战运动日渐扩大；普通民众建立更广泛的联系网络，通过个人交流相互了解。

　　在这得天独厚的20世纪里，科学技术突飞猛进，预示着这星球将要出现一个社会演进的高潮，同时也为人类的实际问题指出了解决方法。诚然，科技进步为这个日趋融合世界错综复杂生活的管理提供了非常有效的手段。然而，障碍依旧存在。怀疑、误解、偏见、猜忌以及自私自利等观念仍然困扰着各国、各民族之间的关系。

值此良机，作为巴哈伊信仰的教务管理人，精神和道义上的深切责任感驱使我们恳请您留意并分享巴哈伊信仰创始人巴哈欧拉在一个多世纪前首次向人类统治者们表达的深刻洞见。

巴哈欧拉写道："绝望之风从四面八人方吹来，分裂和折磨人类的争斗与日俱增。骚动与混乱已迫在眉睫，而现行的制度却显得可悲的无能。"这段带有预言性的判断已经从人类的共同经历中得到了充分的证实。现行的制度显然乏善可陈，由主权国家组成的联合国无法驱除战争的幽灵，无法阻止国际经济秩序崩溃的危机，无法遏制无政府主义与恐怖主义的蔓延，也无法解救蒙受这些痛苦和灾难折磨的千百万生灵。的确，侵略与冲突已经成为我们的社会、经济和宗教系统的显著特征，致使许多人不得不认为，如此行径出自人类与生俱来的天性，因而无法根除。

随着这种看法的扎根立足，人类事务中出现了令人气馁的矛盾现象：一方面，所有国家的人民都宣称，为了结束每日面临的折磨人心的忧惧，他们不仅准备好了，更渴望着和平的到来。而另一方面，人们却不加思辨地附和这种论调，认为人类的自私与侵略本性是无可救药的，因此不可能建立一个既和平又进步，既生动又和谐，既能让个人自由发挥创造性和主动性，又有合作与互惠作基础的社会体制。

和平的需要越来越迫切，然而这种根本矛盾却妨碍了它的实现，这就要求我们对种种由来已久的流行观念所赖以根据的各种假设作重新的检讨。只要冷静和细致地审视即可发现，如此行径绝不是真正人性的反映，而只是对人类精神的歪曲。确信这一点，就能够在全社会发动合乎人性的、能促进和睦与合作而非战争与冲突的建设力量。

这样做不是否定人类的过去，而是更好地理解过去。巴哈伊信仰认为，当前世界在人类事务上所出现的混乱和灾难局面，只是一个有机演进进程的必经阶段，而这一进程最终将不可抗拒地引领全人类团结在同一个社会秩序下，该世界秩序覆盖我们整个星球。作为一个独特的有机体，人类的演进如同其个体成员的成长那样，已历经了婴儿和童年期，目前正处于躁动不安的青春期，并逐渐步入那期盼已久的成年期。

在人类历史的漫长进程中，偏见、战争和剥削都是未成熟阶段的表现；如今人类正在经受无可规避的混乱，它预示着人类集体成熟期的来临。坦率承认这些事实非但不应成为失望的理由，反而是着手缔造世界和平的先决条件。这项千秋大业可以实现，所需的建设力量确实具备，统一的社会结构也一定能建立，这，就是我们恳请您来共同探讨的主题。

无论眼下还会遭受什么苦难和动乱，不管当前的形势怎样黑暗，巴哈伊社团都坚信，人类有能力和勇气迎接这项最重大的考验并一定能取得最终的胜利。人类正前所未有地被急速推入社会的剧变之中，这些剧变绝非是文明末日到来的信号，相反，它们有助于释放"人的内在潜能"，有助于展现"他在尘世的命运和他实在的内在卓越"。

一

人类之所以有别于所有其他生物，是因为人类拥有通常所谓的"人的精神"的禀赋，心智乃其基本品质。这些禀赋使人类创造出文明，成就了物质繁荣。然而，单靠这些成就是不能满足人类精神需要的。精神的神秘本性促使人类倾心于那超凡的境界，向往那不可见的领域，仰慕那终极的实在——那不可知精髓之精髓，即所谓的"上帝"。由历史上依次出现的灵性导师所带给人类的各个宗教，就是人类与那终极实在之间联系的基本纽带，它们激发并完善了人类取得精神成就和社会进步的能力。

凡要认真妥善管理人类事务，实现世界和平，便不可忽视宗教。人类对宗教的认识和实践，构成了人类历史的主干。一位杰出的历史学家称宗教是"人性的一种天赋能力"。对这种天赋能力的滥用加剧了社会混乱和个人之间的冲突，这是无可否认的事实。然而，任何公正的观察者都不能漠视宗教对人类文明的生动表达所起到的主导影响。不仅如此，宗教对社会秩序也是不可或缺的，这已由宗教对法律和道德的直接影响一再得到证明。

巴哈欧拉将宗教描述为一种社会力量，他说："宗教是建立世界秩序和谋求全人类和平幸福的最佳手段。"在谈到宗教的衰落和腐败时他写道："一旦宗教之灯暗淡，混乱与迷惑便继之而来；公平、正义、安宁与和平之光就不再照耀。"巴哈伊著作在谈到这类种种后果时指出："在这种情况下，人性之扭曲，行为之堕落，社会机体之腐败与溃散，将会无以复加。人格被贬低，信心受动摇，纪律神经松弛，良心之声哑然，体面与廉耻被隐蔽，责任、团结、互惠与忠诚的概念被曲解，祥和、欢乐与希望的美好感觉日渐消失。"

因此，要是可怕的冲突真的弄到如此地步，那么人类就必须躬身自问，检讨自己有何过失，听从了哪些诱惑之声，以便找出借宗教之名造成的误解和混乱。那些盲目并自私地坚持自己所谓正统教义的人，那些将其对上帝先知圣言的矛盾诠释强加于信徒的人，应当对这混乱局面承担很大的责任——这混乱局面被人为设立在信仰与理智、科学与宗教之间的障碍所加剧。其实，只要不带偏见地对各伟大宗教创始人的真实言辞和他们从事其使命时所处的社会环境稍加考察，就会发现那些扰乱宗教生活和所有人类事务的争论与偏见都是毫无根据的。

"你愿人怎样待你，你就该怎样待人。"各伟大宗教以不同形式反复强调的这条道德观，从两个具体方面给上述说法提供了支撑：第一，它概括出贯穿这些宗教——无论它们起源于何时何地——的一种道德态度，一种和平动机；第二，它体现出团结是它们的一种基本美德，而这一美德已被那些孤立和片面看待历史的人所漠视。人类幼年期所出现的精神导师们的真正使命是推动文明进程。如果人类认识到这一点，那么毫无疑问，人类就会从这些导师相继教诲的累积影响中获得无可估量的更大裨益。不幸的是，人类没有这么做。

许多地方所发生的宗教狂热的复活，只不过是一种回光返照的表现。随之而来的暴力与破坏现象，恰恰证明了它们所代表之宗教精神的沦丧。当前爆发的宗教狂热已经到了这样一种地步，那就是在每一个事例中，它都不仅损害了有利于团结的价值观，还逐渐削弱了其所支持的宗教所取得的独特道德成就，这的确是它最奇怪也是最可悲的特征之一。

无论在人类历史上宗教曾是何其重要的力量，也不管当前好战的宗教狂热是多么的令人触目惊心，几十年来，越来越多的人认为，宗教与宗教组织对于当今世界所关心的大事来说是无关痛痒的。于是，他们要么转而追求物质满足与享乐，要么摇身变成形形色色人为意识形态的追随者，以为由此就能将社会从罪恶的困扰中拯救出来。人为的意识形态何其之多，可遗憾的是，它们非但不倡导人类一家的理念，不促进人民之间的和睦，反而试图神化国家，使全人类屈从于一个国家、一个种族或一个阶级，压制一切讨论和思想交流，弃千百万忍饥挨饿的人于不顾，任由市场经济机制主宰其命运，而这种市场经济机制显然只会让少数人过上我们的前辈做梦也想不到的富裕生活，同时却加剧大多数人的困境。

在我们这个时代里，那些精通世故者所捏造出来的种种替代信仰留下了何等可悲的记录！从全体民众被教导去顶礼膜拜这些信仰所造成的精神幻灭中，我们能够看出历史已对它们的价值作了不可翻案的判决。经过数十年那些靠这些教条攫取社会事务大权的人不断变本加厉地肆意妄为，这些教条产生出了各种社会与经济的弊病，并在20世纪末期侵害着世界每一个角落。隐藏在这些外在病患之下的则是人类心灵的创伤，这些创伤反映在各国人

民对世事的漠不关心，以及亿万贫穷且痛苦心灵的美好愿望的破灭。

现在，是要那些物质主义教条的鼓吹者，无论来自东方还是西方，无论是资本主义者还是社会主义者，交代清楚他们是如何履行维护道德责任的时候了。这些思想意识所许诺的"新世界"在哪里？他们自称热爱的国际和平在哪里？由某个种族、某个国家或某个阶级的势力扩张而产生之文化新领域的突破成就又在哪里？为什么当今人类事务决断者手中掌握的物质财富，已达到连过去法老王、凯撒大帝乃至19世

纪帝国主义权贵们都难以想象的程度，而世界上绝大多数人却陷入越来越饥饿与不幸的状况之中呢？

值得一提的是，我们发现，对物质追求的吹捧，乃是"人类是无可救药般自私"这种错误观念得以出现的根源。物质追求同时也是所有这类思想意识的肇因和共同特征。如今，必须清理干净这片土地，方能在其上建设一个适合我们后代生存的新世界。

经验证明，物质主义的理想并未满足人类的需求，这一事实要求我们坦率承认，我们必须作出新的努力来找出解决这个星球上各种困扰我们的问题的办法。遍布社会的难以容忍的情状，证明了上述种种理想的破灭，而这种局面在各方面都只会助长而非削弱人们巩固各自的利益与势力。显然，我们亟需作出共同的努力来加以纠正。这首先是一个态度的问题。人类是一意孤行地继续死抱着过时的观念和行不通的假设不放呢？还是其领导者们撇开意识形态，下定决心走到一起，共同探讨与磋商正确的解决办法呢？

关心人类未来的人不妨思量这个建言："如果那些长期信奉的理想和历史悠久的制度，或者某些社会假定和宗教常规，已不再能促进人类大众的福利，不再能适应不断演进之人类的需要，那就将它们清除并扔进过时与遗忘教义的故纸堆里。在一个受'不变则衰、不进则退'永恒法则支配的世界里，人类所设立的每一项制度都必然会逐渐失效，为何唯独上述这些可以例外呢？法律规范、政治和经济理论只是用作保障人类整体利益的，因此绝不可为了维持某项法律或教条的完整而使人类受罪。"

二

禁止核武器，禁止使用毒气或进行细菌战，并不能消除战争的根源。这些实际的措施无疑是和平进程的要素，但无论它们是多么显而易见的重要，都只能治标不治本，无法产生持久的作用。人类的才智足以发明其他形式的武器，还会利用食品、原料、经济、工业力量、思想意识及恐怖主义来相互摧残，以谋求霸权和统治地位。现时人类事务的极度紊乱，也不能靠化解国家之间的某些具体冲突和歧见来解决。有鉴于此，我们无疑急需一个真正的世界性组织。

当然，各国领导人不是没有认识到这一问题的世界性，这在他们每天所面临的越来越多的问题中已很显明。许多热心和开明的团体以及联合国各机构都进行了大量研究，提供了许多建议，以试图消除世人对这一问题的严峻性质的无知。但是，意志的消沉，才是需要认真加以检讨，这还是须下决心予以解决的要害之所在。如上所述，这种意志的消沉源自一种根深蒂固的信念，即人类互相争斗是不可避免的。这种信念使得人们不愿考虑让本国的利益服从于一个世界性体制的需要，也不愿勇敢地正视建立一个世界统权所包含的深远意义。这也说明为什么那些受压制的无知民众无法表达他们的渴望，即能使他们与所有人共同生活在和平、协调与繁荣气氛的新世界秩序中。

尤其自第二次世界大战以来，迈向世界体制的尝试步骤带来了希望的迹象。一些国家集团相互间建立了各种形式的关系，以便在共同利益事项上进行合作，这一有增无减的趋势表明，各国最终将克服意志上的消沉。东南亚国家联盟、加勒比海共同体和共同市场、中美洲共同市场、经济互助委员会、欧洲共同体、阿拉伯国家联盟、非洲统一组织、美洲国家组织以及南太平洋论坛，所有这些组织所作的共同努力都是在为世界秩序铺平道路。

另一个有希望的迹象是，这个星球上一些最为棘手的问题正越来越为人们所重视。尽管联合国有着明显的缺点，但是它所通过的四十多个宣言和公约——哪怕各国政府并未热心投入——还是给普通大众带来了一种新生感。《世界人权宣言》、《防止和惩治灭绝种族罪行公约》，以及杜绝基于种族、性别或宗教信仰的各种形式歧视的措施；维护儿童权益；反对酷刑；消除饥饿和营养不良；使用先进科技来增进和平与人类的福祉；等等。所有这些举措，若能加以大胆执行和扩展，战争的幽灵不再支配国际关系的那一天就会提早到来。这些宣言和公约所涉及的事项之重要性已无需强调。可是，有几个议题因直接关系到世界和平的建立，故仍值得一提。

　　种族主义是最具危害和最顽固的罪恶之一，实为和平的一大障碍。种族主义的行径极大地摧残人类的尊严，因而绝不能以任何借口加以纵容。种族主义使人民深受其害，妨碍了他们发挥无限的潜能，腐化了奉行它的人们，阻挠了人类的进步。若要解决这个问题，人类一家的理念就必须在适当的法律措施下得到全世界的拥护。

　　贫富悬殊是造成深重苦难的根源之一。它使人类社会处于不稳定的状态，几乎濒临战争的边缘。几乎没有一个社会能有效地消除这种状况。解决这个社会问题，需要综合使用精神的、道德的和实际的方法。对这个问题作新的探讨是有必要的。在探讨时要听取各有关领域专家的意见，要避免出现经济学和意识形态上的争执，还要让受这些急需作出的决策直接影响的人们参与。与这个问题息息相关的，不仅是消除极端贫富，还要认识到一些精神原则，这种认识可以培养一样新的普世态度。而养成这种态度，这本身就是解决这个问题的一个重要步骤。

　　狂热、偏激的民族主义，与理智和正当的爱国主义毫无相同之处，它应该让位于一种更宽广的忠诚和对人类整体的博爱。巴哈欧拉说："地球乃一国，人类皆其民。"科学的发展使地球变得越来越小，国与国之间越来越相互依赖，其结果必然导致"世界公民"的概念。爱全人类并不排斥爱自己的国家。在一个世界性的社会中，局部的利益只有通过全局利益的提高才能得到最好的满足。如今在各个领域开展的国际对话活动，在不同民族之间促生了友爱和团结的意识，然而，这类活动仍需极大增多。

　　在整个人类历史上，宗教的纷争导致了无数的战争与冲突，是阻扰人类进步的主要因素，招致越来越多的信仰者及无信仰者的憎恶。各宗教的追随者必须积极面对这些宗教争端所引起的根本问题，并求得明确的解答。如何从理论和实际行动上解决他们之间的分歧呢？各宗教的领袖所面临的挑战是，怀着同情心和求真欲去思量人类的困境。他们应在万能的主面前谦恭地扪心自问：能不能以互相宽容的伟大精神来消除他们在神学上的分歧，从而为促进人类的理解与和平携手努力？

　　女性的解放和男女充分平等的实现，是实现和平的最重要的先决条件之一，尽管承认这一点的人并不多。否认这种平等便是对世界半数人口的不公平，并助长男性的不良态度和习惯，而这些会由家庭延伸到工作场所和政治生活之中，并最终会影响到国际关系。在道德、实践和生理上都找不到任何根据来证明否定男女平等的合理性。只有女性充分与平等地参与人类各方面的努力，才能够营造出有利于建立世界和平的道德与心理环境。

　　教育普及事业虽然已经得到各国和各宗教热心人士的支持，但是，仍然需要各国政府的鼎力扶助。无知确实是民族衰落和偏见产生的主要原因，一个国家若要成功，就必须实施全民教育。资源的缺乏使许多国家满足这一需求的能力受到限制，这就必然要作出轻重缓急次序的适当安排。有关决策机构最好优先考虑妇女和女童的教育，因为正是通过受教育的母亲，知识的利益才能最有效和最迅速地传遍整个社会。为了符合时代的要求，还应该考虑将世界公民的概念纳入儿童的规范教育之中。

　　各国各族人民之间缺乏基本的交往与沟通，这严重地削弱了世界和平的努力。采用一种辅助性的国际语言，对解决这个问题会大有帮助，需要引起人们最迫切的关注。

　　所有这些问题中，有两点需要强调。第一，消除战争不单是一个签署条约和协议的问题，它还是一项复杂的任务，需要作出新的程度的努力来解决那些习惯上被认为与追求和平无直接关联的问题。仅仅立足于政治协议的共同安全意念只不过是一种妄想。第二，处理和平问题所面对的首要挑战是，将这一问题提高到原则的高度，而不能只采取实用主义的态度。这是因为，从本质上来说，和平的信念发自一种基于精神或道德立场的心态，要找到长治久安的解决办法，首先就必须培养出这种心态。

　　精神原则，或所谓的价值观，是能够为任何社会问题提供解答的。一般来说，任何善意的团体都可以制定出解决自身问题的办法。但是，仅有善意和实用知识往往是不够的。精神原则的基本价值在于，它不仅提供了符合人的真正本性的观点，还引发出相应的态度、动力、意愿和抱负，从而促进人们去发现并执行各种实际措施。各政府领导人和所有当权者若能先确定有关的精神原则，然后依照这些原则行事，解决问题的努力就会富有成效。

三

需要解决的主要问题是，如何能将当今这样一个冲突不绝的世界，改变成一个以协调与合作为主导的世界。

世界秩序只能建立在人类一体这个不可动摇的观念之上，这是一个得到科学证实的精神真理。尽管人类的生活千差百异、无穷多样，但人类学、生理学和心理学都只承认一个人种。认同这个真理就必须抛弃形形色色的偏见，包括种族的、阶级的、肤色的、信仰的、国家的、性别的和物质文明程度上的，以及其他所有能使人自以为高人一等的偏见。

接受人类一体的观念，这是将世界改组成同一个国家——全人类的共同家园——并进行管理的先决条件。这个精神原则的举世公认，对成功缔造世界和平是至关重要的。因此，这项原则要在全世界加以倡导，在各学校里讲授，要得到所有国家坚定不移的拥护，以便为这一原则所必然包含的社会结构的系统改革作准备。

巴哈伊信仰认为，人类一体"至少需要重建整个文明世界并实现非军事化，使其在政治机构、精神抱负、贸易金融、语言文字等所有重要方面都得以有机的统一，而又不损害各组成部分的多姿多彩的民族特性。"

巴哈伊信仰的圣护守基·阿芬第在1931年对这条中心原则的含义作了详细的阐述："它（人类一体化原则）的目的绝不是要破坏现有的社会基础，而是拓宽这个基础，改造其体制，以满足一个不断变化世界的需求。它不抵触合法的效忠精神，也不削弱必要的忠诚心。它的目的既不在于压制人们心中正常而理智的爱国热情，也不在于废除民族自治体制——该体制对避免过度中央集权之恶果极其必要。它既不忽视也不会企图抑制种族特性、风俗习惯、历史传统以及语言和思想等诸方面的差异，而这些差异正是造成国家和民族千姿百态、精彩纷呈的因素所在。它要求一种更为宽广的忠诚心，一种比以往任何激励人类进步的抱负更为博大的雄心壮志。它强调国家的意志和利益必须服从于一体化世界的迫切需要。它一方面拒绝过度的中央集权，另一方面也反对所有强求一律的企图。它的口号是'多元一体'。"

实现这些目标需要分几个阶段来调整国家的政治态度。由于缺乏明确的法律以及普世认同并可执行的准则来制约国家间的关系，各国的政治态度已近乎混乱。国际联盟和联合国，加上许多由它们建立的组织和订立的协议，确实有助于消减某些国际冲突的副作用，然而它们本身也表明了它们无法防止战争。事实上，自第二次世界大战结束以来，已经爆发了大量的战争，好些仍在激烈进行中。

这个问题的主要方面在19世纪就已经显露出来了，那时巴哈欧拉首次发出了建立世界和平的倡议。他在向世界各统治者所作的声明中提出了共同安全的原则。守基·阿芬第对他的意旨评述道："这些一言九鼎的话语，除了指明削减不受约束的国家主权，以便为将来所有国家结成世界联邦作好必要的铺垫，还能意味着什么呢？某种形式的世界联邦一定要逐步建立起来。为此，世界各国必须自愿放弃所有战争要求，放弃某些征税权，放弃所有军备权，唯各国用以维护各自内部秩序者除外。这个联邦在其管辖范围内必须设有一个全球执行机构，足以对联邦内任何拒不服从的成员国施加最高的和不可抗拒的权威；这个联邦有一个世界议会，其议员由各国人民在各自的国家内选举产生，并经各自国家的政府批准；它还有一个最高法院，其判决即使在当事双方不情愿将其案件提交它时也具有约束力。

"在这个世界社区里，所有的经济堡垒将被永久地拆除，资本和劳力相互依赖的原则必然得到举世公认；狂热的宗教喧嚣和争端会永远停止；种族仇恨之火终会熄灭；由世界联邦的代表们经过深思熟虑制定出的单一的世界法典，将会授权由各成员国共同组建的联合军队实行迅即的强行干预，以此作为它的制裁手段；变化无常而好战的民族主义狂热将转化为始终不渝的世界公民的意识——这就是巴哈欧拉用粗略的线条所勾勒出的世界体制的蓝图，这就是人类逐步走向成熟的最合理的结果。"

巴哈欧拉在谈到实现这些远大方针时指出："有朝一日，人们一定会普遍认识到召开一个全球综合大会的迫切必要性。世界各国的统治者和国王都必须到会，参加各项审议，研究奠定世界和平基础的方法与手段。"

勇气、决心、纯正的动机、民族间无私的友爱，所有这些为实现这一重大和平步骤所必需的精神与道德品质，都要集中体现在行动的意志上。正是为了激发出这必要的意志力，人的精神实在，即思维，必须得到认真严肃的考虑。要了解这潜在实在的关联意义，就意味着还要认识到，社会迫切需要通过坦率、冷静和诚挚的磋商来体现出它的独特价值，并依磋商的结果去行动。巴哈欧拉曾一再强调磋商对人类事务管理的效用和必要性。他说："磋商有助于明达事理，化推测为确知。在黑暗的世界里，磋商是一盏指路明灯，因为那里的一切事物都有待完善和成熟。天赋理解力通过磋商才能成熟起来。"正是通过他建议的磋商方式而作的和平努力，能够激发出世界民众的精神力量，从而众志成城，排除万难，赢得最终的胜利。

关于这个全球大会的议项，巴哈欧拉之子、他的教义的权威诠释人阿博都-巴哈提出以下的深刻见解："他们必须把和平的大业当作大会商议的主题，尽一切方式和力量建立起世界联邦。他们必须订立一项有约束力的条约并达成盟约，其条款必须是合理、明确和不得违犯的。他们必须向全世界公布这盟约，并求得全人类的认可。地球上所有的居民都要将这项至高无上的伟业——世界和平与福祉的真正泉源——看作是极其神圣的。必须动员人类的一切力量来保证这个伟大盟约的稳定和持久。在这个包罗万象的盟约里，每个国家的疆域和边界必须清楚划定，政府间关系的原则必须明文确立，所有国际协定和义务必须得到确认。同样，应该严格限制各国军事力量的规模，因为一旦某个国家扩军备战，势必引起其他国家的疑虑。这个庄严盟约的基本原则如此严明不误，以致一旦某个政府违背了其中任何一项条款，全球所有其他政府必将群起而伐之。更有甚者，全人类还应决心用一切可以动用的力量去摧毁那个政府。只要将这个至灵疗法用于这个百病缠身的世界，就定能使它康复并永保太平。"

这宏伟的大会早该举行了！

我们满怀热忱地吁请所有国家的领导人，把握良机，毅然决然地召开这个全球大会。所有的历史力量都驱使着人类采取这一行动，不论在什么时候召开，它都标志人类期待已久的成熟期的来临。

得到各成员国完全拥护的联合国，难道不应该为这样一个再好不过的大会所要实现的崇高目标喝彩吗？

要让世界各地的男女老少都认识到这个为了全人类的势在必行之举的永恒价值，并高歌赞美。是啊，就让这一代人来掀开地球上社会生活演进的这辉煌的一页吧！

四

我们的乐观出自一种远非局限于停止战争和创立国际合作组织的远见。国家之间实现永久和平虽然是绝对必要的步骤，但巴哈欧拉指出，那并不是人类社会发展的最终目标。世界会因恐惧核浩劫而被迫实行初步休战，互相猜疑的敌对国之间会勉强达成政治和平，人们为安全共处起见也会作出实用的安排，甚至通过上述步骤试行各种合作，但是，超越这一切的那个最高目标，却是普天之下，结成一家。

地球上的国家和民族再也经受不起分裂失和了，它的后果之可怕不堪设想，之明显也无需证明。巴哈欧拉早在一个多世纪前就写道："唯有且直到牢固地建立团结，人类才有望享得福祉、和平与安全。"在观察到"人类呻吟着，在渴望和睦与团结，渴望结束世世代代的苦难"时，守基·阿芬第说："全人类的团结统一是人类社会正在迈向的新阶段的标志。人类相继尝试并完全确立了家庭、部落、城邦和国家形式的结合。饱受磨难的人类正奋力以求的乃是世界大同。国家的创建已达尾声。主权国家内在的混乱正趋于白热化。一个走向成熟的世界必须放弃对国家主权的迷恋，认清人类关系的同一性和整体性，一劳永逸地建立起能够最完美体现这一人类生活基本原理的制度。"

当代所有的变革力量都证明了这个观点的正确性。前面所列举的现时国际运动和发展中许多有利于世界和平的迹象也同样能证明这一点。在联合国各机构与部门工作的男女大军，实际上来自地球上各种不同的文化、种族和国家，体现出一种"世界公仆"的形象。他们所取得的令人钦佩的成就表明，即使是在令人气馁的情况下，也能做到一定程度的合作。对团结统一的渴望，如灵性的春天，正通过吸聚各领域和各行业人们的无数国际会议竭力寻求表达。它也促使人们呼吁为儿童和青少年开展国际合作计划。事实上，它也是促使历史上曾彼此敌视的各宗教和派别无法抗拒地相互谅解与合作的真正驱动力。未曾间断的世界团结和统一运动，连同对立的战争与自我扩张的趋向，构成了20世纪末期这个星球上人类生活的一个突出和普遍的特征。

巴哈伊社团的经验可被视为这不断扩大之团结的典范。这个团体是由形形色色具有不同民族、文化、阶层和信仰背景的数百万人组成的。它在众多的国家和地区从事满足人们精神、社会和经济需要的各种各样的活动。它是同一个的社会有机体，是人类那多姿多彩大家庭的缩影，按普遍接受的磋商原则管理和运作，一视同仁地珍视人类历史上所有伟大神圣的教谕。它的存在令人信服地证明，它的创立者对大同世界的远见是切实可行和能够实现的；它的存在还表明，人类可以生活在同一个全球社会中，能够经受成熟过程中的种种考验。如果巴哈伊社团的经验能有助于增强对人类团结统一的信心，我们乐于将它呈献出来作为研究的范例。

思及整个世界目前所面临任务的极度重要性，我们谦卑地俯首在神圣造物主的尊前。造物主以无限的爱，用同一原料创生了普世万民，提升了人类珍宝般的实在，赋予人类才华、智慧、高贵和永生，授予人类"认识和敬爱祂的独一无二的特性与能力"，这种能力"必须被视为整个创造界的驱动力和首要目的"。

　　我们坚信，人之所以被创造是为了"推动不断演进的文明"的；坚信"人绝不可形同禽兽"；坚信与人的尊严相称的美德是待人以诚信、克制、仁慈、同情和友爱。我们在此重申以下的信念："人的内在潜能，他在尘世间命运的全部意义，他卓越的天赋，在这个上帝承诺的日子里，必然会尽数显现。"正是出于这些信念，我们毫不动摇地相信，人类正奋力以求的团结与和平，是能够实现的。

　　此时此刻，仍有巴哈伊信徒在其信仰诞生地遭受着迫害，可尽管如此，他们的企盼之声依然不绝于耳。通过笃信的榜样他们证实，凭着巴哈欧拉的启示所具有的变革力量，即将实现的和平夙愿现在已具备了神授的权能。因此，我们所传达给您的不光是用语言描述的理想；我们要激发信念和牺牲的行动力量，我们要传达我们在世界各地所有教友对和平与团结的迫切请求。我们要与所有侵略的受害者，所有渴望结束冲突与争斗的人们，以及所有献身于和平与世界秩序的人们携起手来，为实现慈悲的造物主赋予人类的崇高目标而共同奋斗。

　　我们最诚挚地希望与您分享我们炽热的希望和强烈的信心，谨此奉上巴哈欧拉坚定的承诺："这些无益的冲突，这些毁灭性的战争，都将成为过去，大和平必将到来！"

世界正义院

The Promise of World Peace

French

Octobre 1985

Aux peuples du monde :

La Grande Paix à laquelle ont aspiré profondément les gens de bonne volonté au fil des siècles, dont prophètes et poètes nous offrent la vision depuis d'innombrables générations et dont les livres saints de l'humanité ont toujours renfermé la promesse, se profile enfin à l'horizon mondial. Il est maintenant possible à chacun, pour la première fois dans l'histoire, de voir toute la planète et les innombrables peuples qui l'habitent, dans une perspective globale. La paix mondiale est non seulement possible mais inévitable. C'est la prochaine étape de l'évolution de cette planète, ce qu'un grand penseur [Teilhard de Chardin] a appelé « la planétisation de l'humanité ».

Tous les habitants de la terre doivent décider s'ils parviendront à cette paix en empruntant un chemin pavé d'horreurs inconcevables nées de l'attachement tenace de l'humanité envers d'anciens modèles de comportement ou bien, en optant pour la paix dans une affirmation de volonté conjointe. En ce moment critique, alors que les problèmes très difficiles, affligeant tous les pays, sont devenus la préoccupation commune pour le sort de l'humanité entière, il serait inconsciemment irresponsable de ne point prendre les mesures requises pour enrayer la montée des nombreux conflits et troubles.

Certains signes favorables pointent dans cette direction : la croissance régulière de mesures d'organisation à l'échelle mondiale, commencée par la création de la Société des Nations au début du siècle, et poursuivie avec l'organisation des Nations Unies, qui réunit un nombre plus vaste de pays ; l'accession à l'indépendance, depuis la seconde guerre mondiale, de la plupart des pays de la terre, ce qui a marqué la fin du processus d'édification des nations, et la collaboration de ces nouvelles nations avec les pays plus anciens sur les questions d'intérêt mutuel ; la coopération plus étroite qui s'en est suivie entre des peuples et des groupes auparavant isolés et ennemis, dans le cadre de projets internationaux portant sur les sciences, l'éducation, le droit, l'économie et la culture ; la constitution, depuis quelques dizaines d'années, d'un nombre sans précédent d'organisations humanitaires internationales ; la dissémination de mouvements composés de femmes et de jeunes réclamant la fin des conflits armés et la multiplication spontanée de réseaux de plus en plus grands d'individus tentant de promouvoir la compréhension par des échanges personnels.

Les progrès scientifiques et technologiques marquant ce siècle singulièrement favorisé présagent une avance importante de l'évolution sociale de la planète et indiquent les moyens pour résoudre les problèmes de l'humanité dans leur aspect pratique. Ils fournissent effectivement les moyens d'organiser la vie complexe d'un monde uni. Des barrières n'en persistent pas moins. Les rapports entre les nations et les peuples sont troublés par des doutes, des idées fausses, des préjugés, des soupçons et la recherche d'intérêts égoïstes.

Un sens profond du devoir spirituel et moral nous pousse en ce moment opportun à partager avec vous les pensées intuitives et profondes qui furent déjà communiquées aux gouvernants mondiaux voici plus d'un siècle par Bahá'u'lláh, fondateur de la foi bahá'íe, dont nous sommes les dépositaires et les administrateurs.

Bahá'u'lláh s'exprima en ces termes : « Les vents du désespoir soufflent, hélas, de toutes les directions et les querelles qui divisent et affligent l'humanité s'enveniment chaque jour. Des signes de bouleversements et de chaos imminents peuvent maintenant être discernés dans la mesure où l'ordre établi donne des résultats lamentables ». Ce jugement prophétique a été confirmé maintes et maintes fois par l'expérience commune de l'humanité. L'ordre établi présente des défauts évidents quand on considère l'incapacité des états souverains composant les Nations Unies d'exorciser le spectre de la guerre, la menace d'écroulement de l'ordre économique international, l'extension de l'anarchie et du terrorisme et la souffrance intense que causent ces troubles et d'autres encore à une multitude croissante. Agressions et conflits en sont tellement venus à caractériser nos systèmes sociaux, économiques et religieux que ce comportement est perçu par un grand nombre de personnes comme étant intrinsèque à la nature humaine et, par conséquent, irrémédiable.

Ce point de vue a entraîné des contradictions paralysantes dans les affaires humaines. D'un côté, les peuples de toutes les nations déclarent qu'ils sont non seulement prêts, mais aussi décidés à vivre en paix et en harmonie et à mettre un terme à ces craintes terrifiantes qui tourmentent leurs vies quotidiennes. De l'autre, on accepte trop facilement la thèse selon laquelle les êtres humains sont irrémédiablement égoïstes et agressifs et, par conséquent, incapables de mettre en place un système social qui soit à la fois progressiste et pacifique, dynamique et harmonieux, un système donnant libre cours à la créativité et à l'initiative de l'individu, mais fondé sur une base de collaboration et de réciprocité.

Au fur et à mesure que la paix devient une nécessité impérieuse, cette contradiction fondamentale qui fait obstacle à sa réalisation nous force à réexaminer les hypothèses sur lesquelles repose cette conception courante d'un triste destin de l'humanité. Un examen dénué de passion révèle que cette conduite, loin de traduire la véritable nature de l'homme, représente une déformation de l'esprit humain. Ayant admis ce point, tous les peuples pourront mettre en œuvre des forces sociales constructives qui, étant compatibles avec la nature humaine, favoriseront l'harmonie et la collaboration plutôt que la guerre et les conflits.

L'adoption d'une telle conduite ne revient pas à nier le passé de l'humanité mais plutôt à le comprendre. La foi bahá'íe voit la confusion actuelle du monde et la situation désastreuse des affaires humaines comme une phase normale d'un processus naturel menant inéluctablement à l'unification de la race humaine en un seul ordre social qui ne connaîtra d'autres frontières que la planète. La race humaine, en tant qu'unité organique distincte, est passée par des phases d'évolution qui rappellent les phases de bas âge et d'enfance de la vie des humains et elle se trouve maintenant dans la phase culminante de son adolescence troublée, à la veille de l'âge adulte tant attendu.

Il n'y a pas lieu de se désespérer parce que l'on admet en toute sincérité que les préjugés, la guerre et l'exploitation furent l'expression de phases immatures d'un vaste processus historique et que la race humaine connaît aujourd'hui les tumultes inévitables qui marquent son accession à une maturité collective. Cette reconnaissance constitue plutôt une condition élémentaire préalable à la tâche prodigieuse de construire un monde pacifique. Nous vous demandons instamment de considérer qu'une telle entreprise est possible, que les forces constructives nécessaires sont présentes et que les structures sociales unifiantes peuvent être mises en place.

En dépit des souffrances et des troubles que peuvent nous réserver les quelques prochaines années, en dépit de l'aspect tragique que peuvent revêtir les circonstances immédiates, la communauté bahá'íe estime que l'humanité peut faire face à cette épreuve suprême en ayant confiance en son dénouement. Loin de marquer la fin de la civilisation, les bouleversements vers lesquels l'humanité est toujours plus rapidement poussée permettront de libérer les « potentialités inhérentes à la condition de l'homme » et révèleront « la pleine mesure de son destin sur la terre, l'excellence innée de sa réalité ».

I

Les dons qui distinguent la race humaine de toutes les autres formes de vie se retrouvent dans ce que l'on désigne comme l'esprit humain ; l'intelligence est sa qualité essentielle. Ces dons ont permis à l'humanité de construire des civilisations et de prospérer matériellement. Cependant, ces réalisations à elles seules n'ont jamais comblé l'esprit humain, dont la nature mystérieuse porte à la transcendance, incite à la recherche d'un royaume invisible, de la réalité fondamentale, de l'essence des essences qui échappe à la perception humaine et que l'on appelle Dieu. Les religions offertes à l'homme par une succession de personnes touchées par la ferveur spirituelle ont constitué le principal lien entre l'humanité et cette réalité fondamentale ; elles ont exalté et raffiné la capacité de l'homme à atteindre le succès spirituel tout en réalisant le progrès social.

Aucune tentative sérieuse de remise en ordre des affaires humaines et de réalisation de la paix mondiale ne peut ignorer la religion. La perception qu'en a l'homme et la manière dont il la pratique forment une grand part des matériaux de l'histoire. Un éminent historien [Arnold Toynbee] a décrit la religion comme une « faculté de la nature humaine ». Il est difficile de nier que la perversion de cette faculté a contribué, en grande partie, à la confusion qui règne dans la société et aux conflits touchant et divisant les individus. De la même manière, tout observateur impartial ne peut minimiser l'influence prépondérante exercée par la religion sur les expressions fondamentales de la civilisation. De plus, l'effet direct qu'elle exerce sur les lois et la moralité a amplement démontré qu'elle était indispensable à l'ordre social.

Assimilant la religion à une force sociale, Bahá'u'lláh s'exprima en ces termes : « La religion est le meilleur moyen de faire régner l'ordre dans le monde et de satisfaire, dans un cadre pacifique, tous ceux qui l'habitent ». A propos de la disparition ou de la corruption de la religion, il écrivait : « Si la lampe de la religion faiblit, le chaos et la confusion prévaudront et les lumières de l'équité, de la justice, du calme et de la paix s'éteindront ». Dressant une liste de ces conséquences, les écrits bahá'ís soulignent que la « perversion de la nature humaine, la dégradation de sa conduite, la corruption et le dérèglement des institutions humaines se révèlent, dans de telles circonstances, sous leur aspect le plus sombre et le plus révoltant. La nature humaine est avilie, la confiance est ébranlée, la discipline se relâche, la voix de la conscience humaine est étouffée, la décence et la honte perdent toute signification, les concepts de devoir, de solidarité, de réciprocité et de loyauté sont faussés et le sentiment même de paix, de joie et d'espoir disparaît graduellement ».

Si l'humanité en est ainsi arrivée à un stade de conflits paralysants, elle doit en rechercher la cause en elle-même, en sa propre négligence et dans le fait qu'elle s'est fiée à des apparences trompeuses. C'est là qu'elle trouvera l'origine des malentendus et de la confusion créés au nom de la religion. Ceux qui se sont accrochés aveuglément et égoïstement à leurs orthodoxies particulières, qui ont imposé à leurs adeptes des interprétations erronées et contradictoires des déclarations des prophètes de Dieu, sont grandement responsables de cette confusion, qu'amplifient les barrières artificielles érigées entre la foi et la raison, la science et la religion. En effet, un examen impartial des véritables déclarations des fondateurs des grandes religions et des milieux sociaux dans lesquels ils durent remplir leur mission ne permet pas de soutenir les affirmations et les préjugés semant le trouble dans les communautés religieuses de l'humanité et, par conséquent, dans toutes les affaires humaines.

L'enseignement selon lequel nous devrions traiter les autres comme nous aimerions être traités, qui se retrouve sous des formes diverses dans toutes les grandes religions, vient renforcer cette dernière observation à deux égards : il résume l'attitude morale, l'aspect de recherche de la paix qui existe dans ces religions, quelles que soient leurs origines géographiques ou historiques ; il comporte également un aspect d'unité qui constitue leur vertu essentielle, une vertu que l'homme, dans sa perception incohérente de l'histoire, n'a pas su apprécier.

Si l'humanité avait vu les Educateurs de son enfance collective tels qu'ils étaient en réalité, c'est-à-dire en agents d'un même processus de civilisation, elle aurait sans aucun doute tiré des bénéfices infiniment supérieurs des effets cumulatifs de leurs missions successives. Hélas! elle n'a pas su le faire.

Le regain de ferveur religieuse fanatique qui se produit dans de nombreux pays ne peut être vu comme autre chose qu'une dernière convulsion. La nature même de la violence et des troubles auxquels ce phénomène est associé témoigne de l'échec spirituel qu'il représente. De fait, l'une des caractéristiques les plus étranges et les plus tristes de la vague actuelle de fanatisme religieux est la force avec laquelle, dans chaque cas, il ébranle non seulement les valeurs spirituelles qui favorisent l'unité de la race humaine, mais aussi les victoires morales uniques remportées par la religion dont il se prétend précisément le défenseur.

Malgré le rôle essentiel de la religion dans l'histoire de l'humanité et le caractère dramatique du regain actuel de fanatisme religieux militant, la religion et les institutions religieuses sont depuis plusieurs dizaines d'années considérées, par un nombre croissant de personnes, comme n'ayant aucun rapport avec les principales préoccupations du monde moderne. Ces personnes ont substitué à la religion la recherche hédoniste de satisfactions matérielles ou bien des idéologies créées par l'homme et qui visent à délivrer la société des maux évidents qui la font gémir. Malheureusement, un trop grand nombre de ces idéologies, plutôt que d'adhérer au concept de l'unité de la race humaine et de promouvoir une plus grande harmonie entre les divers peuples, ont eu tendance à déifier l'Etat, à subordonner le reste de l'humanité à une nation, une race ou une classe, à tenter de supprimer toute discussion et tout échange d'idées ou à abandonner sans pitié des millions d'affamés au libre jeu d'un système de marché qui aggrave sans conteste la misère de la majorité de la race humaine, tout en permettant à d'infimes minorités de vivre dans une aisance que nos ancêtres ne pouvaient même pas imaginer.

Combien tragiques sont les résultats des croyances de substitution créées par ces sages selon le monde. L'histoire a rendu un verdict irréversible sur leur valeur, comme en atteste le désenchantement massif de populations entières auxquelles on a appris à prier devant leurs autels. Les fruits qu'ont produits ces doctrines, après de nombreuses années d'un exercice de plus en plus arbitraire du pouvoir par ceux qui s'en servent pour dominer les affaires humaines, sont les plaies sociales et économiques qui affligent toutes les régions du monde, alors que nous nous approchons de la fin du XXe siècle. Toutes ces calamités externes cachent des dommages spirituels sous-jacents qui se reflètent dans l'apathie dont souffre l'ensemble des peuples de tous les pays et dans l'absence d'espoir qui assèche les cœurs de millions de personnes dépourvues et angoissées.

Nous sommes arrivés au stade où ceux qui prêchent les dogmes du matérialisme, que ce soit de l'Est ou de l'Ouest, que ce soit du capitalisme ou du socialisme, doivent rendre compte de la direction spirituelle qu'ils ont prétendu exercer. Où est le « nouveau monde » annoncé par ces idéologies ? Où est la paix internationale dont ils affirment promouvoir les idéaux ? Où sont les percées dans de nouveaux domaines de réalisation culturelle produites par l'exaltation de telle race, nation ou classe ? Pourquoi la vaste majorité des peuples du monde s'enfonce-t-elle sans cesse plus profondément dans la famine et la misère alors que les arbitres actuels des affaires humaines disposent de richesses énormes que n'auraient pu concevoir ni les pharaons, ni les empereurs romains, ni même les puissances impérialistes du XIXe siècle ?

C'est dans la glorification de la poursuite des intérêts matériels, qui est à la fois source et trame commune de toutes ces idéologies, que l'on retrouve les origines de la conception erronée selon laquelle les êtres humains sont irrémédiablement égoïstes et agressifs. Il s'agit là du terrain que l'on devra déblayer pour permettre la construction d'un monde nouveau qui conviendra à nos descendants.

L'histoire montre que les idéaux matérialistes n'ont pas su répondre aux besoins de l'humanité et ceci devrait nous amener à reconnaître en toute honnêteté que de nouveaux efforts doivent maintenant être entrepris pour résoudre les problèmes déchirants de la planète. Les conditions intolérables dans lesquelles vivent certains secteurs de la société traduisent l'échec de tous et chacun, et cet état de choses contribue davantage à provoquer qu'à atténuer la division des camps. Il est évident que des efforts conjoints doivent être entrepris de toute urgence pour remédier à ces problèmes. C'est d'abord et avant tout une question d'attitude. L'humanité continuera-t-elle à s'entêter dans le mauvais chemin, à s'accrocher à des concepts dépassés et à des hypothèses inapplicables ? Ou bien ses leaders iront-ils de l'avant et, faisant fi de leurs idéologies, décideront-ils de se consulter pour rechercher conjointement des solutions appropriées ?

Ceux qui ont à cœur l'avenir de l'humanité feront bien de réfléchir à ce conseil. « Si des idéaux longuement caressés et des institutions dont la réputation n'est plus à faire, si certaines hypothèses sociales et certaines formules religieuses ont cessé de promouvoir le bien-être de l'ensemble de l'humanité, s'ils ne répondent plus aux besoins d'une humanité en constante évolution alors, balayons-les et reléguons-les là où vont les doctrines désuètes et oubliées. Pourquoi, dans un monde soumis aux lois immuables du changement et de l'usure, seraient-ils à l'abri de la dégradation qui doit forcément gagner toute institution humaine ? Car les normes juridiques, les théories politiques et les doctrines économiques sont uniquement destinées à protéger les intérêts de l'humanité vue dans une perspective globale et l'humanité n'a pas à être sacrifiée pour préserver l'intégrité d'une loi ou d'une doctrine particulière ».

II

Le désarmement nucléaire, l'interdiction du recours aux gaz toxiques et aux armes bactériologiques ne supprimeront pas les causes fondamentales de la guerre. Sans vouloir nier l'importance évidente de ces mesures pratiques dans le cadre du processus de paix, elles sont en elles-mêmes trop superficielles pour exercer une influence durable. Les peuples sont assez ingénieux pour inventer d'autres formes de guerre et pour utiliser la nourriture, les matières premières, l'argent, la puissance industrielle, l'idéologie et le terrorisme pour tenter de s'asservir les uns les autres dans leur recherche interminable de suprématie et de pouvoir. De même, la désorganisation massive qui afflige actuellement les affaires de l'humanité ne pourra pas être résolue en mettant fin à des conflits ou désaccords spécifiques entre les nations. Il faut adopter un cadre universel authentique.

On ne peut certainement pas accuser les leaders nationaux d'ignorer l'ampleur mondiale du problème qui se manifeste dans les questions toujours plus pressantes auxquelles ils font face quotidiennement. Et les études et solutions avancées par des groupes concernés et éclairés ainsi que par des organismes des Nations Unies sont trop nombreuses pour que l'on puisse ignorer les défis. On assiste cependant à une paralysie de la volonté, et c'est là le phénomène qu'il faut minutieusement étudier afin d'y apporter une solution ferme. Comme nous l'avons mentionné auparavant, cette paralysie procède d'une croyance profonde en la nature inéluctablement batailleuse de la race humaine ; ceci explique pourquoi on répugne à considérer la possibilité d'assujettir les intérêts nationaux aux exigences d'un ordre mondial et pourquoi on refuse d'envisager courageusement les vastes ramifications de l'établissement d'une autorité mondiale unifiée. Cette paralysie est également attribuable à l'incapacité des masses, en grande partie ignorantes et soumises, d'exprimer clairement leur désir d'un nouvel ordre dans lequel elles pourraient vivre en paix, en harmonie et en prospérité avec toute l'humanité.

Les mesures timides prises, surtout depuis la dernière guerre mondiale, en vue de l'instauration d'un ordre mondial, donnent lieu d'espérer. La tendance croissante de groupes de pays désireux de donner à leurs rapports un cadre formel leur permettant de collaborer sur des questions d'intérêt mutuel, permet de penser qu'un jour ou l'autre tous les pays finiront par surmonter cette paralysie. L'Association des nations de l'Asie du Sud-Est, la Communauté et le Marché commun des Caraïbes, le Marché commun d'Amérique centrale, le Conseil d'assistance économique mutuelle, les Communautés européennes, la Ligue des pays arabes, l'Organisation de l'unité africaine, l'Organisation des états américains, le Forum du Pacifique sud – toutes les initiatives conjointes représentées par ces organisations ouvrent la porte à l'ordre mondial.

Le fait que certains des problèmes les plus enracinés de la planète font l'objet d'une attention plus grande constitue un autre signe d'espoir. En dépit des lacunes évidentes des Nations Unies, la quantité de déclarations et de conventions adoptées par cette organisation, même lorsque les gouvernements ne lui ont pas donné un appui chaleureux, a donné aux populations le sentiment d'un regain de vie. La déclaration universelle des droits de l'homme, la convention sur la prévention et la punition du crime de génocide et les mesures de nature semblable ayant pour but d'éliminer toutes les formes de discrimination basées sur la race, le sexe ou la croyance religieuse ; la défense des droits de l'enfant ; la protection de toutes les personnes contre la torture ; l'élimination de la faim et de la malnutrition ; l'utilisation des découvertes scientifiques et technologiques dans le but de promouvoir la paix et le bien-être de l'humanité – toutes ces mesures, si elles sont mises en application et développées courageusement, nous permettront d'atteindre plus rapidement une ère où le spectre de la guerre cessera de pouvoir dominer les relations internationales. Point n'est besoin d'insister sur l'importance des questions couvertes par ces déclarations et conventions. Cependant, certaines questions, en raison de leur rapport direct avec l'instauration de la paix mondiale, méritent une plus ample élaboration.

Le racisme, l'un des fléaux les plus néfastes et les plus persistants, représente l'un des principaux obstacles à la paix. Sa pratique constitue une violation si scandaleuse de la dignité de l'être humain qu'elle ne peut être justifiée sous aucun prétexte. Le racisme retarde le développement du potentiel illimité de ses victimes, corrompt ceux qui le pratiquent et ruine les espoirs de progrès humain. L'unité de la race humaine doit être reconnue universellement et mise en œuvre par des mesures juridiques appropriées si l'on veut surmonter ce problème.

Le gouffre qui sépare les riches des pauvres, source de grandes souffrances, maintient le monde dans un état d'instabilité, pratiquement au seuil de la guerre. Peu de sociétés ont su apporter une solution efficace à cette situation. La solution requiert l'alliance d'éléments spirituels, moraux et pratiques. Il faut envisager le problème dans une perspective nouvelle, consulter des experts couvrant une vaste gamme de disciplines, à l'abri des polémiques économiques et idéologiques, et s'assurer le concours de gens qui sont directement concernés par les décisions devant être prises d'urgence. Cette question est liée non seulement à la nécessité d'éliminer les extrêmes de richesse et de pauvreté, mais aussi aux vérités spirituelles dont la compréhension pourra donner naissance à une attitude universelle nouvelle. L'encouragement et le développement d'une telle attitude représentent en eux-mêmes un élément-clé de la solution.

Le nationalisme effréné, par opposition à un patriotisme sain et légitime, doit faire place à une loyauté plus vaste, à l'amour de l'humanité dans son ensemble. Comme le dit Bahá'u'lláh : « La terre n'est qu'un pays dont tous les hommes sont les citoyens ». Le concept de citoyenneté mondiale est le produit direct de la contraction du monde en un seul village à la suite des découvertes scientifiques, et d'interdépendance indéniable des nations. On peut aimer tous les peuples du monde tout en aimant son propre pays. Dans une société mondiale, les intérêts de chaque partie concordent avec les intérêts du tout. Il importe de stimuler les activités internationales actuelles qui favorisent, dans divers domaines, l'affection mutuelle et le sens de la solidarité entre les peuples.

Tout au long de l'histoire, les rivalités religieuses ont été cause d'innombrables guerres et conflits et ont constitué un des principaux obstacles au progrès. Elles font de plus en plus horreur aux gens de toutes les croyances ainsi qu'aux incroyants. Les adeptes de toutes les religions doivent être disposés à affronter les questions fondamentales soulevées par ces conflits et à formuler des réponses nettes. Comment les différends qui les opposent seront-ils résolus, tant en théorie qu'en pratique ? Le défi auquel font face les leaders religieux de l'humanité consiste à se pencher, le cœur plein de compassion et animés d'un désir de vérité, sur le triste sort de l'humanité et de se demander s'ils ne peuvent, en toute humilité devant leur Créateur tout puissant, enterrer leurs désaccords théologiques au nom d'un grand esprit d'indulgence mutuelle qui leur permettra d'œuvrer conjointement au progrès de la compréhension humaine et de la paix.

L'émancipation de la femme, c'est-à-dire la complète égalité entre les sexes, est l'une des conditions essentielles à l'avènement de la paix. Pourtant, son importance reste méconnue. Le refus de cette égalité constitue une injustice à l'égard de la moitié de la population mondiale et encourage chez les hommes des attitudes et des habitudes préjudiciables qui se propagent de la famille au lieu de travail, à la vie politique et, en fin de compte, aux relations internationales. Ce refus ne peut se justifier selon aucun critère moral ou biologique, ni sur le plan pratique. C'est seulement lorsque les femmes auront accès, en tant qu'associées à part entière, à tous les domaines de l'activité humaine, qu'il sera possible de créer un climat moral et psychologique propice à la paix internationale.

La cause de l'éducation universelle, qui s'est déjà assurée le concours d'une armée de gens dévoués de toutes croyances et de toutes nations, mérite tout le soutien que les gouvernements du monde peuvent lui donner. En effet, l'ignorance est sans conteste la principale raison du déclin et de la chute des peuples, ainsi que de la persistance des préjugés. Aucun pays ne peut connaître la réussite si tous ces citoyens n'ont pas accès à l'enseignement. Le manque de ressources limite la capacité de nombreux pays à répondre à ce besoin et les oblige à dresser une liste de priorités. Les organismes responsables de ces décisions devraient songer à donner la priorité à l'éducation des femmes et des jeunes filles, car des mères instruites représentent le moyen le plus efficace et le plus rapide de propager les connaissances au sein de la société. Conformément aux exigences de notre époque, il serait également opportun de songer à intégrer le concept de citoyenneté mondiale dans le cadre de l'éducation que reçoit normalement chaque enfant.

Un manque fondamental de communication entre les peuples compromet sérieusement les efforts entrepris pour réaliser la paix mondiale. L'adoption d'une langue auxiliaire internationale constituerait un grand pas dans cette direction et on devrait s'attaquer à cette tâche de toute urgence.

Deux points méritent d'être soulignés à propos de toutes ces questions. Premièrement, l'abolition de la guerre va bien au-delà de la signature de traités et de protocoles ; c'est une tâche complexe exigeant un engagement sans précédent à résoudre des questions qui ne sont habituellement pas reliées à la quête de la paix. Une sécurité collective qui ne reposerait que sur des ententes politiques serait purement illusoire. Deuxièmement, le plus grand défi auquel nous faisons face en traitant des questions de paix consiste à sortir d'une démarche purement pragmatique pour élever le débat au niveau des principes. En effet, la paix découle essentiellement d'un état d'âme reposant sur une attitude morale ou spirituelle et c'est principalement en évoquant cette attitude que l'on pourra parvenir à des solutions durables.

Chaque problème social peut être résolu à l'aide de principes spirituels ou de ce que certains appellent des valeurs humaines. De manière générale, tout groupe bien intentionné peut trouver des solutions pratiques à ses problèmes, mais bonnes intentions et connaissances pratiques ne suffisent généralement pas. Le mérite essentiel du principe spirituel consiste non seulement à présenter une perspective concordant avec l'élément immanent de la nature humaine, mais aussi à stimuler une attitude, une dynamique, une volonté, une aspiration qui permettent la découverte et la mise en œuvre de mesures pratiques. Les chefs d'état et toutes les personnes au pouvoir pourraient trouver plus facilement des solutions aux problèmes s'ils s'efforçaient d'abord d'identifier les principes en cause et se laissaient ensuite guider par ces principes.

III

La principale question à résoudre se pose comme suit : comment le monde actuel, enraciné dans un schème de conflits, peut-il se transformer en un monde où règnent l'harmonie et la collaboration?

L'ordre mondial ne peut se fonder que sur la conscience inébranlable de l'unité de la race humaine, une vérité spirituelle que confirment toutes les sciences humaines. L'anthropologie, la physiologie et la psychologie ne reconnaissent qu'une espèce humaine, même si celle-ci est infiniment variée en ce qui concerne les aspects secondaires de la vie. La reconnaissance de cette vérité est subordonnée à l'abandon de tout préjugé de race, de classe, de couleur, de croyance, de nation, de sexe, de degré de civilisation matérielle, autrement dit, de tout ce qui permet aux gens de se considérer comme supérieurs aux autres.

L'acceptation de l'unité de la race humaine est la condition fondamentale de la réorganisation et de l'administration du monde considéré comme un seul pays, le foyer de l'humanité. Toute tentative d'instauration de la paix mondiale ne peut être couronnée de succès que si ce principe spirituel est universellement accepté. Il devrait donc être proclamé universellement, enseigné dans les écoles et affirmé constamment dans chaque pays pour préparer le terrain au changement organique de structure de la société qu'il implique.

Dans la conception bahá'íe, la reconnaissance de l'unité de la race humaine « n'exige rien de moins que la reconstruction et la démilitarisation de tout le monde civilisé ; elle fait appel à un monde unifié organiquement sous tous les aspects essentiels de sa vie, de ses mécanismes politiques, de ses aspirations spirituelles, de son commerce et de sa finance, de son écriture et de son langage, tout en étant infiniment diversifié dans les particularités nationales de ses unités fédérées ».

Se penchant sur les implications de cette notion cardinale, Shoghi Effendi, le Gardien de la foi bahá'íe s'exprima en ces termes en 1931 : « Loin de viser à détruire les fondations existantes de la société, elle cherche à en élargir la base, à transformer ses institutions pour les rendre compatibles avec les besoins d'un monde en constante évolution. Elle ne peut entrer en conflit avec aucune allégeance légitime de même qu'elle ne peut ébranler les loyautés essentielles. Son objet n'est point d'étouffer dans le cœur humain l'ardeur d'un patriotisme sain et intelligent, ni d'abolir le régime de l'autonomie nationale, indispensable si l'on veut éviter les maux d'une centralisation excessive. Elle n'ignore ni ne tente de supprimer la diversité d'origines ethniques, de climats, d'histoires, de langues et de traditions, de pensée et de coutumes qui distinguent les nations et les peuples du monde. Elle fait appel à une loyauté plus vaste et une aspiration plus élevée que celles qui aient jamais animé la race humaine. Elle insiste sur la nécessité de subordonner les impulsions et les intérêts nationaux aux besoins impérieux d'un monde unifié. Elle répudie toute centralisation excessive, d'une part, et repousse toute tentative d'uniformité, de l'autre. Son mot d'ordre est l'unité dans la diversité ».

Ces objectifs ne peuvent être atteints qu'après plusieurs étapes de transformation des attitudes politiques nationales, qui frisent actuellement l'anarchie du fait de l'absence de lois clairement définies, ou de principes acceptés et applicables à l'échelle mondiale, régissant les rapports entre les nations. La Société des Nations, les Nations Unies et les nombreuses organisations et ententes auxquelles elles ont donné lieu ont sans aucun doute contribué à atténuer certains effets négatifs des conflits internationaux, mais elles se sont avérées incapables d'empêcher les guerres. De fait, il y a eu depuis la fin de la seconde guerre mondiale un grand nombre de conflits armés, dont beaucoup font encore rage.

Les aspects prédominants de ce problème avaient déjà fait leur apparition au dix-neuvième siècle, lorsque Bahá'u'lláh formula pour la première fois ses propositions visant l'instauration de la paix mondiale. Il proposa le principe de la sécurité collective dans des déclarations destinées aux gouvernants du monde. Shoghi Effendi en commenta la signification : « Quel autre sens pourraient avoir ces paroles solennelles si ce n'est l'inévitable limitation de la souveraineté nationale absolue comme condition sine qua non de la formation de la future fédération de toutes les nations du monde ? Une formule de super-État mondial devra nécessairement être élaborée. Super-État en faveur duquel toutes les nations du globe devront abandonner de plein gré toute prétention à faire la guerre, certains droits de lever des impôts et tous droits de maintenir des armements autres que ceux requis pour la sauvegarde de l'ordre à l'intérieur de leurs souverainetés respectives. Un tel État devra comprendre un pouvoir exécutif international capable d'imposer son autorité suprême et incontestable à tout membre récalcitrant de la fédération, un parlement mondial dont les membres seront élus par la population des pays respectifs avec ratification de cette élection par leur gouvernement ; un tribunal suprême dont les décisions auront un effet obligatoire, même dans les cas où les parties impliquées n'auraient pas volontairement consenti à sa juridiction ».

« Une communauté mondiale dans laquelle toutes les barrières économiques auront été supprimées à tout jamais et l'interdépendance du capital et du travail reconnue formellement ; dans laquelle la clameur des rivalités et du fanatisme religieux se sera apaisée pour toujours ; dans laquelle la flamme de l'animosité raciale aura été radicalement éteinte ; dans laquelle un seul code de droit international – issu du jugement réfléchi des représentants fédérés du monde – sera sanctionné par l'intervention immédiate et coercitive des forces conjuguées des unités fédérées ; et, finalement, une communauté universelle dans laquelle la violence d'un nationalisme capricieux et militant aura été convertie en une conscience permanente de la citoyenneté mondiale. C'est ainsi, en vérité, que se présente, dans ses grandes lignes, l'Ordre mondial prévu par Bahá'u'lláh, un Ordre qui sera un jour considéré comme le plus beau fruit d'un âge mûrissant lentement ».

Bahá'u'lláh préconisa la mise en œuvre de ces mesures de grande portée : « Le temps doit venir où sera universellement ressentie l'impérieuse nécessité d'une vaste assemblée représentant le monde entier. Les rois et dirigeants de la terre devront y assister, prendre part à ses délibérations et étudier les moyens et instruments qui permettront d'instaurer la grande paix entre les hommes ».

Le courage, la détermination, la motivation désintéressée, l'amour altruiste d'un peuple pour un autre – toutes les valeurs spirituelles et morales nécessaires pour faire ce pas capital en direction de la paix reposent sur la volonté d'agir. Et c'est dans le but de stimuler la volonté nécessaire qu'il importe de songer sérieusement à la réalité de l'homme, c'est-à-dire à sa pensée. Comprendre la pertinence de cette réalité puissante, c'est aussi se rendre compte de la nécessité sociale de réaliser sa valeur unique au moyen de consultations franches, impartiales et cordiales et de mettre en application les résultats de ce processus. Bahá'u'lláh insistait sur les vertus et la nécessité de la consultation pour mettre de l'ordre dans les affaires humaines: « La consultation rehausse la conscience et transforme la conjecture en certitude. C'est une lumière éclatante qui, dans un monde sombre, guide et indique le chemin. Il y a et il y aura toujours pour chaque chose un degré de perfection et de maturité. La maturité du don de la compréhension se manifeste par la consultation ».

A elle seule, la tentative de réaliser la paix au moyen de l'action consultative qu'il proposa peut faire naître, entre les peuples de la terre, un esprit si salutaire qu'aucune puissance ne pourra résister au dénouement triomphal.

'Abdu'l-Bahá, fils de Bahá'u'lláh et interprète autorisé de son enseignement, nous fit part de la manière dont il concevait les procédures requises pour cette assemblée mondiale : « Ils doivent tenir une consultation générale sur la cause de la paix et tenter par tous les moyens en leur possession de mettre sur pied une union des nations du monde. Ils doivent conclure un traité ayant force de loi et rédiger un pacte dont les dispositions seront équitables, inviolables et précises. Ils doivent le proclamer à la face du monde et le faire ratifier par la race humaine tout entière. Cette entreprise suprême et noble – la véritable source de paix et de bien-être pour le monde entier – devra être tenue pour sacrée par tous les habitants de la terre. Toutes les forces de l'humanité doivent être mobilisées pour assurer la stabilité et la permanence de ce pacte suprême. Dans ce pacte universel, les limites et les frontières de chaque pays devront être délimitées clairement, les principes régissant les relations réciproques entre gouvernements, établis avec précision et tous les accords et engagements internationaux bien définis. De même, l'importance des armements de chaque État devra être strictement limitée car, si l'on permettait à une nation d'augmenter son potentiel de guerre et d'accroître ses forces militaires, cela rendrait les autres nations méfiantes. Le principe fondamental servant de base à ce pacte solennel devra être établi de manière à ce que, si quelque État que ce soit violait l'une de ses dispositions, tous les autres devraient agir pour le réduire à la soumission la plus totale, mieux encore, la race humaine dans son ensemble devrait faire tout ce qui est en son pouvoir pour abattre ce gouvernement. Si ce remède suprême était appliqué au corps malade du monde, il guérirait sûrement de ses maux et ne connaîtrait plus aucun danger ».

Cette importante assemblée aurait dû être convoquée depuis longtemps.

C'est avec toute la ferveur dont nous sommes capables que nous demandons aux dirigeants du monde entier de saisir ce moment opportun et de prendre des mesures irréversibles pour convoquer cette assemblée mondiale. Toutes les forces de l'histoire poussent la race humaine vers cet acte qui marquera à jamais l'aube de sa maturité tant attendue.

Les Nations Unies avec l'appui total de leurs membres, sauront-elles se mettre à la hauteur d'un événement si grandiose?

Que tous, hommes et femmes, jeunes et enfants de tous les coins du monde reconnaissent le mérite éternel de cet acte impérieux et proclament leur assentiment ! Qu'il revienne à la présente génération d'inaugurer cette phase glorieuse de l'évolution de la vie sociale de notre planète !

IV

L'optimisme que nous ressentons procède d'une vision qui se situe au-delà de la fin des guerres et de la création d'organismes de coopération internationale. La paix permanente entre les nations est une étape essentielle mais, comme l'affirmait Bahá'u'lláh, ne constitue pas le but fondamental du développement social de l'humanité. Au-delà de l'armistice initial qu'aura imposé au monde la crainte de l'holocauste nucléaire, au-delà de la paix politique conclue à regret par des nations rivales se méfiant les unes des autres, au-delà des accords pragmatiques de sécurité et de coexistence et des nombreuses expériences de collaboration que ces mesures rendront possibles se trouve le but ultime : l'unification de tous les peuples du monde en une famille universelle.

La discorde est un danger que les nations et les peuples de la terre ne peuvent plus endurer, les conséquences en sont si terribles qu'on ne veut point les envisager et si évidentes qu'elles ne nécessitent aucune démonstration. Bahá'u'lláh a affirmé à ce sujet il y a plus d'un siècle : « Le bien-être de l'humanité, sa paix et sa sécurité ne pourront être obtenus si son unité n'est pas fermement établie ». Observant que « l'humanité tout entière se lamente, se meurt du désir d'être unifiée et de mettre un terme à son long martyre », Shoghi Effendi poursuivit en ces termes : « L'unification du genre humain est la caractéristique du stade dont s'approche l'humanité. L'unité de la famille, de la tribu, de la cité-état et de la nation ont été successivement tentées et réalisées dans toute leur ampleur. L'unité du monde est maintenant le but vers lequel tend une humanité accablée. Le processus d'édification de la nation est complété. L'anarchie inhérente à la souveraineté d'un État approche de son point culminant. Un monde qui se dirige vers la maturité doit renoncer à ce fétiche, il doit reconnaître l'unité et l'intégrité des relations humaines et mettre en place une fois pour toutes le mécanisme le plus apte à incarner ce principe fondamental de son existence ».

Tous les courants de changement contemporains soutiennent cette conception. A preuve les nombreux exemples déjà cités de signes s'orientant en direction de la paix mondiale et que l'on retrouve dans les mouvements et développements internationaux actuels. L'armée d'hommes et de femmes originaires de pratiquement chaque culture, race et nation de la terre et œuvrant au sein des divers organismes des Nations Unies représente une « fonction publique » à l'échelle de la planète. Ses réalisations impressionnantes témoignent du degré de collaboration qu'il est possible d'atteindre même dans des circonstances décourageantes. Un besoin impérieux de réaliser l'unité, que l'on pourrait assimiler à un printemps spirituel, lutte désespérément pour s'exprimer à travers d'innombrables congrès internationaux réunissant des spécialistes des disciplines les plus variées. Il motive les appels lancés pour des projets internationaux impliquant des enfants et des jeunes. Il constitue effectivement la source même du mouvement remarquable vers l'œcuménisme qui semble attirer irrésistiblement l'un vers l'autre les membres de religions et sectes historiquement opposées. Tout comme la tendance à la guerre et au développement égoïste qui lui est opposé et contre laquelle elle lutte sans relâche, l'impulsion vers l'unité mondiale constitue l'un des traits dominants et envahissants de la vie de notre planète au cours des dernières années du vingtième siècle.

L'expérience de la communauté bahá'íe peut être un des exemples de cette unité grandissante. Cette communauté regroupe de trois à quatre millions de personnes originaires de nombreuses nations, cultures, classes et croyances et engagées dans une vaste gamme d'activités couvrant les besoins spirituels, sociaux et économiques des peuples de nombreux pays. Il s'agit d'un organisme social unique qui reflète la diversité de la famille humaine, mène ses activités sur la base de principes consultatifs admis par tous et vénère, sans marque de préférence, toutes les grandes manifestations de l'influence divine de l'histoire humaine. Son existence même prouve que la foi de son fondateur en un monde unifié n'était pas chimérique et confirme que l'humanité peut vivre comme une société mondiale et qu'elle peut relever les défis inhérents à son passage à la maturité. Si l'expérience bahá'íe peut contribuer de quelque manière que ce soit à renforcer l'espoir en l'unité de la race humaine, nous sommes heureux de la soumettre à votre étude.

Conscients de l'importance suprême de la tâche que doit maintenant entreprendre le monde entier, nous nous inclinons humblement devant la majesté imposante du divin Créateur qui, dans son amour infini, a créé l'humanité entière de la même souche, a exalté la réalité précieuse de l'homme, lui a accordé les dons inestimables de l'intelligence et de la sagesse, de la noblesse et de l'immortalité, et lui a conféré « en privilège unique, par l'opération de sa volonté libre et souveraine, la capacité de le connaître et de l'aimer, le dotant ainsi d'une faculté dont l'exercice doit être considéré comme la raison d'être et le but fondamental de toute la création ».

Nous sommes fermement convaincus que tous les êtres humains ont été créés « pour promouvoir le progrès de la civilisation », qu' « agir comme le font les bêtes des champs est indigne de l'homme », et que les vertus propres à la dignité humaine sont la loyauté, l'indulgence, la pitié, la compassion et la bonté à l'égard de tous les peuples. Nous réaffirmons notre conviction que « les potentialités inhérentes à la condition de l'homme, la pleine mesure de son destin sur la terre et l'excellence innée de sa réalité, tout cela doit se manifester en ce jour promis de Dieu ». Voilà ce qui motive notre croyance inébranlable que l'unité et la paix sont des objectifs réalistes vers lesquels tend l'humanité.

Au moment où nous écrivons ces lignes, les voix pleines d'espoir des Bahá'ís retentissent en dépit des persécutions dont ils sont toujours victimes dans le pays où est née leur foi. En donnant l'exemple d'un espoir inébranlable, ils témoignent de la conviction que la réalisation imminente de ce vieux rêve de paix est maintenant, en vertu des effets métamorphosants de la révélation de Bahá'u'lláh, investi de la force du pouvoir divin. Notre message représente donc plus qu'une vision exprimée par des mots : nous faisons appel à la puissance évocatrice des actes de foi et de sacrifice ; nous vous communiquons l'appel angoissé à la paix et à l'unité de nos coreligionnaires du monde entier. Nous nous associons à tous ceux qui sont victimes d'agressions, à tous ceux qui aspirent à un monde sans conflit ni lutte, à tous ceux qui, par leur dévouement aux principes de la paix et de l'ordre mondial, se font les promoteurs des causes ennoblissantes pour lesquelles l'humanité fut créée par Dieu dans son amour infini.

Dans notre désir ardent de vous communiquer la ferveur de notre espoir et la profondeur de notre confiance, citons la promesse formelle de Bahá'u'lláh : « Ces luttes stériles, ces guerres ruineuses passeront et la Paix suprême viendra ».

LA MAISON UNIVERSELLE DE JUSTICE

The Promise of World Peace

Hindi

अक्तूबर 1985

विश्व के लोगों को:

वह महान शांति, जिसकी ओर सद्भावनासंपन्न लोगों ने शताब्दियों से अपने हृदय की आशा को केन्द्रित किया है, जिसकी परिकल्पना अगणित पीढ़ियों के द्रष्टाओं और कवियों ने की है, और जिसका वचन युग—युग में मानवजाति के पवित्र धर्मग्रंथों ने दिया था, अब, अन्ततः, राष्ट्रों की पहुँच के भीतर दिखाई देती है। इतिहास में पहली बार प्रत्येक व्यक्ति के लिये यह संभव हो सका है कि वह विविध राष्ट्रों और जनसमूहों वाला इस समूची पृथ्वी को एकता की दृष्टि से देख सके। विश्व शांति न केवल सम्भव है, अपितु अवश्यम्भावी है। इस धरती के विकास का यह अगला चरण है। एक महान विचारक के शब्दों में ''मानवजाति का सार्वभौमीकरण''।

क्या शांति की मंजिल तक हम तभी पहुँच पायेंगे, जब मानवजाति द्वारा व्यवहार और आचरण के पुराने ढर्रे और पुराने तौर तरीकों पर हठपूर्वक अड़े रहने के कारण हम अकल्पनीय यातनायें भोग चुके होंगे ? या फिर आपसी परामर्श के परिणामस्वरूप स्वेच्छापूर्वक हम शांति को अपनायें ? यह एक ऐसा विकल्प है जो इस धरती के सभी निवासियों के सामने खुला है। इस नाजुक मोड़ पर जबकि राष्ट्रों के सामने खड़ी अनेक असाध्य समस्यायें एक असामान्य रूप लेकर पूरे विश्व की चिंता बन गई हैं, संघर्ष और अव्यवस्था के ज्वार को रोकने में असफलता, एक घोर गैरजिम्मेदारी का काम होगा।

कुछ अनुकूल लक्षण भी सामने आ रहे हैं। उनमें से एक है, एक विश्व—व्यवस्था की ओर बढ़ते हुए कदमों का निरंतर अधिक सशक्त होते जाना। इस दिशा में पहली शुरूआत लीग ऑफ नेशन्स के निर्माण के द्वारा इस शताब्दी के प्रारम्भिक काल में हुई थी और लीग ऑफ नेशन्स का उत्तराधिकारी है संयुक्त राष्ट्र संघ जो उसकी अपेक्षा कहीं अधिक व्यापक आधार पर खड़ा है। दूसरे विश्वयुद्ध के बाद से संसार के अधिकांश राष्ट्रों ने स्वतंत्रता पा ली है। यह राष्ट्रनिर्माण की प्रक्रिया के पूरे होने का संकेत है। एक—दूसरे से संबंधित मामला. में इन नवोदित राष्ट्रों की पुराने राष्ट्रों से संलग्नता। अब तक जो जातियां अथवा राष्ट्र अलग—थलग और एक—दूसरे के प्रति विरोधीभाव रखते थे, वे वैज्ञानिक, शैक्षणिक, आर्थिक और सांस्कृतिक क्षेत्रों में अंतर्राष्ट्रीय कार्यकलापों के माध्यम से एक—दूसरे से सहयोग करने लगे हैं। हाल के दशकों में अंतर्राष्ट्रीय मानवतावादी संगठनों की संख्या में अभूतपूर्व वृद्धि हुई है। युद्धों को समाप्त करने की पुकार उठाने वाले, महिलाओं और युवाओं के आंदोलनों का प्रसार हो रहा है। व्यक्तिगत

संपर्क और संवाद द्वारा आपसी समझ बढ़ाने के आकांक्षी साधारण जनों के निरंतर बढ़ते हुए ताने बाने का स्वतः ही विकास हो रहा है।

इस असाधारण रूप से सौभाग्यशाली शताब्दी में होने वाली वैज्ञानिक और तकनीकी, प्रगति, इस धरती पर सामाजिक विकास के क्षेत्र में एक भारी उन्नति का पूर्वाभास देती और उन साधनों की ओर इशारा करती है जिनके द्वारा मानवज. ाति की व्यावहारिक समस्यायें सुलझाई जा सकती हैं। वस्तुतः वे एक संयुक्त संसार के जटिल जीवन प्रशासन के साधन प्रस्तुत करते हैं। फिर भी मार्ग में बाध गायें बनी हुई हैं। शंकायें, गलत धारणायें, पूर्वाग्रह, संदेह और संकीर्ण निहित स्वा. र्थ राष्ट्रों और जातियों के आपसी संबंधों में अड़चनें बने हुए हैं।

इस उपयुक्त अवसर पर एक आध्यात्मिक और नैतिक दायित्व से प्रेरित होकर हम आपका ध्यान उन गहन अन्तर्दृष्टि सम्पन्न तथ्यों की ओर आकर्षित कर रहे हैं, जो बहाई धर्म के संस्थापक बहाउल्लाह ने एक सदी से भी पहले मानवज. ाति के शासनकर्ताओं तक प्रेषित किये थे। उनके धर्म के न्यासधारी होने के कारण हम इसे अपना कर्त्तव्य समझते हैं।

बहाउल्लाह ने लिखा था ''शोक का विषय है कि निराशा के झंझावात प्रत्येक दिशा से चल रहे हैं और मानवजाति को विभाजित तथा आहत करने वाले झगड़े दिन–प्रतिदिन बढ़ते जा रहे हैं। भविष्य में होने वाली उथल–पुथल और संकट के चिह्न अब पहचाने जा सकते हैं, क्योंकि वर्तमान व्यवस्था अत्यधिक दयनीय रूप से दोषपूर्ण है।'' इस भविष्यद्रष्टा के इस निष्कर्ष का पर्याप्त प्रमाण मानवजाति के सामान्य अनुभव से मिल जाता है। वर्तमान व्यवस्था की कमियां इस तथ्य से स्पष्ट हो जाती हैं कि संयुत राष्ट्रसंघ के रूप में संगठित संसार के प्रभ. ुत्तासंपन्न राष्ट्र, युद्ध की मंडराती प्रेतछाया को अभी तक दूर नहीं हटा सके हैं, अंतर्राष्ट्रीय अर्थव्यवस्था के ढह जाने का संकट सामने खड़ा है, अराजकता और आतंकवाद फैलते जा रहे हैं और इनके तथा अन्य व्याधियों के कारण करोड़ों लोगों के भीषण कष्ट भी निरंतर बढ़ते जा रहे हैं। दरअसल आक्रामकता और संघर्ष हमारी सामाजिक, आर्थिक और धार्मिक व्यवस्थाओं का इस हद तक मूल स्वभाव बन गये हैं कि बहुत से लोग इस दृष्टिकोण के आगे घुटने टेक चुके हैं–कि ऐसा व्यवहार मानव स्वभाव का एक स्वाभाविक अंग है और इसलिये इसे दूर नहीं किया जा सकता।

इस दृष्टिकोण के गहरे जड़ जमा लेने के कारण मानवजाति के कार्यकलापों में एक ऐसा विरोध उत्पन्न हो गया है जो उसे जड़ और गतिहीन बना रहा है। एक ओर तो सभी राष्ट्रों के लोग न केवल शांति और समन्वय के लिये अपनी स्वीकृति बल्कि अपनी प्रबल लालसा का ढिंढोरा पीटते हैं, और उनकी

रोजमर्रा की जिन्दगी पर मंडराती भय और शंकाओं की इस यंत्रणा का अंत चाहते हैं। दूसरी ओर इस सिद्धांत को भी बिना सोचे–समझे स्वीकार कर लेते हैं कि मनुष्य एक इतना स्वार्थी और आक्रामक जीव है कि उसके इन दुर्गणों को दूर नहीं किया जा सकता और इसलिए वह एक ऐसी समाज–व्यवस्था के निर्माण के अयोग्य है जो एक साथ ही प्रगतिशील तथा शांतिमय हो, गतिशील और सामंजस्यपूर्ण हो, एक ऐसी व्यवस्था जिसमें व्यक्ति की सृजनात्मकता और व्यक्तिगत पहल के लिए उन्मुक्त अवसर हों, लेकिन वह सहयोग और आपसी आदान–प्रदान पर भी आधारित हो।

जैसे–जैसे शांति की अधिक से अधिक आवश्यकता महसूस हो रही है। यह आधारभूत विरोध जो शांति के सपने के साकार होने में बाधक है, उन धारणाओं पर पुनर्विचार की मांग करता है जिन पर आज का सामान्य दृष्टिकोण आधारित है। अनासक्त भाव से तथ्यों की परीक्षा से यह प्रमाणित हो जाता है कि ऐसा आचरण मनुष्य के सच्चे स्वरूप को प्रकट करने की बात तो दूर, मानव–चेतना के एक विकृत रूप को सामने रखता है। इस विचार से संतुष्ट होने पर सभी मनुष्य ऐसी रचनात्मक सामाजिक शक्तियों को गतिमान कर सकेंगे जो मनुष्य के मूल स्वभाव के अनुकूल होंगी और युद्ध तथा विरोध को बढ़ावा देने के स्थान पर सामंजस्य और सहयोग को प्रोत्साहन देंगी।

एक ऐसे मार्ग को चुनने का अर्थ मानवता के अतीत को नकारना नहीं, बल्कि उसको समझना है। बहाई धर्म वर्तमान विश्व में व्याप्त अव्यवस्था और मानव क्रियाकलापों में रची–बसी संकटमय स्थिति को उस जीवन्त प्रक्रिया का एक स्वाभाविक चरण मानता है जो अन्ततः और अबाध्यरूप से मानवजाति को एक ऐसी सामाजिक व्यवस्था तक ले जाएगी जिसकी अंतिम सीमायें वही होंगी जो इस धरती की हैं। मानवजाति एक जैविक इकाई के रूप में विकास के उन सभी चरणों से गुजरी है जो मनुष्य के शैशव और बाल्यकाल के समान्तर हैं और अब इस विकास की परिणति इसके उथल–पुथल भरे किशोरकाल में हो रही है जो स्वयं चिर प्रतीक्षित युग की ओर बढ़ रहा है।

इसे बेझिझक स्वीकार कर लेना कि पूर्वाग्रह, युद्ध और शोषण उस विराट ऐतिहासिक प्रक्रिया में अपरिपक्वता के चरण थे और मानवजाति आज जिस उथल–पुथल की स्थिति से गुजर रही है वह उसके सामूहिक रूप से वयस्कता तक पहुँचने का चिहन है, निराशा का कोई कारण नहीं बल्कि एक शांतिपूर्ण विश्व के निर्माण के महत्तर दायित्व को निभाने की एक जरूरी शर्त है। ऐसा महत्तर कार्य संभव है, इसके लिये आवश्यक रचनात्मक शक्तियों का अस्तित्व है, और एक एकीकरण करने वाले सामाजिक ढांचे का निर्माण किया जा सकता है — यही वह विषय है जिसका हम निवेदन करते हैं कि आप परीक्षण करें।

जो कुछ भी पीड़ा और उथल-पुथल निकट भविष्य में मानवता को भोगने हैं, तात्कालिक परिस्थितियाँ चाहे कितनी ही अंधकारमय हों, बहाई समुदाय का विश्वास है कि मानवजाति इसके अंतिम परिणाम के प्रति पूर्णतया आश्वस्त रहते हुए, इस महान परीक्षा का सामना कर सकती है। सभ्यता के अंत की ओर इंगित करने की बात तो दूर, वे उथल-पुथल भरे परिवर्तन जिनकी ओर मानवता अधिकाधिक तीव्रगति से बढ़ने को बाध्य है, ''मानव में अन्तर्निहित संभावनाओं को उन्मुक्त करने में'' और ''इस धरती पर इसकी नियति की संपूर्णता को, उसके यथार्थ की नैसर्गिकता को प्रकट करने में सहायक होंगी''।

1

वे ईश्वरप्रदत्त गुण जो मानवजाति को अन्य सभी जीवरूपों से अलग करते हैं, उस एक शब्द में साररूप में निहित हैं, जिसे मानवचेतना कहा जाता है। मस्तिष्क इसका एक सारभूत गुण है। इन्हीं नैसर्गिक गुणों ने मानवजाति को सभ्यताओं के निर्माण और भौतिक समृद्धि की क्षमता दी है। लेकिन केवल इन्हीं उपलब्धियों से मानवचेतना संतुष्ट नहीं हो सकी है। इसका रहस्यमय स्वरूप इसे एक सर्वातीत भाव की ओर, एक अदृश्य लोक की ओर बढ़ने को, उस अंतिम यथार्थ की ओर सभी सारतत्त्वों के उस सारतत्त्व की ओर जिसे ईश्वर कहा जाता है, पहुँचने की प्रवृत्ति देता है। एक के बाद एक आने वाली आध्यात्मिक प्रतिभ. ाओं ने जो धर्म मानवजाति को प्रदान किये थे, व मानवता और उस अंतिम यथार्थ के बीच प्राथमिक संबंध-सूत्र रहे हैं। और उन्होंने मानवजाति की क्षमता को इस तरह से अनुप्राणित और सुसंस्कृत किया है कि वह सामाजिक प्रगति के साथ-साथ आध्यात्मिक उत्कर्ष की उपलब्धि भी कर सके।

मानव क्रियाकलापों को व्यवस्थित करने के, विश्वशांति को प्राप्त करने के कोई भी गंभीर प्रयास धर्म को अनदेखा नहीं कर सकता। मानवजाति का धर्म के प्रति दृष्टिकोण और आचरण अधिकांश में इतिहास का विषय है। एक प्रमुख इतिहासकार ने धर्म को ''मानव स्वभाव का एक गुण'' कहा है। इस गुण की विकृति ने ही समाज में होने वाली अव्यवस्था तथा व्यक्तियों के बीच होने वाले संघर्षों को जन्म दिया है, इसे इन्कार नहीं किया जा सकता है। लेकिन कोई भी निष्पक्ष विचारों वाला पर्यवेक्षक धर्म द्वारा सभ्यता पर पड़ने वाले प्रबल प्रभावों से भी इन्कार नहीं कर सकता। इसके अतिरिक्त, कानूनों और नैतिकता पर पड़ने वाले इसके सीधे प्रभाव द्वारा सामाजिक व्यवस्था के लिए इसकी अनिवार्यता, स्वतः प्रमाणित है।

धर्म की सामाजिक शक्ति के बारे में बहाउल्लाह ने कहा है : ''इस संसार में व्यवस्था की स्थापना और इसमें जो भी रहते हैं उनकी शांतिपूर्ण संतुष्टि के

लिए धर्म सभी साधनों में सबसे महान है।'' धर्म के सच्चे स्वरूप के छिप जाने या भ्रष्ट होने के विषय में उन्होंने लिखा है – ''यदि धर्म का दीपक अंधकार में छिप जाये तो अव्यवस्था उत्पन्न होगी, और औचित्य की, न्याय की और शांति की ज्योति प्रकाश देना बंद कर देगी।'' ऐसे परिणामों को गिनते हुए बहाई पवित्र ग्रंथों में यह इंगित किया गया है कि ''मानव–स्वभाव की विकृति, मानवीय आचरण का पतन, मानवीय संस्थाओं की भ्रष्टता और विघटन, ऐसी परिस्थितियों में स्वयं को अपने सबसे निकृष्ट रूपों में प्रकट करते हैं। मानव चरित्र का अधःपतन होता है, आत्मविश्वास विचलित हो जाता है। शिष्टता और लज्जा की भावना तिरोहित हो जाती है। मानव अन्तःकरण की आवाज को कुचल दिया जाता है। कर्त्तव्य, सुदृढ़ता, पारस्परिक आदान–प्रदान और निष्ठा की धारणायें विकृत हो जाती हैं और शांति, आनंद और आशा की मूल संवेदना ही धीरे–धीरे समाप्त हो जाती है।''

अतः यदि मानवता एक ऐसे बिन्दु तक आ पहुँचे जब विरोध और संघर्ष ने उसे जड़ और गतिहीन कर दिया हो तो गलतफहमियों और भ्रम के उस मूलस्रोत को खोजने के लिए जो धर्म के नाम पर उसे आहत कर रहा है, उसे स्वयं अपनी ओर, अपनी उपेक्षा की ओर, और उन तीखी पुकारों की ओर ध्यान देना चाहिए। और जो लोग अंधेपन और स्वार्थ के साथ अपनी विशिष्ट कट्टरपंथी धारणाओं पर अड़े हुए हैं, जिन्होंने अपने अनुयायियों पर ईश्वरीय संदेशवाहकों की वाणी की परस्पर विरोधी और गलत धारणायें थोपी हैं, वे भी इस भ्रम और व्यवस्था के लिये अधिक जिम्मेदार हैं – एक ऐसा भ्रम और एक ऐसी अव्यवस्था जिन्हें धर्म और तर्क, विज्ञान और धर्म के बीच नकली दीवारें खड़ी करके और अधिक बढ़ा दिया गया है। क्योंकि महान धर्मसंस्थापकों की वास्तविक वाणी के एक न्यायपूर्ण परीक्षण से और उस सामाजिक परिवेश पर दृष्टि डालने से जिसके बीच उन्हें अपने ईश्वरीय उद्देश्य को निभाने के लिए बाध्य होना पड़ा था, यह निष्कर्ष निकाला जा सकता है कि विभिन्न मानवीय धर्मसमुदायों को विश्रृंखलित कर देने वाले विवादों और पूर्वाग्रहों का कोई भी आधार नहीं है।

यह शिक्षा कि हमें दूसरों से भी वैसा ही व्यवहार करना चाहिए जैसा व्यवहार हम स्वयं अपने प्रति चाहें, ऐसा नैतिक सिद्धांत है जिसे सभी महान धर्मों में अनेक रूपों में दोहराया गया है। यह सिद्धान्त हमारे इस बाद के कथन को दो विशिष्ट संदर्भों में और अधिक बल देता है। यह इन धर्मों में व्याप्त उनके नैतिक रवैये, उनके शांति को प्रोत्साहन देने वाले पक्ष का सार रूप प्रस्तुत करता है, चाहे वे धर्म किसी भी युग और किसी भी स्थान में उदभूत हुए हों। यह एकता के उस पहलू की ओर भी संकेत करता है जो उनकी सारभूत अच्छाई है, एक ऐसी अच्छाई जिसे अपने असंबद्ध ऐतिहासिक परिप्रेक्ष्य में समझने में मानवजाति असफल रही है।

यदि मानवजाति ने अपने सामूहिक बाल्यकाल के शिक्षकों को उनकी वास्तविक विशिष्टता के परिप्रेक्ष्य में, एक ही सभ्यता के निर्माण की प्रक्रिया के माध्यमों के रूप में देखा होता, तो यह अवश्य ही उनके उत्तरोत्तर आने वाले ईश्वरीय प्रयोजनों के समग्र अभावों से इतने महान रूप से लाभान्वित होती जिसका अनुमान नहीं लगाया जा सकता। लेकिन शोक, कि यह ऐसा करने में असमर्थ रही।

कई देशों में धर्मांध धार्मिक उत्साह का फिर से उमड़ पड़ना, बुझने से पहले दिये की लौ के भड़कने के अतिरिक्त और कुछ नहीं समझा जा सकता। इस धर्मान्धता की लहर के साथ हिंसा और विघटनकारी घटनाओं का आना इनके आध्यात्मिक दिवालियापन की गवाही देता है। निश्चय ही धार्मिक धर्मान्धता के इस वर्तमान उत्थान का एक सबसे विचित्र और सबसे दुखजनक पहलू यह है कि इसने, जिस धर्म में भी यह प्रकट हुआ है, उस धर्मविशेष के मानवीय एकता से संबंधित आध्यात्मिक मूल्यों को ही खोखला नहीं कर दिया है, बल्कि जिस धर्म की यह धर्मान्धता सेवा करना चाहती है उस धर्म के द्वारा प्राप्त अनूठी नैतिक विजयों को भी इसने निःशेष कर दिया है।

मानवजाति के इतिहास में धर्म चाहे जितनी ही महत्वपूर्ण शक्ति के रूप में उभरा हो और उग्रवादी धार्मिक कट्टरता का वर्तमान पुनरूत्थान कितना ही नाटकीय हो, धर्म और धार्मिक संस्थाओं को पिछले कुछ दशकों से अधिकाधिक संख्या में लोगों ने आधुनिक विश्व की प्रमुख समस्याओं के संदर्भ में अप्रासंगिक समझा है। धर्म के स्थान पर लोग या तो भौतिकवादी संतुष्टि की ओर मुड़े हैं या उन मानवनिर्मित वादों का अनुसरण करने में लगे रहे हैं जो उन बुराइयों को दूर करने के लिए रचे गये हैं जिनके कारण ऊपरी तौर पर समाज संत्रस्त दिखाई पड़ता है। इनमें अधिकांश वादों की प्रवृत्ति मानवजाति की एकता को बढ़ावा देने और विभिन्न राष्ट्रों के बीच सहमति और मेलमिलाप की अभिवृद्धि करने के बजाय या तो राजतंत्र को ही ईश्वर की जगह बिठाने अथवा सारी मानवता को एक राष्ट्र, नस्ल या धर्म के अधीन करने अथवा सभी प्रकार के विचारविमर्श और विचारों के आदान–प्रदान के दमन का प्रयास करने तथा करोड़ों भूखे मरते लोगों को एक ऐसी बाजार व्यवस्था की दया पर छोड़ देने की ओर है जो स्पष्टतया ही बहुसंख्यक मानवता की दुर्दशा को और अधिक बढ़ा रही है जबकि कुछ थोड़े से वर्गों को समृद्धि की ऐसी स्थिति में जीवन बिताने की सामर्थ्य दे रही है जिसकी कल्पना भी हमारे पूर्वजों ने शायद ही की हो।

कितना दुःखद है इन स्थानापन्न धर्मों का लेखा–जोखा जिन्हें हमारे युग के बुद्धिमान लोगों ने दिया है। जिन विशाल जनसमूहों को इन वादों की वेदिक. ओं पर आराधना करने की शिक्षा दी गई थी, आज उनका पूर्णतया भ्रमभंग हो

चुका है। इन वादों और सिद्धांतों ने जो फल उत्पन्न किये हैं, वे हैं अनेक ऐसी सामाजिक और आर्थिक बुराइयां जो बीसवीं सदी के इन अंतिम वर्षों में संसार के प्रत्येक क्षेत्र को संत्रस्त कर रही हैं। इन सभी ऊपरी व्याधियों के मूल में है एक आध्यात्मिक क्षति; और यह क्षति प्रतिबिंबित होती है सभी राष्ट्रों के जनसमूहों पर छाई हुई निष्क्रियता की भावना में। इसने करोड़ों उपेक्षित और पीड़ित लोगों के हृदयों में प्रकाशित आशा की सभी किरणों को बुझा डाला है।

अब वह समय आ गया है जब भौतिकवादी सिद्धांतों को उपदेश देने वाले लोगों को चाहे वे पूर्व के हों या पश्चिम के, पूंजीवादी हों या समाजवादी, चाहिये कि उस नैतिक नेतृत्व का हिसाब पेश करें, जो अपनी धारणा के अनुसार उन्होंने अब तक संचालित किया है। कहां है वह नई दुनिया जिसका वायदा इन वादों ने किया था ? कहां है सांस्कृतिक उपलब्धि के वे नये आयाम जो इस या उस राष्ट्र या नस्ल के द्वारा या विशेष वर्गों के द्वारा शक्ति और समृद्धि हथियाकर उत्पन्न हुई ? क्यों संसार के लोगों का विशाल बहुमत अधिक से अधिक भूख और दुर्दशा के दलदल में फंसता जा रहा है ? जबकि इतनी धनसंपत्ति आज मानवजाति के भाग्य के निर्णायकों के हाथों में है, जिसकी कल्पना फैरो (मिस्र के सम्राट) सीजरा या उन्नीसवीं शताब्दी की साम्राज्यवादी शक्तियों ने भी न की होगी।

विशेषरूप से इन सभी वादों में भौतिक उपलब्धियों की जो महिमा गाई गई है, वही इन सब वादों की जननी भी है और उनकी एक सामान्य विशेषता भी। वही इस मिथ्या भावना को पोषित करती है कि मनुष्य इतना स्वार्थी और आक्रामक स्वभाव का है कि उसके स्वभाव को बदला नहीं जा सकता। यहीं से उस आधारभूमि को निष्कंटक बनाना है जहाँ से हमारी आने वाली पीढ़ियों के लिए एक नये विश्व का निर्माण शुरू होगा।

अनुभव के निष्कर्ष के रूप में यह स्पष्ट हो जाता है कि भौतिकवादी आदर्श मनुष्यजाति को संतुष्टि देने में असफल रहे हैं। और इसी कारण से यह ईमानदारी से स्वीकार किया जाना चाहिए कि अब इस धरती की यातनामयी समस्याओं के हल के लिए एक नया प्रयास किया जाना आवश्यक है। आज समाज में व्याप्त असहनीय परिस्थियाँ सभी की सामान्य असफलताओं का उद्घोष करती हैं। यह एक ऐसी स्थिति है जो प्रत्येक दिशा से घिरी हुई मानवता को राहत देने के बजाय उस विकट परिस्थितियों के घेरे को और भी अधिक घातक बनाती है। स्पष्ट है कि सामान्य उपचार के लिए तुरन्त प्रयास किया जाना आवश्यक है। मूलरूप से यह मामला हमारे रवैये से संबंधित है। क्या मानवता अपने पथभ्रष्ट तौर–तरीकों पर चलती रहेगी, घिसी पिटी धारणाओं और अव्यावहारिक मान्यताओं पर अड़ी रहेगी ? या इसके नेतागण अपने–अपने वादों पर ध्यान न देते हुए, दृढ़

निश्चय के साथ आगे बढ़ेंगे और उचित समाधानों की एक साझी खोज के लिए आपस में परामर्श करेंगे ?

जिन्हें मानवजाति के भविष्य की चिन्ता है वे इन शब्दों पर भी कुछ विचार करने का कष्ट करें ''यदि लम्बे समय से प्रतिष्ठित आदर्श, और समय की कसौटी पर खरी उतरने वाली संस्थायें, कुछ सामाजिक धारणायें और धार्मिक फार्मूले सामान्य मानवता का कल्याण करने में अब असमर्थ हो गये हैं, यदि वे अब निरंतर विकसित होती हुई मानवता की आवश्यकताओं को पूरा नहीं कर पाते, तो उन्हें बुहार कर दकियानूसी और विस्मृत सिद्धांतों के कबाड़खाने में फेंक दिया जाना चाहिए। एक ऐसी दुनिया में जो परिवर्तन और ह्रास के अपरिवर्तनीय नियम के अधीन है, ये सिद्धांत ह्रास से मुक्त क्यों रहें और प्रत्येक मानव संस्था से आगे क्यों बढ़ जायें ? क्योंकि वैधानिक मानदंडों और राजनीतिक तथा आर्थिक सिद्धांतों की रचना, मात्र मानवजाति के हितों की समग्ररूप से रक्षा के लिए हुई है और इसलिए नहीं कि किसी विशिष्ट नियम, विधान या सिद्धांत की अखंडता को बनायें रखने के लिये सारी मानवता को सूली पर चढ़ा दिया जाये।''

2

अणअस्त्रों पर पाबंदी लगाने से, जहरीली गैसों के इस्तेमाल को रोकने से या कीटाणु युद्ध का गैरकानूनी करार देने से लड़ाई के मूल कारण समाप्त नहीं होंगे। किन्तु ऐसे महत्वपूर्ण व्यावहारिक उपाय स्पष्ट रूप से शांति की प्रक्रिया के ही अंग हैं। अपने आप में वे इतने सतवी नहीं हैं कि कोई स्थायी प्रभाव नहीं डाल सकते। लोग इतने चतुर हैं कि वे युद्ध के कोई दूसरे तरीके खोज लेंगे और एक—दूसरे के ऊपर आधिपत्य पाने के लिए खुराक, कच्चे माल, आर्थिक शक्ति, औद्योगिक शक्ति, सिद्धांतवाद या आतंकवाद का उपयोग करेंगे। साथ ही राष्ट्रों के बीच विशेष झगड़ों या असहमति का निपटारा करके मानवजाति के कार्यकलापों में आई वर्तमान विराट अव्यवस्था को भी नहीं दूर किया जा सकता। उसके लिए एक प्रामाणिक सार्वभौम ढांचे को अपनाये जाने की आवश्यकता है।

निश्चय ही राष्ट्रीय नेताओं ने इस समस्या के उस सार्वभौम स्वरूप को जो उनके सामने दिन—प्रतिदिन अधिक प्रबल रूप से उठने वाली समस्याओं के द्वारा स्वतः स्पष्ट हो जाता है, समझने में कोई कोताही नहीं की है और इसके साथ ही अनेक चिन्तित और प्रबुद्ध लोगों द्वारा किये गये अध्ययनों और समाधानों की संख्या भी निरंतर बढ़ती जा रही है। इसके अतिरिक्त संयुक्त राष्ट्र के अनेकों अभिकरणों ने भी इस विषय में कार्य किया है, जिससे कि इन चुनौतीभरी आवश्यकताओं के विषय में किसी प्रकार की जानकारी के अभाव की संभावना न रहे। लेकिन इस दिशा में कुछ करने की इच्छा को ही जैसे काठ मार गया हो।

और इसी समस्या का सावधानीपूर्वक परीक्षण और दृढ़ निश्चय के साथ उसका निराकरण होना चाहिए। जैसाकि हम पहले कह चुके हैं, इस निष्क्रियता की जड़ है इस धारणा में कि मनुष्यजाति अनिवार्यतः झगड़ालू है। और इसी कारण से एक विश्व व्यवस्था के हित में राष्ट्रीय हितों को गौण मानने के प्रति अनिच्छा उत्पन्न है और एक संयुक्त विश्व अधिकरण के दूरगामी परिणामों का साहसपूर्वक सामना करने के प्रति अनिच्छा उत्पन्न हुई है। इसका एक कारण इस तथ्य में भी खोजा जा सकता है कि अधिकांश में अज्ञान में डूबे हुए और गुलामी में पड़े हुए जनसमूह एक ऐसी नई व्यवस्था के प्रति अपनी कामना को प्रकट कर पाने में असमर्थ हैं, जिसमें वे शांति, सामंजस्य और खुशहाली से सारी मानवता के साथ रह सकें।

विश्व व्यवस्था की ओर बढ़ते कदम, विशेष रूप से दूसरे विश्व युद्ध के बाद से, आशाजनक संकेत देते हैं। राष्ट्रों के समूहों द्वारा ऐसे संबंधों को औपचा. रिक रूप देने की प्रवृत्ति जो उन्हें आपसी हितों के मामलों में सहयोग देने योग्य बनाते हैं, यह संकेत देते हैं कि अन्तोगत्वा सभी राष्ट्र इस निष्क्रियता पर काबू पा सकते हैं। दक्षिण पूर्वी राष्ट्रों के संगठन, कैरेबियन समुदाय तथा साझाबाजार, केन्द्रीय अमरीकी साझा बाजार, पारस्परिक आर्थिक सहयोग की परिषद, योरोपीय समुदाय, अरब राष्ट्रों का संघ, अफ्रीकी एकता संगठन, अमेरिकन राष्ट्रों का संगठन, दक्षिण प्रशांत संस्था तथा वे सभी संयुक्त प्रयास जो ऐसे संगठनों के द्वारा किये जाते हैं एक विश्व व्यवस्था के लिए मार्ग तैयार करते हैं।

इस धरती की सबसे अधिक जड़ जमा लेने वाली समस्याओं की ओर जो लगातार ज्यादा से ज्यादा ध्यान दिया जा रहा है वह भी एक दूसरा आशाजनक संकेत है। संयुक्त राष्ट्र की कुछ साफ दिखाई देने वाली कमियों के बावजूद, उस संगठन द्वारा चालीस से भी अधिक अपनाये गये घोषणा पत्रों तथा सिद्धांतों ने उस स्थिति में भी जबकि कुछ सरकारें उनके प्रति प्रतिबद्धता के विषय में बहुत अधिक उत्साही नहीं हैं, आम लोगों में एक नई उम्र पाने जैसी भावना दी है। मानव अधि. कारों की सार्वभौम उद्घोषणा, जातिनाश के अपराध को रोकने और दंडित करने पर समझौता, लिंगभेद, या धार्मिक विश्वास, नस्ल आदि पर आधारित सभी प्रकार के भेदभाव को समाप्त करने से संबंधित उसी प्रकार के उपाय, बच्चों के अधिक. रों की रक्षा, यंत्रणा के शिकार सभी लोगों का बचाव, भूख और कुपोषण को मि. टाना, शांति और मानव कल्याण के लिये वैज्ञानिक तथा तकनीकी विकास का उपयोग – ऐसे सभी उपायों को यदि साहसपूर्वक लागू किया जाये और विस्तार दिया जाये, तो ये उस दिन को और निकट ले आएंगी जब युद्ध की प्रेतछाया अंतर्राष्ट्रीय संबंधों पर अपने आधिपत्य को खो चुकी होगी। इन घोषणाओं और समझौतों में जिन समस्याओं की ओर संकेत किया गया है, उनके महत्व पर बल देने की कोई आवश्यकता नहीं है। फिर भी ऐसी कुछ समस्यायें, विश्व शांति की

स्थापना के विषय में तात्कालिक रूप से प्रासंगिक होने के कारण कुछ अतिरिक्त टिप्पणी की मांग करती हैं।

नस्लवाद, जो सभी बुराइयों में सबसे अधिक घातक और रूढ़िबद्ध है, शांति की राह में एक प्रमुख रूकावट है। इसका अब भी व्यवहार में लाया जाना मानवता के गौरव का इतना अपमानजनक उल्लंघन है कि उसको किसी भी बह. ाने से सहन नहीं किया जा सकता। नस्लवाद अपने शिकार लोगों की असीम आंतरिक संभावनाओं को प्रकट होने से रोकता है, इसको व्यवहार में लाने वाले को भ्रष्ट करता है और मानव प्रगति को अवरुद्ध कर देता है। मानवजाति की एकता की स्वीकृति की, जिसे समुचित वैधानिक उपायों से लागू किया जाये, सार्वभौम रूप से रक्षा होनी चाहिए, यदि इस समस्या पर काबू पाया जाना है।

धनी और निर्धनों के बीच बेहिसाब असमानता महान कष्टों का एक मूलस्रोत है और संसार को अस्थिरता की स्थिति में, वस्तुतः लड़ाई के कगार पर बनाये रखता है। बहुत थोड़े समाज इस स्थिति से प्रभावशाली रूप से निपट पाये हैं। इसका समाधान आध्यात्मिक, नैतिक और व्यावहारिक तरीकों की मांग करता है। इस समस्या पर एक नये पहलू से नजर डाले जाने की आवश्यकता है जिसका अर्थ है ज्ञान के अत्यधिक विस्तृत क्षेत्रों के विशेषज्ञों के साथ ऐसे विचार—विमर्श जो आर्थिक बहस और वादों की पेचीदगियों से मुक्त हों और जिसमें उन लोगों की भी पूरी साझेदारी हो जो इन निर्णयों से, जिन्हें शीघ्र ही किया जाना बहुत आवश्यक है, सीधे रूप से प्रभावित होते हों। यह एक ऐसा मामला है जो न केवल अत्यधिक धनाढ्यता और अत्यधिक गरीबी को समाप्त करने की आवश्यकता से जुड़ा हुआ है, बल्कि जिसका संबंध उन आध्यात्मिक सत्यों से भी है जिन के समझ लेने पर एक नये सार्वभौमिक रवैये का जन्म हो सकता है। एक ऐसी प्रवृत्ति को बढ़ावा देना स्वयं इस समाधान का एक प्रमुख हिस्सा है।

अनियंत्रित राष्ट्रवाद, जिसे एक समझदारी भरी और औचित्यपूर्ण देशभक्ति से अलग समझा जाना चाहिए, एक व्यापक निष्ठा, संपूर्ण मानवता के प्रति प्रेम का रूप ले। यह अत्यन्त आवश्यक है। बहाउल्लाह का कथन है ''धरती एक देश है, और मानवजाति इसके नागरिक।'' विश्व नागरिकता की धारणा का सीधा संबंध वैज्ञानिक प्रगति और राष्ट्रों की आपसी निर्भरता के कारण पूरे संसार के एक ही पड़ोस के रूप में बदल जाने से है। सारे संसार के लोगों से प्रेम में किसी के अपने देश के प्रति प्रेम को वर्जित नहीं किया गया है। विश्व समाज का एक अंग होने के लाभ को संपूर्ण के लाभ को बढ़ावा देकर और अधिक बढ़ाया जा सकता है। विभिन्न क्षेत्रों में ऐसे अंतर्राष्ट्रीय क्रियाकलाप जिनसे आपसी स्नेह और विभिन्न देशों के लोगों के बीच एकजुटता की भावना को पोषण मिलता हो, बेहद बढ़ावा देने की जरूरत है।

पूरे इतिहास के दौरान धार्मिक मतभेद अनगिनत युद्धों और संघर्षों के कारण बने रहे हैं, प्रगति के मार्ग में एक प्रमुख बाधा बन रहे हैं और सभी धर्मों के मानने वालों और किसी धर्म को भी न मानने वाले लोगों के लिए भी वह अधिक से अधिक घृणित बन गये हैं। सभी धर्मों के अनुयायियों को अवश्य ही उन आधारभूत प्रश्नों का सामना करने के लिए तैयार रहना चाहिए जो यह मतभेद खड़ा करते हैं, और स्पष्ट उत्तरों तक पहुँचने के लिए प्रस्तुत रहना चाहिए। कैसे उनके बीच के मतभेद सैद्धान्तिक और व्यावहारिक रूप से दूर हों ? आज के धार्मिक नेताओं के सामने जो चुनौती है, उस पर मानवीय संवेदना की भावना और सत्य की कामना से पूर्ण हृदयों के साथ मानवजाति की दुर्दशा पर उन्हें विचार करना चाहिये और अपने आप से यह प्रश्न पूछना चाहिये कि क्या उन्हें अपने सर्वशक्तिमंत स्रष्टा के सम्मुख विनीत भाव से, पारस्परिक धर्मशास्त्रीय मतभेदों को डुबो नहीं देना चाहिए जो उन्हें मानवीय समझ और शांति की प्रगति के लिए कार्य करने के योग्य बना सके ?

स्त्रियों का उद्धार, स्त्रियों और पुरुषों के बीच पूर्ण समानता की उपलब्धि शांति की सबसे महत्वपूर्ण, यद्यपि कम स्वीकृत मूल आवश्यकताओं में से है। ऐसी समानता को अस्वीकार करना संसार की आधी आबादी के विरूद्ध एक अन्याय को जारी रखता है और पुरुषों के बीच ऐसी हानिकारक प्रवृत्तियों और आदतों को बढ़ावा देता है जो परिवार से आगे बढ़कर काम की जगह, राजनीतिक जीवन, और अंततः अंतर्राष्ट्रीय संबंधों तक पहुंचती है। ऐसा कोई भी नैतिक, व्यावहारिक अथवा जैवशास्त्रीय आधार नहीं है जिस पर अधिकारों की यह अस्वीकृति न्यायपूर्ण ठहराई जा सके। मानवीय प्रयास के सभी क्षेत्रों में जब महिलाओं की पूरी साझेदारी का स्वागत किया जाएगा, केवल तभी वह नैतिक और मनोवैज्ञानिक वातावरण तैयार किया जा सकेगा जिसमें से अंतर्राष्ट्रीय शांति का जन्म होगा।

सब के लिये शिक्षा का लक्ष्य, जिसके लिए पहले से ही प्रत्येक धर्म और राष्ट्र के निष्ठावान लोगों का एक विशाल दल अपनी सेवायें समर्पित कर चुका है, संसार की सरकारों के अधिक से अधिक समर्थन का अधिकारी है। क्योंकि अज्ञान ही अकाट्यरूप से वह प्रमुख कारण है जो लोगों के पतन और ह्रास का और पूर्वग्रहों के लगातार बने रहने का आधार है। कोई भी राष्ट्र तब तक सफलता नहीं प्राप्त कर सकता जब तक उसके सभी नागरिकों को शिक्षा नहीं प्रदान की जाती। संसाधनों का अभाव अनेक राष्ट्रों की क्षमता को सीमित कर देता है और उन्हें वरीयताओं का एक क्रम निश्चित करने के लिए विवश करता है। इस संबंध में निर्णय लेने का अधिकार जिन संस्थाओं को है, वे यदि महिलाओं और लड़कियों की शिक्षा को पहली वरीयता देने के संबंध में विचार करें, तो बहुत अच्छा होगा। क्योंकि, शिक्षित माताओं के माध्यम से ही ज्ञान के लाभों का प्रभावशाली रूप से और तेजी के साथ पूरे समाज में प्रसार किया जा सकता है। समय की

आवश्यकताओं का लिहाज रखते हुए विश्व नागरिकता की मान्यता को प्रत्येक बालक की सामान्य शिक्षा के एक भाग के रूप में पढ़ाये जाने के संबंध में भी विचार होना चाहिए।

विभिन्न देशों के बीच संचार का अभाव भी विश्वशांति के प्रयासों को गंभीर हानि पहुँचाता है। एक अंतर्राष्ट्रीय सहायक भाषा को अपनाने से इन समस्याओं को सुलझाने में बड़ी हद तक सफलता मिलेगी और इस विषय पर तत्काल ध्यान दिया जाना आवश्यक है।

इन सभी मामलों में दो बातों पर विशेष बल दिया जाना आवश्यक है। पहली यह कि युद्ध की समाप्ति महज संधियों और समझौतों पर हस्ताक्षर करने की ही बात नहीं है, यह एक बहुत ही जटिल पर शांति की प्राप्ति के साथ नहीं जोड़ा जाता। दूसरी बात यह है कि शांति से संबंधित समस्याओं का सामना विशुद्ध व्यावहारिकता से बिल्कुल अलग चीज हो। क्योंकि मूलरूप में, शांति एक आंतरिक मनःस्थिति स उपजती है जिसका आधार होती है आध्यात्मिक, नैतिक वृत्ति और प्रमुखतः इस वृत्ति को जगाने पर ही चिरस्थायी समाधानों की संभावना हो सकती है।

कुछ ऐसे आध्यात्मिक सिद्धांत हैं, जिन्हें कुछ लोग मानवीय मूल्य कहते हैं। आध्यात्मिक सिद्धांत का सारभूत गुण यह है कि यह न केवल एक ऐसा दृष्टिकोण प्रस्तुत करता है जो मानव प्रकृति के अंतर्निहित स्वभाव के साथ सामंजस्य रखता है, बल्कि यह एक ऐसी वृत्ति की प्रेरणा देता है – एक गतिशीलता की, एक इच्छाशक्ति की, एक आकांक्षा की – जो व्यावहारिक उपायों की खोज और उन्हें लागू करने के रास्ते को सुगम बनाती है। सरकारों के अध्यक्ष और सत्ताधीन सभी लोग, यदि वे पहले इस समस्या के मूल में निहित सिद्धांतों को पहचान लेंगे और फिर उनसे मार्गदर्शन प्राप्त करेंगे, तो इन समस्याओं को सुलझाने में उनके प्रयासों को अच्छी सहायता मिलेगी।

3

जिस आधारभूत प्रश्न को सुलझाना है, वह यह है कि आज की दुनिया, जिसमें संघर्ष की बद्धमूल रूढ़ियां बरकरार हैं, क्या एक ऐसी दुनिया के रूप में बदल सकती है जिसमें सामंजस्य और सहयोग का बोलबाला हो।

विश्वव्यवस्था केवल मानवजाति की एकता की अडिग चेतना के आधार पर खड़ी की जा सकती है। यह एक ऐसा आध्यात्मिक सत्य है जिसकी पुष्टि सभी मानवीय विज्ञान करते हैं। मानवशास्त्र, शरीर विज्ञान, मनोविज्ञान, आदि स्वीकार

करते हैं कि मानव की एक ही नस्ल है, चाहे वह जीवन के गौणतर पहलुओं में अनंत विविधता रखती हो। इस सत्य की स्वीकृति के लिए सभी प्रकार के पूर्वाग्रहा. के परित्याग की आवश्यकता है – नस्ल, वर्ग, रंग, धर्म, राष्ट्र, लिंग तथा भौतिक सभ्यता के स्तर से संबंधित सभी पूर्वाग्रहों के परित्याग की आवश्यकता है, उस सभी कुछ के परित्याग की आवश्यकता है जो लोगों द्वारा स्वयं को दूसरों से श्रेष्ठ समझे जाने का कारण बनते हैं।

मानवजाति की एकता की स्वीकृति इस संसार को एक देश के रूप में, समस्त मानवता के घर के रूप में पुनर्गठित करने और प्रशासित करने की पहली आधारभूत आवश्यकता है। इस आध्यात्मिक सिद्धांत की सार्वभौमिक स्वीकृति विश्व शांति स्थापित करने के किसी भी सफल प्रयास के लिये अत्यन्त अनिवार्य है। अतः इसकी सार्वभौम उद्घोषणा की जानी चाहिए। इसे स्कूलों में पढ़ाया जाना चाहिए और समाज के ढांचे में, उस जीवंत परिवर्तन के लिए जो इसका निहितार्थ है, प्रत्येक राष्ट्र में इस पर निरंतर बल दिया जाना चाहिए।

बहाई दृष्टिकोण के अनुसार मनुष्य जाति की एकता की स्वीकृति यह मांग करती है कि ''संपूर्ण सभ्य संसार का पुनर्निर्माण व असैन्यीकरण हो।'' इससे कम कुछ नहीं – एक ऐसा संसार जो जीवन के सभी सारभूत पक्षों में, अपनी राजनीतिक प्रणाली में, अपनी आध्यात्मिक आकांक्षाओं में, अपने व्यापार और अर्थव्यवस्था में, अपनी लिपि और भाषा में जीवंत रूप से एकता के सूत्र में बंधा हुआ हो, और फिर भी इस संघ की सभी संघभूत इकाइयों की राष्ट्रीय विविधताओं की विशिष्टता अनंत हो।

इस मूल सिद्धांत के प्रभावों को स्पष्ट करते हुए बहाई धर्म के संरक्षक, शोगी एफेंदी ने 1931 में विचार व्यक्त किये थे कि : ''समाज के वर्तमान आध ारों को तोड़ने की बात तो दूर, यह (बहाई धर्म) को व्यापक बनाने का और इसकी संस्थाओं को इस रूप में पुनःनिर्मित करने का इच्छुक है जो इस निरंतर बदलती हुई दुनिया की आवश्यकताओं के अनुकूल हों। इसका विरोध किसी भी प्रकार की सही उद्देश्यों वाली संस्था के साथ नहीं हो सकता और न ही यह अनिवार्य वफादारी को ओछा दिखलाना चाहता है, इसका उद्देश्य न तो मानव हृदयों में जलने वाली प्रबुद्ध और समझदारी भरी देशभक्ति की दीपशिखाओं को दबाना है, न ही राष्ट्रीय स्वायत्तता की उस प्रणाली को समाप्त करना है जो अत्यधिक आवश्यक है, इसका उद्देश्य सीमा से अधिक केन्द्रीकरण से बचना है। यह नस्ली मूलों, जलवायु, इतिहास, भाषा और परम्परा, विचार और स्वभाव, तथा स्वभाव की उन विविधताओं को भी दबाना नहीं चाहता जो संसार के राष्ट्रों और लोगों को अलग करते हैं। इसकी पुकार है कि अब तक मानवजाति में जिन निष्ठाओं और आकांक्षाओं को अनुप्राणित किया गया है उससे कहीं अधिक व्यापक और विशालतर

आकांक्षायें हमारी हों। इसका आग्रह है कि एकता के सूत्र में बंधे हुए संसार के अनिवार्य दावों के सम्मुख राष्ट्रीय आवेगों और हितों को गौण माना जाये। एक ओर तो यह अत्यधिक केन्द्रीकरण का खंडन करता है और दूसरी ओर एकरूपता लाने के सभी प्रयासों को स्वीकार करता है। इसका मूल स्वर है विविधता में एकता।"

ऐसे लक्ष्यों की प्राप्ति के लिए राष्ट्रीय, राजनैतिक रवैयों का कई कारणों से व्यवस्थित किया जाना आवश्यक है, जो इस समय स्पष्ट रूप से परिभाषित कानूनों या राष्ट्रों के बीच संबंधों को नियंत्रित करने वाले स्वीकृत सार्वभौम सिद्धान्तों के अभाव के कारण अराजकता के सीमान्त पर स्थित हैं। लीग ऑफ नेशन्स, संयुक्त राष्ट्र तथा अनेक वे संगठन या समझौते जिनको इन दोनों संस्थाओं ने जन्म दिया है, अन्तर्राष्ट्रीय संघर्षों के कुछ नकारात्मक प्रभावों को क्षीण करने में सहायक अवश्य हुए हैं लेकिन उन्होंने स्वयं को युद्ध रोकने में असमर्थ प्रमाणित किया है। वास्तव में दूसरे विश्व युद्ध के समाप्त होने के बाद से बीसियों लड़ाइयाँ हो चुकी हैं और बहुत सी इस समय भी चल रही हैं।

इस समस्या के प्रमुख पहलू उन्नीसवीं सदी में भी सामने आ चुके थे। जब बहाउल्लाह ने पहले पहल विश्वशांति की स्थापना के अपने प्रस्तावों को सामने रखा था, तब विश्व के शासकों को संबोधित एक वक्तव्य में उन्होंने सामूहिक सुरक्षा के सिद्धान्त का प्रतिपादन किया था। शोगी एफेंदी ने उनके आशय पर टिप्पणी करते हुए लिखा है : "और किस आशय की ओर ये गुरुत्तर शब्द संकेत करते हैं, यदि उन्होंने उस अबाधित राष्ट्रीय प्रभुसत्ता की अनिवार्य कटौती की ओर संकेत नहीं किया है जो संसार के सभी राष्ट्रों के भावी राष्ट्रसंघ के निर्माण के लिए एक अनिवार्य शर्त है। यह जरूरी है कि एक विश्व की सर्वोपरि सरकार के किसी रूप का विकास अवश्य किया जाये जिसके पक्ष में संसार के सभी राष्ट्र स्वेच्छा से युद्ध करने, कर लगाने के कुछ अधिकारों और शस्त्रास्त्र रखने के सभी अधिकारों का स्वेच्छा से परित्याग कर चुके होंगे, सिवा अपने—अपने अधिकार क्षेत्रों में आंतरिक व्यवस्था बनाये रखने के उद्देश्य से शस्त्र रखने के अधिकारों के। ऐसे एक राज्य की परिधि में, एक ऐसी अंतर्राष्ट्रीय कार्यकारिणी भी सम्मिलित होगी जो उस राष्ट्रसंघ के प्रत्येक झगड़ालू सदस्य पर सर्वोपरि और चुनौती न दी जा सकने वाले अधिकार को लागू करने के लिए पर्याप्त रूप में सक्षम हो, एक विश्व संसद, जिसके सदस्य सम्बद्ध राष्ट्रों के लोगों द्वारा चुने जायेंगे और जिसके चुनाव की पुष्टि वहाँ की सरकारों द्वारा की जायेगी और इसके साथ ही एक सर्वोपरि न्यायाधिकरण भी होगा जिसका निर्णय ऐसे मामलों में भी बाध्यकारी प्रभाव रखता होगा जिन मामलों में संबंधित पक्ष अपने मामले को विचारार्थ उसके समक्ष प्रस्तुत करने के लिए स्वेच्छापूर्वक सहमत नहीं भी हुए होंगे।

"एक ऐसा विश्व समाज जिसमें सारी आर्थिक दीवारें स्थायी रूप से ढहाई जा चुकी होंगी और जिसमें पूंजी और श्रम की पारस्परिक निर्भरता निश्चित रूप से स्वीकार की जा चुकी होंगी, जिसमें धार्मिक धर्मान्धता और झगड़ों का शोरगुल सदा के लिये खामोश किया जा चुका होग, जिसमें नस्ली दुश्मनी की ज्वाला को अंतिम रूप से बुझाया जा चुका होगा, जिसमें अंतर्राष्ट्रीय कानून की एक संहिता – संसार के संघरूप में संगठित प्रतिनिधियों के सुविचारित निर्णय के निष्कर्ष लागू किये जा सकेंगे – जिसमें दंड के रूप में (पाबंदियों के रूप में) संघीभूत इकाइयों की सम्मिलित शक्तियों के तत्काल दौर दमनकारी हस्तक्षेप का प्रयोग हो सकेगा, और अंत में एक ऐसा विश्व समाज जिसमें एक सनकी और आक्रामक राष्ट्रवाद की उग्रता को विश्व नागरिकता की एक स्थायी चेतना के रूप में परिवर्तित किया जा चुका होगा – निश्चय ही बहाउल्लाह द्वारा दी गई व्यवस्था की व्यापक रूपरेखा ऐसी ही प्रतीत होती है, एक ऐसी व्यवस्था जो धीरे–धीरे वयस्क होते हुए युग के श्रेष्ठतम फल के रूप में मानी जाएगी।

इन दूरगामी उपायों के क्रियान्वयन की ओर बहाउल्लाह ने संकेत किया था, "वह समय अवश्य आयेगा जब एक सर्वव्यापी अधिकारों वाली मानव सभा की आवश्यकता को सार्वभौम रूप से अनुभव किया जायेगा। आवश्यक है कि इस दुनिया के शासक और राजा लोग इसमें भाग लें, और इसके कार्यकलापों में भाग लेते हुए, अवश्य ही ऐसे तरीकों और उपायों पर विचार करें जो मनुष्यों के बीच संसार की महानतम शांति की नींव रखे।

साहस, दृढ़ संकल्प, विशुद्ध उद्देश्य, एक देश के लोगों का दूसरे देश के लोगों के प्रति निःस्वार्थ प्रेम – वे सभी आध्यात्मिक और नैतिक गुण जिनकी शांति की ओर बढ़ने वाले इस युगांतरकारी कदम के लिए आवश्यकता है, मुख्य रूप से एक ही तथ्य की ओर इशारा करते हैं – काम करने के दृढ़ संकल्प की ओर। और इस आवश्यक संकल्प शक्ति को जगाने के लिए जरूरत है कि मनुष्य के मूल यथार्थ पर अर्थात् उसके 'विचार' पर तत्काल ध्यान दिया जाये। इस बात को समझने का अर्थ है स्पष्ट आवेग रहित और सौहार्दपूर्ण परामर्श के द्वारा इस प्रक्रिया के परिणामों पर आचरण करने की सामाजिक आवश्यकता को यथार्थ रूप देना। बहाउल्लाह ने मानव क्रियाकलापों को व्यवस्थित करने के लिये परामर्श की अनिवार्यता और गुणों पर ध्यान दिलाया है। उन्होंने कहा है, "परामर्श अधिक व्यापक जागरूकता प्रदान करता है और मात्र अनुमान को निश्चितता में परिवर्तित करता है। यह एक ऐसी जगमगाती ज्योति है जो, इस अंधेरी दुनिया में हमारा पथप्रदर्शन करती है। प्रत्येक कार्य के लिए एक पूर्णता और वयस्कता की स्थिति है और सदा रहेगी। बोध की शक्ति की परिपक्वता परामर्श के द्वारा मूर्त होती है।" उन्होंने जिस शांति का प्रस्ताव किया है उसकी प्राप्ति के लिए मात्र परामर्श करने का प्रयास ही इस संसार के लोगों के बीच एक ऐसी मंगलमय भावना को

उन्मुक्त कर सकता है कि कोई भी शक्ति उसके अंतिम, विजयपूर्ण परिणाम को रोक नहीं सकती।

इस विश्व सभा के कार्यकलापों के संबंध में, बहाउल्लाह के सुपुत्र और उनकी शिक्षाओं के अधिकृत व्याख्याता, अब्दुलबहा ने यह अंतर्दृष्टि संपन्न बातें सामने रखी हैं "यह आवश्यक है कि वे शांति के उद्देश्य को सामान्य परामर्श का विषय बनायें और अपनी सामर्थ्य के अनुसार प्रत्येक साधन के द्वारा संसार के राष्ट्रों का एक संगठन (संघ) स्थापित करने का प्रयास करें। यह आवश्यक है कि वे एक बाध्यकारी संधि करें और एक ऐसे समझौते की स्थापना करें जिसके प्रावधान समुचित, अनुलंघनीय और सुनिश्चित होंगे। यह आवश्यक है कि ये समस्त मानवजाति की स्वीकृति प्राप्त करें। यह सर्वोपरि और उदात्त दायित्व जो संसार की शांति और कल्याण का मूलस्रोत है – इस धरती के समस्त निवासियों के द्वारा एक पवित्र दायित्व माना जाये। इस परम महान समझौते के स्थायित्व और स्थिरता के लिये मानवता की सभी शक्तियों को गतिशील किया जाये। इस सर्वव्यापी समझौते में प्रत्येक राष्ट्र की सीमाओं और सरहदों को स्पष्ट रूप से निश्चित किया जाये। एक-दूसरे के साथ सरकारों के संबंधों के आधारभूत सिद्धांतों को निश्चित किया जाए और सभी अंतर्राष्ट्रीय समझौतों और दायित्वों को सुनिश्चित रूप दिया जाए। उसी प्रकार से प्रत्येक सरकार के शस्त्रास्त्रों को कड़ाई के साथ सीमित किया जाये, क्योंकि यदि युद्ध के लिए तैयारियों और किसी राष्ट्र की सैनिक शक्तियों को बढ़ने दिया जायेगा तो उससे दूसरों का संदेह बढ़ेगा। इस पवित्र समझौते के आधारभूत सिद्धांतों को इस प्रकार से निश्चित किया जाये कि यदि कोई सरकार बाद में इसके किसी भी प्रावधान को भंग करे, तो इस संसार की सारी सरकारें उसे पूरी तरह अधीनस्थ करने के लिए उठ खड़ी हों, बल्कि मानवजाति को एक समग्र इकाई के रूप में अपने अधिकार में उपलब्ध सभी शक्ति का उपयोग करते हुए उस सरकार को नष्ट कर देना चाहिए। यदि सभी उपायों में से इस महानतम उपाय को इस विश्व के रोगी शरीर पर प्रयुक्त किया जाये तो यह निश्चय ही अपनी बुराइयों से मुक्त हो जाएगा और चिरंतन रूप से सुरक्षित और स्थायी रहेगा।

इस प्रबल सम्मेलन के आयोजन में पहले ही बहुत विलम्ब हो चुका है।

हम अपने हृदयों की प्रखरतम भावना के साथ सभी राष्ट्रों के नेताओं से अपील करते हैं कि इस उपयुक्त क्षण का लाभ उठाते हुए, ऐसे उपाय करें जिनसे कि यह विश्व सभा एक वास्तविकता बन सके। इतिहास की सभी शक्तियाँ मानवजाति को इस कार्य के लिए बाध्य कर रही हैं और यह सदा-सदा के लिए उस चिर अपेक्षित वयस्कता के उदय का सूचक होगा।

क्या संयुक्त राष्ट्र अपने सभी सदस्यों के पूर्ण समर्थन के साथ इस सवा.
'परि घटना के उच्च उद्देश्य को पूरा करने के लिए नहीं उठ खड़ा होगा ?

सभी स्थानों के महिलाओं और पुरुषों, युवकों और बालकों को हमारा
आह्वान है कि सभी देशों के लोगों के लिए इस आवश्यक कदम के शाश्वत महत्व
को स्वीकार करें और अपने स्वर स्वेच्छापूर्वक स्वीकृति में उठायें। निश्चय ही इस
पीढ़ी को ही इस धरती के सामाजिक जीवन के विकास के इस नये चरण को
शुभारंभ करने का अवसर प्रदान किया जाना चाहिए।

4

हम यह अनुभव करते हैं कि इस आशावाद का मूलस्रोत एक ऐसी दृष्टि
है जो युद्धों की समाप्ति और अंतर्राष्ट्रीय सहयोग की संस्थाओं के निर्माण की
स्थिति से आगे झांकती है। राष्ट्रों के बीच स्थायी शांति एक आवश्यक चरण है,
लेकिन बहाउल्लाह बलपूर्वक कहते हैं कि यह मानवजाति के सामाजिक विकास
का अंतिम लक्ष्य नहीं है। आणविक महाविनाश के भय से विवश होकर अपनाये
गये शस्त्र त्याग से भी पूरे, एक—दूसरे पर संदेह करने वाले प्रतिद्वन्दी राष्ट्रों द्वारा
अनिच्छापूर्वक स्थापित की गई राजनीतिक शांति से परे, सुरक्षा और सह अस्तित्व
की व्यावहारिक व्यवस्थाओं से परे, ये उपाय सहयोग के जिन प्रयोगात्मक प्रयासों
को संभव बनायेंगे, उनसे भी परे है वह सर्वोपरि लक्ष्य — एक सार्वभौम परिवार के
रूप में संसार भर के राष्ट्रों और जातियों का एक सूत्र में गठन।

एकता का अभाव वह खतरा है जिसे इस धरती के राष्ट्र और लोग और
देर तक सहन नहीं कर सकते, इसके परिणाम इतने भयंकर हैं कि उनके विषय
में सोचा भी नहीं जा सकता और इतने प्रत्यक्ष हैं कि उनका वर्णन करने की
कोई आवश्यकता नहीं है। बहाउल्लाह ने एक शताब्दी से भी पहले लिखा था, —
''मानवजाति का कल्याण, उसकी शांति और सुरक्षा, तब तक प्राप्त नहीं की जा
सकती जब तक कि उसकी एकता सुदृढ़ रूप से स्थापित न हो जाये''। और यह
उद्गार व्यक्त करते हुए कि ''मानवजाति कराह रही है, एकता की मंजिल तक
पहुँचने का मार्गदर्शन पाने को और अपनी युगों से चलती आ रही शहादत को
समाप्त करने के लिए छटपटा रही है'' शोगी एफेंदी ने इससे आगे कहा है कि :
''संपूर्ण मानवजाति की एकता उस स्थिति का संकेत है जहां मानव समाज अब
पहुंच रहा है। परिवार की, कबीले की, नगर राज्य की ओर राष्ट्र की एकता का
उत्तरोत्तर प्रयास किया गया और वह पूरी तरह से स्थापित हो चुकी है। विश्व
एकता वह लक्ष्य है जिसकी ओर संत्रस्त मानवता अब प्रयासरत है। राष्ट्र निर्माण
की स्थिति अब समाप्त हो चुकी है। राज्य की प्रभुसत्ता में निहित अराजकता अब
चरम परिणति पर पहुँच रही है। वयस्कता की ओर विकसित होती हुई इस दुनिया

को यह दकियानूसी विचार छोड़ देना चाहिए और मानव संबंधों की एकता और समग्रता को स्वीकार करना चाहिए और सदा के लिए उस प्रणाली को स्थापित कर देना चाहिए जो जीवन के इस आधारभूत सिद्धांत को सर्वोत्तम रूप में मूर्त कर सकें।''

परिवर्तन की सभी समकालीन शक्तियाँ इस दृष्टिकोण को प्रामाणिकता प्रदान करती है। वर्तमान अंतर्राष्ट्रीय आंदोलनों और घटनाओं में इस विश्वशांति की ओर संकेत करने वाले इन प्रमाणों को हम देख सकते हैं। स्त्री–पुरुषों की एक विशाल सेना, जिसमें वस्तुतः प्रत्येक संस्कृति, नस्ल और राष्ट्र के लोग हैं और जो संयुक्त राष्ट्र की अनेकानेक संस्थाओं में कार्य करते हैं, एक ऐसी सार्वभौम ''नागरिक सेवा'' का ही रूप हैं जिसकी प्रभावशाली उपलब्धियाँ यह संकेत देती हैं कि निरुत्साहित करने वाली परिस्थितियों में भी सहयोग और सहकार को बहुत बड़ी सीमा तक उपलब्ध किया जा सकता है। एक आध्यात्मिक वसंत के समान ही एकता की आकांक्षा अपने आपको अनगिनत अंतर्राष्ट्रीय सम्मेलनों के रूप में अभिव्यक्त करने के लिए संघर्षरत है। ये सम्मेलन अत्यन्त व्यापक और विविध विषयों और विधाओं से संबंधित लोगों को एक स्थान पर इकट्ठा करते हैं। निश्चय ही यह सार्वभौमता की ओर गतिशील प्रवृत्ति का एक वास्तविक स्रोत है जिसके माध्यम से ऐतिहासिक रूप से एक–दूसरे के विरोधी धर्म और पंथ भी एक–दूसरे की ओर खिंचते दिखाई देते हैं। युद्ध और स्वार्थपरता की उस विरोधी प्रवृत्ति के साथ–साथ एकता की प्रवृत्ति इस विश्व एकता की ओर गतिशीलता 20वीं सदी के अंतिम वर्षों के दौरान इस धरती के जीवन की प्रमुख और व्यापक विशेषताओं में से एक है।

बहाई समुदाय का अनुभव इस बढ़ती हुई एकता के एक उदाहरण के रूप में देखा जा सकता है। यह तीस से चालीस लाख लोगों का एक समुदाय है जो अनेकों राष्ट्रों, संस्कृतियों, वर्गों और धर्मों से संबंधित हैं और जो ऐसी बहुमुखी क्रियाकलापों में लगे हुए हैं जिनसे अनेकों देशों की जनता की आध्यात्मिक, सामाजिक और आर्थिक आवश्यकताओं की पूर्ति होती है। यह एक सूत्र में बंधा हुआ जीवन्त समुदाय है जो मानव परिवार की विविधता का प्रतीक है और अपने क्रियाकलापों को सामान्य रूप से स्वीकृत परामर्श के आधार पर अपनाये गये सिद्ध ांतों की एक प्रणाली के द्वारा संचालित करता है और मानव इतिहास में दिव्य पथप्रदर्शन के जो भी महान प्रेरणास्रोत हुए हैं उनका समान रूप से आदर करता है। इसका अस्तित्व इसके प्रवर्त्तक की दृष्टि की व्यावहारिकता का एक और प्रमाण है। यह एक और साक्ष्य है कि मानवता एक विश्वव्यापी समाज के रूप में जीवन बिता सकती है और इसकी वयस्कता–प्राप्ति के मार्ग में जो भी चुनौतियाँ आयें उनका सफलतापूर्वक सामना कर सकती है। यदि बहाई अनुभव मानवजाति की

एकता को सुदृढ़ करने में किसी भी मात्रा में योगदान दे सकता हो, तो हम इसे अध्ययन के एक मॉडेल के रूप में प्रस्तुत करने में प्रसन्नता का अनुभव करेंगे।

इस समय सारे विश्व के सम्मुख जो चुनौतीपूर्ण दायित्व है, जब उसकी सर्वोपरि महत्ता पर हम विचार करते हैं, तो हम उस दिव्य सृष्टा की विराट भव्यता के सामने विनम्रता के सर झुका लेते हैं जिसने अपने अनंत प्रेम के कारण सारी मानवता को एक भी तत्व से उत्पन्न किया है, मनुष्य को रत्न जैसे यथार्थ की उदात्तता दी है, इसे प्रज्ञा, उच्चता और अमरता से सम्मानित किया है, और मानव को ''उस प्रभु को जानने और उससे प्रेम करने की क्षमता'' प्रदान की है, जो अपने आप में अद्वितीय है। यह एक ऐसी क्षमता है जिसे समस्त दृष्टि के उद्देश्य के मूल में स्थित सृजनात्मक प्रेरणा कहा जा सकता है।''

हमारा यह सुदृढ़ विश्वास है कि मानव की सृष्टि ''एक निरंतर प्रगतिशील सभ्यता को आगे बढ़ाने के लिए हुई है'', कि जंगल के पशुओं की तरह व्यवहार करना मनुष्य के लिए अशोभनीय है, ''कि मनुष्य के लिये तो विश्वसनीयता, सहनशीलता, दया, करुणा, स्नेहमय सौहार्द जैसे सद्गुण ही शोभा देते हैं। हम पुनः इस विश्वास की पुष्टि करते हैं कि मानव के पद में अंतर्निहित सामर्थ्य, इस धरती पर उसकी नियति की पूर्णता, उसके यथार्थ की स्वाभाविकता श्रेष्ठता, परमेश्वर के इस प्रतिश्रुत दिवस में अवश्य ही प्रकट होने चाहिए'' हमारी यह अडिग आस्था है कि एकता और शांति वे लक्ष्य हैं जो प्राप्त किये जा सकते हैं और जिसके लिये समस्त मानवता प्रयत्नशील है।

इन पंक्तियों के द्वारा बहाईयों की आशा भरी वाणी सुनी जा सकती है, बावजूद उस उत्पीड़न के जो अभी–अभी भी इस धर्म की जन्मभूमि में उन्हें दिया जा रहा है। अडिग आशा के उनके इस उदाहरण के द्वारा वे अपने इस विश्वास के साक्षी हैं कि शांति का युगों पुराना वह स्वप्न अब शीघ्र ही साकार होने वाला है। बहाउल्लाह द्वारा प्रकट किये गये उस धर्म के परिवर्तनकारी प्रभाव के कारण, ईश्वरीय सत्ता से सम्पन्न होने के कारण यह दिव्य शक्ति से अनुप्राणित है। इस प्रकार हम न केवल शब्दों के द्वारा आप तक एक विराट दृष्टि को संप्रेषित कर रहे हैं अपितु हम कर्म में आस्था तथा त्याग की शक्ति का भी आह्वान करते हैं। हम अपने सहधर्मियों की शांति और एकता की आतुर पुकार को सम्प्रेषित करते हैं। हम उन सब के साथ हैं जो आक्रमण के शिकार हैं, हम उन सब के साथ हैं जो संघर्ष और विवाद की समाप्ति की इच्छा रखते हैं, हम उन सब के साथ हैं जो शांति के सिद्धांतों में और एक विश्व व्यवस्था में निष्ठा रखते हैं क्योंकि इनसे उन उच्च आदर्शों को बढ़ावा मिलता है, जिनके लिए सर्वप्रिय सृष्टा ने मानवजाति को अस्तित्व दिया था।

अपनी तीव्र आशा और अपने गहन विश्वास को आप तक पहुँचाने की उत्कट कामना के साथ यहाँ हम बहाउल्लाह के बलशाली वचन को उद्धृत करते हैं : ''ये निरर्थक विवाद, ये विनाशकारी युद्ध समाप्त हो जायेंगे और परम महान शांति आयेगी।''

–विश्व न्याय मन्दिर

The Promise of World Peace

Persian

اکتبر 1985

خطاب به مردم جهان:

صلح بزرگ که طیّ قرون و اعصار آرزوی قلبی نیک‌اندیشان جهان بوده است، صلحی که نسل‌های بی‌شماری از عارفان و شاعران در باره‌اش سخن گفته‌اند، صلحی که کتب مقدّسه در ادوار متوالی نویددهندهٔ آن بوده‌اند، سرانجام دست‌یابی به آن برای ملل جهان ممکن گشته است. برای اوّلین بار در تاریخ بشر برای هر فرد این امکان وجود دارد که تمامی کرهٔ زمین را با میلیاردها مردم متنوّع‌اش در یک چشم‌انداز واحد مشاهده نماید. صلح جهانی نه تنها امکان‌پذیر بلکه اجتناب‌ناپذیر است. استقرار این صلح، مرحلهٔ بعدی تکاملِ کرهٔ زمین و به قول یکی از متفکّرین بزرگ، مرحلهٔ "جهانی شدن نوع بشر" (ترجمه) است.

گزینش اینکه آیا صلح تنها پس از وقوع بلایای وحشتناکِ ناشی از تمسّکِ سرسختانهٔ نوع بشر به روش‌های دیرینه تحقّق خواهد پذیرفت و یا از طریق یک اقدام ارادی و مشورتی در این زمان به دست خواهد آمد، در دست تمامی ساکنان کرهٔ زمین است. در این لحظهٔ بحرانی و حسّاس که مشکلات سرسخت ملّت‌ها به یک نگرانی مشترک برای همهٔ جهانیان مبدّل گشته، کوتاهی و قصور در متوقّف ساختن امواج اختلاف و بی‌نظمی کمالِ بی‌مسئولیّتی خواهد بود.

امّا نشانه‌های امیدبخشی نیز موجود است از جمله: تحکیم فزایندهٔ گام‌هایی به سوی نظمی جهانی که اوّل بار در اوایل این قرن با تأسیس جامعهٔ ملل برداشته شد، جامعه‌ای که بعداً سازمان ملل متّحد با بنیانی وسیع‌تر جای‌گزین آن گردید؛ کسب استقلال توسّط اکثر ملل جهان بعد از جنگ جهانی دوم که نمایانگر اتمام فرایند ملّت‌سازی است و تعامل این ملل نوخاسته با کشورهای کهن در علایق مشترک؛ گسترش وسیع همکاری‌های متعاقب در زمینه‌های علمی، آموزشی، حقوقی، اقتصادی و فرهنگی در بین ملّت‌ها و گروه‌هایی که تا به حال جدا از هم و دشمن یکدیگر بودند؛ فزونی یافتن بی‌سابقهٔ تعداد سازمان‌های انسان‌دوستانهٔ بین‌المللی در دهه‌های اخیر؛ افزایش جنبش‌های زنان و جوانانِ خواستار پایان جنگ؛ و ازدیاد خودجوشِ شبکه‌های در حال گسترشِ مردمِ عادیِ در جستجوی تفاهم از طریق مراودات شخصی.

پیشرفت‌های علمی و تکنولوژیکی حاصله در این قرنِ فوق‌العاده نجسته بر جهش عظیمی در تکامل اجتماعی کرهٔ زمین دلالت دارد و ابزاری را ارائه می‌دهد که می‌تواند راه حلّی برای مشکلات عملی نوع بشر فراهم آورد. این پیشرفت‌ها براستی وسایل لازم برای ادارهٔ زندگیِ پیچیدهٔ یک دنیای متّحد را فراهم می‌سازند. با این حال هنوز موانع بسیاری وجود دارد. شک و تردید، برداشت‌های غلط، تعصّبات، بدگمانی‌ها و خودخواهی‌های کوته‌نظرانه، بر روابط بین ملل و اقوام سایه افکنده‌اند.

ما امنای امر بهائی بنا بر احساسی عمیق از مسئولیّت روحانی و وجدانی، خود را موظّف می‌دانیم که در این فرصت مغتنم توجّه شما را به بینش‌های نافذی معطوف داریم که اوّل بار بیش از یک قرن پیش حضرت بهاءالله، مؤسس دیانت بهائی، به فرمانروایان جهان ابلاغ فرمود.

حضرت بهاءالله خاطرنشان می‌کنند که طوفان ناامیدی از هر سو می‌وزد و اختلافاتی که نوع بشر را به تفرقه و فلاکت می‌کشاند روز به روز در ازدیاد است و نشانه‌های تشنّج و هرج و مرج مشاهده می‌شود زیرا نظام کنونی به نحوی اسف‌بار ناقص و نارسا به نظر می‌رسد. تجارب عمومیِ جامعهٔ بشری این قضاوت آینده‌بینانه را کاملاً تأیید نموده است. نواقص نظم رایج را می‌توان در عدم تواناییِ کشورهای مستقلّ عضو سازمان ملل متّحد برای پاک‌سازی عالم از کابوس جنگ، در استمرار خطر فرو ریختن نظم اقتصادی بین‌المللی، در شیوع هرج و مرج و تروریسم، و در مصائب شدیدی که این بلایا و دیگر عوارض بی‌شمار برای میلیون‌ها نفر از افراد بشر ایجاد کرده‌اند به وضوح مشاهده نمود. تهاجم و تعارض در حقیقت چنان در تار و پود نظام‌های اجتماعی و اقتصادی و دینی موجود را فراگرفته که بسیاری به این باور تن در داده‌اند که این گونه کردار و رفتار جزء لاینفکِ طبیعت بشری است و ریشه‌کن کردن آن غیر ممکن می‌باشد.

با تثبیت این باور در اذهان عمومی، تضادّی فلج‌کننده در امور بشری به وجود آمده است. از یک سو مردمِ تمام کشورها نه تنها آمادگیِ خود را برای استقرار صلح و آشتی و برای پایان یافتن نگرانی‌های جان‌کاهی که زندگیِ روزمرّهٔ آنان را معذّب می‌سازد اعلان می‌کنند. از سوی دیگر بی‌دریغ مُهرِ قبول بر این نظر نهاده می‌شود که نوع انسان ذاتاً خودپرست، ستیزه‌جو و اصلاح‌ناپذیر است و در نتیجه قادر نیست نظامی اجتماعی بنا نهد که در عین حال هم پیشرو و صلح‌آمیز باشد و هم پویا و هماهنگ، نظامی که آزادیِ ابتکار و خلّاقیت فردی را ترویج کند ولی بر تعاون و تعاضد مبتنی باشد.

با فوریّت یافتن نیاز به صلح، وجود این تضادِّ بنیادین که مانع حصول صلح می‌شود ایجاب می‌کند که پیش‌فرض‌هایی که مبنای نظر عامّه در بارهٔ مشکلات تاریخی نوع بشر است مورد ارزیابی مجدّد قرار گیرد. شواهد موجود نشان می‌دهد که اگر این ارزیابی به نحوی منصفانه صورت پذیرد آشکار خواهد شد که رفتار ستیزه‌جویانه نه تنها نمایان‌گر فطرت واقعی نوع بشر نیست بلکه تصویری کَذِّنما از حقیقت انسان است. رضایت ناشی از این نکته مردم را قادر خواهد ساخت تا قوای اجتماعی سازنده‌ای را به حرکت در آورند که به خاطر هم‌خوانی‌اش با طبیعت بشری، به جای جنگ و ستیز، هماهنگی و همکاری را ترویج خواهد داد.

گزینش چنین مسیری به معنای انکار گذشتهٔ بشریّت نیست بلکه نشانهٔ درک آن است. آیین بهائی اغتشاش کنونی جهان و وضع مصیبت‌بار حاکم بر امور انسانی را مرحله‌ای طبیعی از یک فرایند ارگانیک مشاهده می‌نماید که مآلاً به طور قطع به وحدت نوع انسان در ظلِّ یک نظم اجتماعی واحد منجر خواهد شد، نظمی که حدود و ثغورش تمامی کرهٔ زمین خواهد بود. نوع بشر به عنوان یک واحد متمایز و ارگانیک از مراحل تکاملی مشابه با مراحل شیرخوارگی و کودکی در زندگی هر فرد گذشته است و اکنون در اوج مرحلهٔ متلاطم نوجوانی قرار گرفته و به مرحلهٔ بلوغی که مدّت‌ها انتظارش را می‌کشیده نزدیک می‌شود.

اذعان صادقانه به اینکه تعصّب و جنگ و استثمار جلوه‌هایی از مراحل قبل از بلوغ نوع بشر در طیِّ یک فرایند گستردهٔ تاریخی بوده‌اند و قبول اینکه نوع انسان امروز شاهد آشوب اجتناب‌ناپذیری است که نشانهٔ فرا رسیدن مرحلهٔ بلوغ جمعی او می‌باشد، دلیلی برای یأس و ناامیدی نیست بلکه شرط لازم برای قبول مسئولیّت خطیر و مهمِّ ساختن دنیایی صلح‌آمیز است. مطلبی که بررسی‌اش را صمیمانه به شما توصیه می‌نماییم اینست که انجام چنین امر عظیمی امکان‌پذیر است، قوای سازندهٔ لازم موجود است و ساختارهای اجتماعی متّحدکننده را می‌توان بنا نهاد.

هر قدر آیندهٔ نزدیک مشحون از رنج و اغتشاش و هر قدر افق کنونی تیره و تار باشد، جامعهٔ بهائی معتقد است که نوع بشر می‌تواند با اطمینان از نتایج نهایی با این امتحان و افتتان عظیم مقابله نماید. تحوّلات تشنّج‌آمیزی که عالم انسانی به سرعت به سوی آن سوق داده می‌شود نه تنها به هیچ وجه نشانهٔ پایان تمدّن بشری نیست بلکه سبب خواهد شد که باید در این یوم موعود مقام و رتبهٔ انسان ظاهر شود، قوا و استعدادات

مکنونه‌اش به منصّهٔ ظهور رسد، سرنوشت درخشانش به خوبی آشکار گردد و فضایل عالیهٔ فطری‌اش به عرصهٔ شهود در آید.

1

استعدادها و مواهبی که نوع انسان را از سایر موجودات زنده ممتاز می‌کند در لطیفه‌ای مکنون است که روح انسانی نامیده شده و عقل خصیصهٔ اساسی آنست. این مواهب، نوع بشر را قادر به بنیان نهادن تمدّن‌ها و ایجاد رفاه مادّی نموده است. امّا این قبیل دست‌آوردها به تنهائی هرگز سبب ارضای روح انسانی نگشته است، روحی که ماهیّت اسرارآمیزش او را به سوی جهان بالا سوق می‌دهد، به سوی عالمی غیبی، به سوی حقیقتی مطلق و به سوی ذاتی منیع و لایدرک و به سوی جوهر الجواهری که خدا نامیده می‌شود. ادیانی که از طریق یک سلسله پیامبران روحانی به بشر داده شده‌اند حلقه‌های اوّلیّهٔ ارتباط بین انسان و آن حقیقت مطلق بوده‌اند و قابلیّت نوع بشر را برای حصول به ترقّیات روحانی توأم با پیشرفت‌های اجتماعی شکل بخشیده و تلطیف نموده‌اند.

هیچ اقدام جدّی برای اصلاح امور جامعهٔ انسانی و تأسیس صلح جهانی نمی‌تواند دین را نادیده بگیرد. درک و پیروی بشر از دین قسمت اعظم محتوای صفحات تاریخ را تشکیل می‌دهد. یک مورّخ بزرگ، دین را به عنوان "قوّه‌ای از طبیعت انسان" (ترجمه) توصیف کرده است. البتّه نمی‌توان منکر شد که سوء استفاده از این قوّه در بروز بسیاری از اغتشاشات در اجتماع و ظهور جنگ و جدال بین افراد سهمی بسزا داشته است ولی در عین حال هیچ ناظر منصفی نمی‌تواند نفوذ غالبهٔ دین در جنبه‌های حیاتی مدنیّت انسانی را انکار نماید. به علاوه لزوم دین برای نظم اجتماع از طریق تأثیر مستقیمی که بر قوانین و اخلاقیّات داشته مکرّراً به ثبوت رسیده است.

حضرت بهاءالله در وصف دین به عنوان یک قوّهٔ اجتماعی می‌فرمایند: "...اوست سبب بزرگ از برای نظم جهان و اطمینان مَنْ فی الامکان." و در بارهٔ تیرگی و یا فساد دین چنین می‌فرمایند: "اگر سراج دین مستور ماند هرج و مرج راه یابد نیّر عدل و انصاف و آفتاب اَمن و اطمینان از نور باز مانند." آثار بهائی در توضیح پیامدهای انحطاط دین چنین متذکّر می‌شوند که: "انحراف طبیعت انسانی، تدنّی رفتار آدمی و انحطاط مؤسّسات بشری پست‌ترین و زننده‌ترین جنبه‌های خود را نشان می‌دهند. خلق و خوی بشری فاسد می‌گردد، اعتماد و اطمینان سلب می‌شود، قیود انضباط سست می‌گردد، ندای وجدان خاموش می‌شود، شرم و حیا از میان رخت برمی‌بندد، مفاهیمی چون حسّ

مسئولیّت، همبستگی، تعاضد و وفاداری تحریف می‌گردد و احساس آرامش و سرور و امیدواری به تدریج نابود می‌شود." (ترجمه)

پس اگر بشریّت به ورطه‌ای از اختلافات فلج‌کننده رسیده است برای یافتن سرچشمهٔ سردرگمی و سوءتفاهماتی که بنام دین تداوم یافته باید به خویشتن، به غفلت خود، و به ندای‌ گمراه‌کننده‌ای که به آنها گوش فرا داده است بنگرد. کسانی که کورکورانه و خودخواهانه بر معتقدات سنّتی خود اصرار ورزیده‌اند و تفاسیری غلط و ضدّ و نقیض از کلام پیامبران خدا را به مریدان خویش تحمیل نموده‌اند مسئولیّت سنگینی در ایجاد این اغتشاش به دوش دارند، اغتشاشی که با ایجاد سدهای مصنوعی میان خِرد و ایمان، و بین علم و دین تشدید شده است. زیرا بررسی منصفانه‌ای از اصل کلامِ مؤسّسین ادیان بزرگ و اوضاع اجتماعی محیطی که هر یک از این مظاهر الهی موظّف به اجرای رسالت خویش در آن بودند نشان می‌دهد که هیچ مطلبی در تأیید مشاجرات و تعصّباتی که سبب انحراف جوامع دینی و در نتیجه، تدنّی جمیع شئون انسانی گردد وجود ندارد.

آموزهٔ "آنچه به خود نمی‌پسندی به دیگران مپسند" که در تمام ادیان بزرگ به اشکال گوناگون و به طور مکرّر آمده است، از دو جهتِ خاصّ مؤیّد این نظر می‌باشد: یکی آنکه جوهر و چکیدهٔ مفاهیم اخلاقی و جنبهٔ صلح‌آفرین همهٔ ادیان را، فارغ از زمان و مکانی که در آن ظاهر شده‌اند، نشان می‌دهد و دیگر آنکه بر جنبه‌ای از وحدت دین دلالت می‌کند که خصلت ذاتی تمام ادیان است، خصلتی که نوع بشر در چشم‌انداز غیر منسجم خود از تاریخ، از درک آن قاصر مانده است.

اگر نوع بشر مربّیان روحانی عصر طفولیّتِ جمعی خویش را طبق خصلت واقعی آنان، در مقام عاملین یک فرایند تمدّن‌ساز مشاهده می‌نمود، یقیناً از اثرات تکاملی ظهورات پی در پیِ آنان بهره‌ای صدچندان می‌گرفت. افسوس که در این مورد قصور نمود.

بازگشت التهابات افراطی مذهبی در بسیاری از نقاط جهان را نمی‌توان جز تلاشی مذبوحانه به شمار آورد. نفس خشونت و اخلاق‌گری پدیده‌هایی که با این التهابات همراه است خود نمایانگر ورشکستگی روحانی عقاید وابسته به آنها است. براستی یکی از عجیب‌ترین و غم‌انگیزترین خصوصیّات شیوع تعصّب‌گرایی مذهبی کنونی آنست که تا چه حدّ در تمام موارد نه تنها موجب تضعیف مـوازین روحانی لازم برای وحدت نوع انسان می‌شود بلکه همچنین باعث بی‌ارزش نمودن موفقیّت‌های بی‌نظیر اخلاقی همان دینی می‌گردد که مدّعی ترویج آن است.

هرچند دین نیروی حیاتی و مهمّی در تاریخ بشری بوده و هرچند بازگشت التهابات ستیزه‌گر مذهبی شدید است، با این حال مدّت‌هاست که دین و مؤسّسات دینی، از جانب عدّهٔ روزافزونی از مردم، پدیده‌ای بی‌ربط با مسائل مهمّ دنیای مدرن انگاشته شده‌اند. به جای تمسّک به دین، مردم یا به ارضای شهوات مادّی روی آورده‌اند و یا ایدیولوژی‌هایی را دنبال می‌کنند که به دست بشر ساخته شده و برای رهایی اجتماع از بلاهای آشکاری که از آنها رنج می‌برد طرح‌ریزی گردیده‌اند. متأسّفانه بسیاری از این ایدیولوژی‌ها به جای آنکه مفهوم وحدت نوع انسان را در بر گیرند و توافق و هماهنگی بیشتری را در میان مردم مختلف ترویج دهند، گرایش‌شان بر آنست که حاکمیّت ملّی را خدایگون سازند، بقیّهٔ نوع بشر را تابع و فرمان‌بردار یک ملّت، یک نژاد و یا یک طبقه قرار دهند، در سرکوب کردن هر نوع مباحثه و تبادل افکار بکوشند، و یا بی‌رحمانه میلیون‌ها مردم گرسنه را رها نمایند تا قربانی عملیّات یک سیستم بازار اقتصادی گردند، سیستمی که به وضوح باعث تشدید مصائب اکثریّت نوع بشر گشته و در عین حال عدّهٔ قلیلی را قادر ساخته است که در چنان وفور نعمتی غوطه‌ور شوند که نسل‌های پیشینِ ما آن را حتّی در خواب هم نمی‌دیدند.

چه اسف‌بار است کارنامهٔ مرام‌هایی که عقلای دنیا بین عصر حاضر برای جای‌گزینی دین خلق کرده‌اند. قضاوت قطعی تاریخ در بارهٔ ارزش این مرام‌ها را می‌توان در یأس و سرخوردگی گستردهٔ انبوه مردمانی مشاهده نمود که تعلیم یافته‌اند تا در محراب آنها به پرستش پردازند. ثمرات این مکتب‌ها — پس از ده‌ها سال اِعمال قدرتِ روزافزون و بلامانع از طرف کسانی که برتری قدرت و مقام‌شان در امور بشری را مدیون این عقاید می‌باشند — امراض اقتصادی و اجتماعی کشنده‌ایست که در واپسین سال‌های قرن بیستم هر گوشهٔ جهان را مبتلا ساخته است. ریشهٔ تمامی این مصائب ظاهری، صدماتی معنوی است که در بی‌علاقگی و بی‌تفاوتیِ مستولی بر توده‌های مردم همهٔ ملّت‌ها و در خاموش شدن شعلهٔ امید در قلوب میلیون‌ها نفر از افراد محروم و رنج‌دیده منعکس است.

وقت آن فرا رسیده است که مروّجین عقاید مکتب مادّی‌گرایی — چه از شرق و چه از غرب، چه منسوب به کاپیتالیسم و چه وابسته به سوسیالیزم — به ادّعای رهبری اخلاقی‌ای که از آنِ خود می‌دانند پاسخ دهند. کجاست آن "دنیای جدیدی" که این ایدیولوژی‌ها وعده داده‌اند؟ کجاست آن صلح بین‌المللی که مدّعی پای‌بندی به آرمان‌های آن هستند؟ کجاست آن پیروزی‌های عظیم در عرصه‌های تازهٔ پیشرفتِ فرهنگی که با بزرگ نمایاندن این نژاد، آن کشور و یا طبقهٔ خاصّی از مردم حاصل شده است؟ چرا اکثریّت عظیم مردم جهان بیش از پیش در گرسنگی و بدبختی فرو می‌روند در حالی که

ثروت‌های نامحدودی که فراعنه و قیاصره یا حتّی امپراطوری‌های پرقدرت قرن نوزدهم در خواب هم نمی‌دیدند، اینک در دست دلّالان امور بشری انباشته شده است؟

ریشهٔ مغذّی این باور غلط را که نوع انسان خودپرست، ستیزه‌جو و غیر قابل اصلاح است، می‌توان علی‌الخصوص در تجلیل از علایق مادّی که هم منشأ و هم خصیصهٔ مشترک تمام این ایدیولوژی‌هاست یافت. اینجاست که زمینه برای ساختن جهانی جدید و درخور نسل‌های آیندهٔ بشری باید هموار گردد.

از آنجا که تجربه نشان می‌دهد که آرمان‌های مادّی در برآوردن نیازهای بشری شکست خورده‌اند، می‌بایستی صادقانه قبول کرد که برای یافتن راه حلِّ مشکلاتِ دردناک کرهٔ زمین کوشش‌های تازه‌ای باید به عمل آید. شرایط تحمّل‌ناپذیری که جامعهء بشری را فرا گرفته همه از شکستی مشترک حکایت می‌کند و وضعی به وجود آورده است که به جای کاهش جبهه‌گیریِ همه‌جانبه، موجب تحریک آن می‌شود. واضح است که کوششی همگانی و فوری برای علاج دردها مورد نیاز است و درمان این درد در وهلهٔ اوّل مربوط به مسئلهٔ گرایش و طرز فکر است. آیا نوع بشر همچنان به غفلت خود ادامه خواهد داد و به مفاهیم کهنه و فرضیّات غیر عملی تمسّک خواهد جست یا آنکه رهبران جهان، فارغ از ایدیولوژی، قدم همّت پیش خواهند نهاد و با عزمی راسخ در جستجویِ متّحدانه برای یافتن راه حلّی مناسب با یکدیگر به مشورت خواهند پرداخت؟

کسانی که به فکر آیندهٔ نوع انسانند سزاوار است به این پند توجّه کنند: "اگر گرامی‌ترین آمال دیرینه و مشروعات و مؤسّسات جلیلهٔ قدیمه و برخی از شئون اجتماعیّه و قواعد دینیّه از ترویج منافع عمومیّهٔ عالم انسانی باز مانده‌اند و اگر از عهدهٔ رفع حوایج نوع بشری که پیوسته در حال تحوّل و تکامل است دیگر بر نمی‌آیند، باید به دور انداخته شوند و در خاموش‌کدهٔ آموزه‌های منسوخ و فراموش شده سپرده شوند. چرا در جهانی که تابع قانون لایتغیّرِ تغییر و تحلیل است این اعتقادات و مؤسّسات باید از زوالی که ضرورتاً باید بر جمیع مؤسّسات انسانی غلبه نماید مستثنی و معاف باشند؟ باید به خاطر داشته باشیم که موازین حقوقی و نظریّه‌های سیاسی و اقتصادی صرفاً برای آن به وجود آمده‌اند که منافع عموم بشر محفوظ ماند نه آنکه به خاطر حفظ اصالت یک قانون یا یک عقیده، نوع انسان قربانی شود." (ترجمه)

2

تحریم سلاح‌های اتمی، منع استفاده از گازهای سمّی، و غیر قانونی ساختن جنگ‌های میکروبی علل بنیادی جنگ را از بین نخواهد برد. گرچه این قبیل اقداماتِ عملی به عنوان عناصری از فرایند صلح به وضوح از اهمّیت خاصّی برخوردارند امّا به خودی خود سطحی‌تر از آنند که بتوانند اثر عمیق و پایداری داشته باشند. مردم جهان با زیرکی و ابتکار در تلاشی بی‌پایان برای کسب سلطه و برتری، باز آلات جنگی دیگری اختراع خواهند کرد و از غذا، موادّ خام، منابع مالی، قدرت صنعتی، ایدیولوژی و تروریسم برای براندازی یکدیگر استفاده خواهند نمود. به علاوه عظیم کنونی در امور بشری را نمی‌توان از طریق رفع درگیری‌ها و یا اختلاف نظرهای خاصّ بین ملّت‌ها از میان برداشت. یک چارچوب واقعاً جهانی باید اتّخاذ گردد.

رهبران ملّی مطمئنّاً از جهانی بودن مشکلات باخبرند، واقعیّتی که در انبوه فزایندهٔ مسائلی که هرروزه با آن رو به رو هستند به چشم می‌خورد. به علاوه مطالعات و راه‌حلّ‌های پیشنهادی از جانب بسیاری از گروه‌های علاقه‌مند و روشن‌ضمیر و از طرف دوایر وابسته به سازمان ملل متّحد به قدری زیاد و بی‌شمار است که دیگر هیچ کس نمی‌تواند ادّعا کند که از احتیاجات خطیری که باید برآورده شود بی‌خبر است. امّا فلج ارادهٔ گریبانگیر شده و همین بی‌ارادگی است که باید با دقّت مورد بررسی قرار گیرد و با قاطعیّت چاره شود. ریشهٔ این فلج و بی‌ارادگی، چنان‌که ذکر نمودیم، این اعتقاد عمیق است که نوع انسان ذاتاً ستیزه‌خوست و در نتیجه مایل نیست مصالح نظم جهانی را بر منافع خصوصی ملّی ترجیح دهد و نمی‌خواهد با شجاعت به استقرار یک حاکمیّت متّحد جهانی با تمام مزایای عظیم آن بپردازد. آثار این فلج را هم‌چنین می‌توان در توده‌های مردم ناآگاه و تحت انقیاد مشاهده نمود که نمی‌توانند آرزوی خود را برای زیستن در ظلّ نظمی جدید همراه با آرامش و رفاه و صلح و صفا با تمام مردم دنیا به راحتی بر زبان رانند.

گام‌های محتاطانه‌ای که به خصوص پس از جنگ جهانی دوم در جهت نظم جهانی برداشته شده بارقه‌های امیدبخش هستند. تمایل روزافزون گروه‌هایی از ملل به رسمی نمودن روابطی که آنها را قادر به همکاری در امور مورد علاقهٔ مشترک می‌کند بیانگر این نکته است که مآلاً تمام ملل خواهند توانست بر این ضعف اراده فایق آیند. اتّحادیّهٔ کشورهای جنوب شرقی آسیا، جامعه و بازار مشترک کارائیب، بازار مشترک امریکای مرکزی، شورای همکاری متقابل اقتصادی، جامعهٔ اقتصادی اروپا، اتّحادیّهٔ کشورهای

عرب، سازمان وحدت افریقا، سازمان کشورهای امریکایی، شورای جنوب پاسیفیک، هر یک نمونه‌ای از مساعی مشترکی است که راه را برای نظم جهانی هموار می‌سازد.

توجّه روزافزونی که به بعضی از عمیق‌ترین مشکلات کرهٔ زمین معطوف می‌گردد نشانهٔ امیدبخش دیگری است. علی‌رغم نارسایی‌های آشکار سازمان ملل متّحد، بیش از چهل بیانیّه و عهدنامه که این سازمان به تصویب رسانده، حتّی در مواقعی که دولت‌ها در تعهّد خود نسبت به آنها اشتیاق نشان نداده‌اند، جان تازه‌ای به مردم عادی بخشیده است. اعلامیّهٔ جهانی حقوق بشر، کنوانسیون منع و مجازات کشتار دسته‌جمعی و اقدامات مشابهی مربوط به رفع کلّیّهٔ تبعیضات بر مبنای نژاد، جنسیّت، و عقیدهٔ مذهبی، رعایت حقوق کودک، حفظ همهٔ افراد انسانی علیه شکنجه، ریشه‌کنی گرسنگی و سوء تغذیه، استفاده از پیشرفت‌های علمی و تکنولوژیکی در راه صلح و به سود بشریّت، تمامی این قبیل اقدامات، اگر دلیرانه تنفیذ گردد و گسترش یابد، به فرارسیدن روزی سرعت خواهد بخشید که کابوس جنگ دیگر نخواهد توانست بر روابط بین‌المللی سایه افکند. نیازی نیست که بر اهمیّت مطالبی که در این بیانیه‌ها و میثاق‌ها مورد توجّه قرار گرفته تأکید شود امّا برخی از این مطالب به دلیل ارتباط مستقیم‌شان با استقرار صلح جهانی، درخور توضیح بیشتری هستند.

نژادپرستی که یکی از زیانبارترین و مزمن‌ترین مفاسد و شُرور است سدّی عمده در راه استقرار صلح می‌باشد. نژادپرستی چنان هَتک حرمت شرم‌آوری نسبت به مقام انسان است که به هیچ دلیلی و تحت هیچ شرایطی نمی‌توان آن را توجیه نمود. تبعیض نژادی ظهور استعدادهای نهفتهٔ بی‌کران قربانیانش را معوّق و عاطل می‌سازد، مرتکبینش را به فساد و تباهی می‌کشاند و پیشرفت انسان را مختل می‌کند. فایق آمدن بر این مشکل مستلزم پذیرفتن یگانگی نوع بشر و تنفیذ آن از طریق اقدامات قانونیِ مناسب در سراسر جهان است.

اختلاف مفرط میان غنی و فقیر که سرچشمهٔ مصائب شدیدی است جهان را در حالتی از بی‌ثباتی نگاه می‌دارد و عملاً آن را به ورطهٔ جنگ می‌کشاند. معدودند اجتماعاتی که به نحوی مؤثّر به این مسئله پرداخته باشند. حلّ این مشکل اتّخاذ هم‌زمان رویکردهای روحانی، اخلاقی و عملی را ایجاب می‌کند. باید با نگاهی تازه بر این مشکل نگریست، نگاهی که راه‌گشای مشورتِ عاری از مجادلات اقتصادی و ایدیولوژیکی با متخصّصین طیف وسیعی از رشته‌های مختلف باشد و مردم را در اخذ تصمیماتِ فوری که مستقیماً بر زندگیِ آنها اثرگذار است مشارکت دهد. این مسئله تنها به ریشه‌کن کردن

فقر شدید و غنای بیش از حدّ منحصر نمی‌شود بلکه هم‌چنین با آن حقایق روحانیه‌ای مرتبط است که درک آنها می‌تواند طرز فکر و گرایش بین‌المللی جدیدی را به وجود آورد. پروردن چنین طرز فکر و گرایشی خود قسمت عمده‌ای از راه حلّ است.

ملّی‌گرایی افراطی که با وطن‌پرستی معقول و مشروع کاملاً متفاوت است باید جای خود را به یک وفاداری وسیع‌تر یعنی محبّت به تمامی نوع انسان بدهد. حضرت بهاءالله می‌فرماید: "عالم یک وطن محسوب است و مَن علی الارض اهل آن." مفهوم جهان‌وطنی یا شهروندی جهانی نتیجهٔ مستقیم کاهش یافتن کرهٔ ارض به یک سرزمین واحد از طریق پیشرفت‌های علمی و وابستگی غیر قابل انکار ملّت‌ها به یکدیگر است. محبّت ورزیدن نسبت به تمام مردم دنیا با عشق به میهن مغایرت ندارد. در یک اجتماع جهانی، منافع جزء از طریق ترویج منافع کل بهتر تأمین می‌گردد. فعالیّت‌های جاری بین‌المللی در زمینه‌های مختلف که محبّت متقابل و حس هم‌بستگی در میان مردم را تقویت می‌کند باید به مراتب افزایش یابد.

اختلافات دینی، در سراسر تاریخ، باعث حدوث جنگ‌ها و نزاع‌های بی‌شمار گردیده، آفت عمده‌ای برای پیشرفت بوده، و روز به روز در نزد همهٔ مردم چه دین‌دار و چه بی‌دین، پدیده‌ای مبغوض‌تر و منفورتر جلوه می‌کند. پیروان تمام ادیان باید مایل به بررسی مسائل اساسی ناشی از این منازعات باشند و جواب‌های روشنی بیابند که چگونه می‌توان اختلافات بین پیروان ادیان، اعمّ از تئوری و عملی را برطرف ساخت؟ چالشِ پیشِ روی رهبران مذهبی جهان آنست که با قلبی سرشار از رأفت و شفقت و با اشتیاقی برای یافتن حقیقت، به وضع اسف‌بار بشر تفکّر نمایند و از خود بپرسند که آیا نمی‌توانند خاضعانه در برابر خالق توانای خویش اختلافات تئولوژیکی خود را با روح بزرگواری و حلم و مدارای متقابل به کنار افکنند تا بتوانند برای پیشبرد حسن تفاهم و ایجاد صلح در بین ابنای بشر با یکدیگر هم‌کاری نمایند.

آزادی زنان و حصول تساوی کامل میان زن و مرد، هرچند اهمیّت آن کمتر اذعان شده، یکی از مهم‌ترین لوازم استقرار صلح است. انکار این تساوی، ظلم و ستم به نیمی از جمعیّت جهان است و گرایش‌ها و عادات زیان‌بخشی را در مردان به وجود می‌آورد که از محیط خانواده به محلّ کار و به حیات سیاسی و مآلاً به روابط بین‌المللی منتقل می‌گردد. هیچ دلیل اخلاقی، عملی و یا بیولوژیکی وجود ندارد که بتوان بر اساس آن این عدم تساوی را توجیه نمود. تنها زمانی که زنان در جمیع مساعی بشری سهمی کامل

و مساوی داشته باشند جوّ اخلاقی و روانی مساعدی برای پدید آمدن صلح بین‌المللی به وجود خواهد آمد.

امر تعلیم و تربیت عمومی که هم‌اکنون بسیاری از مردمِ متعهّد از تمام ادیان و ملل عالم را بر خدمت خویش گماشته، سزاوار حدّ اکثر حمایت دول جهان است. جهل و نادانی بدون تردید علّت اصلی تدنّی و سقوط ملّت‌ها و تداوم تعصّبات است. هیچ کشوری به موفّقیّت دست نخواهد یافت مگر آنکه تمام شهروندانش از آموزش و پرورش برخوردار باشند. فقدان منابع مالی، توانایی بسیاری از کشورها را در ایفای این امر ضروری محدود می‌نماید و رعایت اولویّت‌های خاصّی را ایجاب می‌کند. شایسته است که دوایر تصمیم‌گیرندهٔ مربوطه، اولویّت اوّل را به آموزش و پرورش زنان و دختران اختصاص دهند زیرا از طریق مادران تحصیل کرده و تعلیم یافته است که ثمرات علم و دانش می‌تواند به سریع‌ترین و مؤثّرترین وجه در سراسر اجتماع انتشار یابد. احتیاجات عصر حاضر ایجاب می‌کند که تدریسِ مفهومِ شهروندی جهانی نیز به عنوان بخشی از آموزش معمولیِ هر کودک در نظر گرفته شود.

مسئلهٔ فقدان اساسی مراوده و ارتباط بین ملّت‌ها مساعی بشر را برای حصول صلح جهانی به شدّت تضعیف می‌کند. اتّخاذ یک زبان کمکی بین‌المللی تا حدّ زیادی سبب حلّ این مشکل خواهد شد و درخور توجّه فوری است.

در تمام موارد مذکور دو نکته نیاز به تأکید دارد. یکی اینکه منسوخ کردن جنگ صرفاً عبارت از امضای قراردادها و قطعنامه‌ها نیست بلکه کار پیچیده‌ای است که مستلزم تعهّدی عمیق‌تر برای حلّ مسائلی است که معمولاً مرتبط با استقرار صلح به شمار نمی‌آیند. این تصور که امنیّتِ جمعی صرفاً بر مبنای پیمان‌های سیاسی حاصل خواهد شد، خیالی پوچ و واهی است. نکتهٔ دیگر آنکه، چالش اوّلیه در پرداختن به مسائل مربوط به صلح آنست که به جای بررسی آن صرفاً از جوانب عملی، مسئله به سطح یک اصل بنیادین ارتقا یابد زیرا صلح اساساً از حالتی درونی مبتنی بر گرایشی روحانی و اخلاقی منبعث می‌شود و عمدتاً با برانگیختن این گرایش است که امکانِ یافتن راه حلّ‌های پایدار میسّر می‌گردد.

اصولی روحانی، یا به قولی ارزش‌هایی انسانی، وجود دارد که به وسیلهٔ آن می‌توان راه حلّی برای هر مشکل اجتماعی پیدا کرد. هر گروه خیراندیشی به طور کلّی می‌تواند برای حلّ مشکلات خود راهی عملی طرح نماید ولی خیراندیشی و دانش منطقی معمولاً کافی

نیست. ارزش اساسی اصول روحانی در آنست که نه تنها چشم‌اندازی ارائه می‌دهد که با آنچه در طبیعت انسان مستور است توازن و هماهنگی دارد بلکه طرز فکر، تحرّک، اراده و آرمانی را نیز برمی‌انگیزد که موجب تسهیل یافتن و به کار بستن اقدامات عملی می‌گردد. رهبران دول و تمام صاحبان قدرت در صورت موفقیّت بیشتری برای حلّ مشکلات خواهند داشت که ابتدا اصول مربوطه را شناسایی کنند و سپس در پرتو آنها به اقدام بپردازند.

3

نخستین سئوالی که جواب آن را باید یافت این است که چگونه جهان کنونی را با الگوی تثبیت شدهٔ محاصماتش می‌توان به جهانی دیگر تبدیل نمود که در آن همکاری و هماهنگی حکمفرما باشد.

نظم جهانی فقط می‌تواند بر پایهٔ یک آگاهی تزلزل‌ناپذیر از وحدت نوع بشر — حقیقتی روحانی و مورد تأیید همهٔ علوم انسانی — بنیان شود. علوم مردم‌شناسی، فیزیولوژی و روان‌شناسی همگی فقط یک نوع انسان را می‌شناسند اگرچه این انسان در جنبه‌های ثانوی حیاتش بی‌نهایت متنوّع است. قبول این حقیقت مستلزم ترک تعصّب است — همهٔ تعصّبات — نژادی، طبقاتی، رنگی، مذهبی، ملّی، جنسیّتی، میزان تمدّن مادّی و هر چیز دیگری که موجب شود مردم خود را از دیگران برتر بدانند.

قبول وحدت نوع انسان اوّلین شرط اساسی برای تجدید سازمان و ادارهٔ جهان به صورت یک کشور و وطن همهٔ نوع انسان است. پذیرش همگانی این اصلِ روحانی برای موفقیّت هر کوششی در راه تأسیس صلح جهانی ضروری است. بنا بر این اصل یگانگی نوع بشر را باید به طور عمومی اعلان نمود، در مدارس تعلیم داد، و مستمرّاً آن را در تمام کشورها به عنوان تمهیدی برای تغییری اساسی در ساختار اجتماع تأکید کرد، تغییری که از ملزمات این یگانگی است.

از نظر آیین بهائی "اصل وحدت عالم انسانی خواهان تجدید ساختار و خلع سلاح تمام جهان متمدّن است نه چیزی کمتر از آن، جهانی زنده و پویا که در جمیع جنبه‌های اصلی حیاتش — دستگاه سیاسی‌اش، آمال روحانیش، تجارت و اقتصادش، و خطّ و زبانش — متّحد باشد و در عین حال تنوّع بی‌کران خصایص ملّی اجزای هم‌پیمانش را حفظ کند." (ترجمه)

حضرت شوقی افندی، ولیِّ امر بهائی، مقتضیات این اصل محوری را در سال ۱۹۳۱ میلادی در توقیعی به زبان انگلیسی چنین توضیح فرمود: "[هدف این احکام] به هیچ وجه تخریب بنیان کنونی جامعه نیست بلکه توسعهء اساس و تجدید مؤسّسات آن به نحوی موافق با مقتضیات و حوایج این جهانِ دائم التّغییر است. نه با هیچ تعهّد مشروعی در تضاد است و نه هیچ یک از وابستگی‌های اساسی را تضعیف می‌کند. قصدش نه آن است که شعلهء وطن‌دوستی موجّه و عاقلانه را در دل مردمان خاموش کند و نه آنکه نظام حاکمیّت ملّی را منسوخ نماید، نظامی که بنفسه برای دفع مفاسد حاصله از تمرکز مفرطِ امور به غایت ضروری است. مقصدش این نیست که نسبت به تنوّع نژادی، اقلیمی، تاریخی، زبان و سنّت، افکار، و عادات، که وجه التّمایز مردم و ملّت‌های دنیا است بی‌اعتنایی نموده و یا سعی در سرکوبی آنها کند. ندایش دعوت به یک وفاداری وسیع‌تر و آمالی عظیم‌تر از آن است که تا به حال تحرّک‌بخش نوع بشر بوده است. تأکیدش بر آن است که امیال و منافع ملّی تابع نیازهای ضروریِ یک جهان متّحد قرار گیرد. از یک طرف تمرکز مفرط امور را مردود می‌شمارد و از طرف دیگر هر کوششی را برای ایجاد یک‌نواختی رد می‌نماید. شعارش وحدت در کثرت است." (ترجمه)

حصول این مقاصد نیازمندِ آنست که فرایند تعدیل گرایش‌های سیاسیِ ملّی چندین مرحله را طیّ کند، گرایش‌هایی که در حال حاضر، در غیاب قوانینی واضح و معیّن و یا اصولی قابل تنفیذ و مورد قبول عام برای تنظیم روابط بین ملل، در آستانهء هرج و مرج است. جامعهء ملل، سازمان ملل متّحد، نهادها و موافقت‌نامه‌های بسیاری که این دو به وجود آورده‌اند البتّه در تخفیف بعضی از اثرات منفی اختلافات بین‌المللی مفید بوده‌اند امّا نتوانسته‌اند از بروز جنگ جلوگیری نمایند. از پایان جنگ جهانی دوم تا کنون در واقع جنگ‌های بسیاری رخ داده است و هنوز هم این روند ادامه دارد.

جنبه‌های عمدهٔ این مشکل در قرن نوزدهم زمانی که حضرت بهاءالله برای اوّلین بار توصیه‌های خویش را برای استقرار صلح جهانی اعلان فرمود ظاهر شده بود. اصل امنیّت جمعی از طرف آن حضرت در مکتوباتی خطاب به فرمانروایان جهان مطرح گردید. حضرت شوقی افندی در نامه‌ای به زبان انگلیسی منظور حضرت بهاءالله را چنین بیان می‌فرمایند: "این بیانات متین جز اشاره به محدود کردن اجتناب‌ناپذیر قدرت مطلق حاکمیّت ملّی — به منزلهٔ مقدّمه‌ای ضروری برای تشکیل یک جامعهء مشترک المنافع از تمام ملل جهان در آینده — چه مفهوم دیگری می‌تواند داشته باشد؟ نوعی ابرحکومت جهانی باید بالضّروره تدریجاً ایجاد شود که تمام ملل عالم به طیب خاطر به نفع آن حکومت از حقّ اعلان جنگ، از برخی اختیارات در مورد وضع مالیات و از

کلّیهء حقوق مربوط به اندوختن تسلیحات، به جز برای حفظ نظم داخلی در قلمرو خود، خواهند گذشت. چنین حکومتی باید شامل یک قوّهٔ مجریهٔ بین‌المللی مقتدر باشد که بتواند حاکمیّت نهایی و بلامنازع خویش را نسبت به هر عضو متمرّد کشورهای مشترک المنافع اِعمال نماید؛ یک پارلمان جهانی که اعضایش به وسیلهٔ مردم در هر کشور انتخاب شده و انتخاب‌شان مورد تأیید دولت‌های متبوعه آنان قرار گرفته باشد؛ یک محکمهٔ کبری که رأیش حتّی در مواردی که کشورهای مربوطه داوطلبانه با ارجاع موضوع خود به آن محکمه موافقت ننموده‌اند قاطع و مطاع باشد. یک جامعهٔ جهانی که در آن تمام موانع اقتصادی برای همیشه برطرف شده و وابستگی متقابل سرمایه و کارگر به طور قطع پذیرفته شده باشد؛ جامعه‌ای که در آن هیاهوی تعصّب و جدال دینی برای ابد ساکت گشته و شعله‌ٔ خصومت نژادی نهایتاً خاموش شده باشد؛ جامعه‌ای که در آن مجموعهٔ واحدی از قوانین بین‌المللی که نتیجهٔ قضاوت دقیق نمایندگان فدرال جهانی است تدوین شده و ضامن اجرایش مداخله‌ٔ فوری و قهری قوای مرکّب از نیروهای کشورهای همپیمان باشد؛ و بالاخره، یک جامعهٔ جهانی که در آن آگاهی مستمر از مفهوم شهروندی جهانی جای‌گزین ملّی‌گرایی افراطی و ستیزه‌جو شده باشد. این است طرحی اجمالی از نظمی که حضرت بهاءالله پیش‌بینی فرموده‌اند، نظمی که در آینده به منزلهٔ اعلی ثمرهٔ عصری شناخته خواهد شد که تدریجاً رو به بلوغ می‌رود." (ترجمه)

اجرای این اقدامات پردامنه را حضرت بهاءالله چنین پیش‌بینی فرمود: "لابّد بر این است مجمع بزرگ در ارض برپا شود و ملوک و سلاطین در آن مجمع مفاوضه در صلح اکبر نمایند."

شجاعت، عزم راسخ، خلوص نیّت، محبّتِ بی‌شائبهٔ یک ملّت نسبت به ملّت دیگر — همهٔ صفات معنوی و اخلاقی لازم برای برداشتن این قدم بزرگ تاریخی به سوی صلح جهانی — بر اِعمال اراده استوارند. و برای برانگیختن این اراده، لازم است که توجّهی جدّی به حقیقت انسان یعنی به تفکّر او معطوف گردد. علاوه بر درک اهمّیّت این حقیقت پرقدرت، باید به این ضرورت اجتماعی نیز پی برد که ارزش بی‌نظیر نیروی تفکّر باید از طریق مشورت صادقانه و صمیمانه و خالی از تعصّب، و با عمل بر طبق نتایج مشورت به عرصهٔ شهود در آید. حضرت بهاءالله توجّه بشر را مؤکّداً به محسّنات مشورت و ضرورت آن در تنظیم امور انسانی جلب نموده می‌فرماید: "مشورت بر آگاهی بیفزاید و ظنّ و گمان را به یقین تبدیل نماید. اوست سراج نورانی در عالم ظلمانی راه نماید و هدایت کند. از برای هر امری مقام کمال و بلوغ بوده و خواهد بود و بلوغ و ظهور خرد به مشورت ظاهر." نفس کوشش برای حصول صلح از طریق اقدامی مشورتی که آن حضرت توصیه فرموده

می‌تواند چنان جوّ مساعد و مناسبی را در میان مردم جهان به وجود آورد که هیچ نیرویی نخواهد توانست مانع نتیجهٔ موفّقیت‌آمیز نهایی آن گردد.

حضرت عبدالبهاء، فرزند حضرت بهاءالله و مبیّن منصوص تعالیم آن حضرت، در بارهٔ دستورالعمل این مجمع جهانی چنین می‌فرمایند: "مسئلهٔ صلح عمومی را در میدان مشورت گذارند و به جمیع وسایل و وسایط تشبّث نموده عقد انجمن دول عالم نمایند و یک معاهدهٔ قویّه و میثاق و شروط محکمهٔ ثابته تأسیس نمایند و اعلان نموده به اتفاق عموم هیئت بشریّه مؤکّد فرمایند. این امر اتمّ اقوم را که فی‌الحقیقه سبب آسایش آفرینش است کلّ سکّان ارض مقدّس شمرده جمیع قوای عالم متوجّه ثبوت و بقای این عهد اعظم باشد و در این معاهدهٔ عمومیّه تعیین و تحدید حدود و ثغور هر دولتی گردد و توضیح روش و حرکت هر حکومتی شود و جمیع معاهدات و مناسبات دولیّه و روابط و ضوابط مابین هیئت حکومتیّهٔ بشریّه مقرّر و معیّن گردد. و کذلک قوّهٔ حربیّهٔ هر حکومتی به حدّی مخصّص معلوم شود چه اگر تدارکات محاربه و قوای عسکریّهٔ دولتی ازدیاد یابد سبب توهّم دول سایره گردد. باری اصل مبنای این عهد قویم را بر آن قرار دهند که اگر دولتی از دول من‌بعد شرطی از شروط را فسخ نماید کلّ دول عالم بر اضمحلال او قیام نمایند بلکه هیئت بشریّه به کال قوت بر تدمیر آن حکومت برخیزد. اگر جسم مریض عالم به این داروی اعظم موفّق گردد البته اعتدال کلّی کسب نموده به شفای باقی دائمی فایز گردد."

انعقاد این مجمع عظیم خیلی به تأخیر افتاده است.

با قلوبی مشتاق از رهبران تمام کشورها تمنّا می‌نماییم که این فرصت مناسب را مغتنم شمارند و برای تشکیل این مجمع جهانی گام‌های برگشت‌ناپذیری بردارند. تمام نیروهای تاریخ، نوع بشر را به سوی این اقدام که نشانهٔ ابدی طلوع صبح بلوغ عالم انسانی خواهد بود سوق می‌دهد، بلوغی که بشریّت قرن‌ها در انتظار آن بسر برده است.

آیا سازمان ملل متّحد، با پشتیبانی کامل تمام اعضایش، برای تحقّق مقاصد عالیهٔ این والاترین مجمع قیام نخواهد کرد؟

سزاوار است که زنان و مردان، جوانان و کودکان در همه جا فواید جاودانه‌ای را که این اقدام ضروری برای تمام مردمان در بر خواهد داشت دریابند و بانگ موافقت مشتاقانهٔ خویش را به گوش جهانیان رسانند. امید وطید ما آنست که نسل حاضر آن

نسلی باشد که این مرحلهٔ شکوه‌مند در فرایند تکامل حیات اجتماعی بر روی کرهٔ زمین را آغاز می‌نماید.

4

سرچشمهٔ خوش‌بینی این جمع بینشی است که فراتر از پایان دادن به جنگ و ایجاد سازمان‌های همکاری بین‌المللی می‌رود. حضرت بهاءالله تأکید می‌فرمایند که صلح پایدار در بین ملّت‌ها هرچند مرحله‌ای مهم و ضروری است امّا هدف غائی تکامل اجتماعی نوع انسان نیست. ورای متارکهٔ اجباری اوّلیّهٔ جنگ از ترس فاجعهٔ جنگ اتمی، ورای امضای پیمان صلح سیاسی از روی اکراه در بین کشورهای رقیب و مظنون به یکدیگر، ورای ترتیبات عملی برای امنیّت و هم‌زیستی، و ورای حتّی آزمون‌های بسیاری در زمینهٔ همکاری که در اثر این اقدامات میسّر خواهد شد، متعالی‌ترین هدف غائی، اتّحاد اهل عالم در یک خانوادهٔ جهانی است.

انشقاق و عدم اتّحاد خطری است که مردم جهان دیگر تاب تحمّلش را ندارند، عواقبش آن‌چنان وخیم است که در تصوّر نگنجد و چنان واضح است که احتیاج به اثبات ندارد. حضرت بهاءالله بیش از یک قرن پیش چنین مرقوم فرمود: "مقصود اصلاح عالم و راحت امم بوده این اصلاح و راحت ظاهر نشود مگر به اتّحاد و اتّفاق." حضرت شوقی افندی با بیان اینکه "حنین انسان بلند است و منتها آمالش آنست که به شطر اتّحاد هدایت گردد و رنج و مشقّت دیرینه‌اش پایان پذیرد"، فرموده‌اند: "اتّحاد نوع بشر ما به الامتیاز مرحله‌ای است که حال اجتماع انسانی به آن نزدیک می‌شود. وحدت خانواده، قبیله، دولت‌شهر و ملّت، یکی پس از دیگری با کوشش فراوان کاملاً تحقّق یافته است. حال اتّحاد جهانی هدفی است که بشر پریشان تلاش‌کنان به سویش روان است. دوران ملّت‌سازی به پایان رسیده است. هرج و مرج منبعث از حاکمیّت ملّی به اوج خود نزدیک می‌شود. جهانی که در حال رسیدن به مرحلهٔ بلوغ است باید این بُت را بشکند، وحدت و جامعیّت روابط نوع انسان را بپذیرد و نهایتاً تشکیلاتی برپا نماید که بتواند این اصل اساسی حیاتش را به بهترین وجه متجسّم سازد." (ترجمه)

این نظر مورد تأیید تمام نیروهای تحوّل‌آفرینِ معاصر است و شواهد آن را در بسیاری از علایم امیدبخشِ صلح جهانی و در نهضت‌ها و تحوّلات جاری بین‌المللی که قبلاً ذکر شد می‌توان یافت. مردان و زنان بی‌شمار، از هر فرهنگ و نژاد و ملّت دنیا، که در دوایر گوناگون سازمان ملل متّحد مشغول به خدمت‌اند نمودارای از یک "کادر خدمات

مدنی" سراسری کرهٔ زمین هستند که موفقیّت‌های قابل توجّه‌شان میزان همکاری و تعاونی است که می‌توان حتّی در شرایطی دل‌سردکننده به آن نائل شد. اشتیاق شدید به وحدت و یگانگی همانند بهاری روحانی، خود را به صورت کنگره‌های بین‌المللی بی‌شمار شامل مردمانی از طیف وسیعی از رشته‌های مختلف، جلوه‌گر می‌سازد. همین اشتیاق محرّک تقاضاهای بی‌شمار برای پروژه‌های بین‌المللی مربوط به کودکان و جوانان می‌باشد و در حقیقت همین اشتیاق مصدر واقعی نهضتی شگفت‌انگیز در جهت هم‌گرایی دینی است که به نظر می‌رسد از طریق آن پیروان ادیان و مذاهب همیشه‌دشمن، حال به نحو مقاومت‌ناپذیری به سوی هم کشیده می‌شوند. در کنار گرایش‌های متضادّ جنگ‌جویی و خودبزرگ‌نمایی که مستمرّاً با وحدت در نبردند، حرکت در جهت اتّحاد بین‌المللی یکی از ویژگی‌های غالب و فراگیر حیات بر روی کرهٔ زمین در سال‌های پایانی قرن بیستم می‌باشد.

مَثَل جامعهٔ بهائی را می‌توان به منزلهٔ نمونه‌ای از این اتّحادِ در حال گسترش مشاهده نمود. جامعهٔ بهائی جامعه‌ای متشکّل از سه تا چهار میلیون نفر مردمانی از کشورهای مختلف، از فرهنگ‌ها، طبقات و مذاهب متفاوت است که با طیف وسیعی از اقدامات، به برآوردن نیازهای روحانی، اجتماعی و اقتصادی سکنهٔ سرزمین‌های متعدّدی خدمت می‌کنند. جامعهٔ بهائی در مقام یک ارگانیسم اجتماعیِ واحد، نمایانگر تنوع خانوادهٔ نوع انسان است که امورش را به وسیلهٔ سیستمی مبتنی بر اصول پذیرفته شدهٔ مشورتی اداره می‌نماید و تمام فیضان‌های عظیم هدایت الهی در طول تاریخ بشری را به طور مساوی گرامی می‌دارد. وجود جامعهٔ بهائی دلیل قانع‌کنندهٔ دیگری است بر عملی بودن بینش مؤسّس آن از جهانی متّحد، و شاهد دیگری است بر اینکه نوع انسان قادر است به مثابهٔ یک جامعهٔ جهانی واحد زندگی کند و می‌تواند از عهدهٔ رویارویی با هر چالشی که با فرارسیدن دوران بلوغش همراه است برآید. اگر تجربهٔ جامعهٔ بهائی بتواند به نحوی از انحا در تقویت امید به ایجاد وحدت نوع بشر کمک کند، ما با کمال سرور آن را به عنوان یک الگو برای مطالعه و بررسی تقدیم می‌کنیم.

چون به اهمّیت عظیم وظیفه‌ای که اکنون پیشِ رویِ تمامی جهان قرار دارد می‌اندیشیم، با کمال خضوع سر تعظیم به پیشگاه خالق متعال فرود می‌آوریم، خالقی که با محبّت بی‌منتهایش جمیع بشر را از یک سلاله خلق فرمود، جوهر ثمین حقیقت انسانی را در او به ودیعه نهاد، به شرف هوش و دانایی و کرامت و جاودانگی مفتخر فرمود، "انسان را از بین امم و خلایق برای معرفت و محبّت خود که علّت غایی و سبب خلقت کائنات بود اختیار نمود."

ایمان راسخ ما بر آنست که انسان "برای اصلاح عالم خلق شده" و "شئونات درنده‌های ارض لایق انسان نبوده و نیست" و کالات و فضایلی که شایستهٔ مقام شامخ انسان است امانت‌داری، بردباری، رحمت، شفقت و مهربانی به تمام نوع بشر است. بر این باور تأکید می‌کنیم که باید در این یوم موعود مقام و رتبهٔ انسان ظاهر شود، قوا و استعدادات مکنونه‌اش به منصّهٔ ظهور رسد، سرنوشت درخشانش به خوبی آشکار گردد و فضایل عالیهٔ فطری‌اش به عرصهٔ شهود در آید. اینست انگیزه و منشأ ایمان راسخ ما بر اینکه صلح و یگانگی مقصدیست ممکن الحصول که نوع انسان تلاش‌کنان به سوی آن پیش می‌رود.

همزمان با تحریر این سطور، ندای مشتاقانهٔ بهائیان را می‌توان شنید که با وجود مظالمی که هنوز در زادگاه آیین خویش متحمّل می‌شوند با امید تزلزل‌ناپذیر خویش بر این باور شهادت می‌دهند که بر اثر قوای تقلیب‌کنندهٔ ظهور حضرت بهاءالله که مؤیّد به تأییدات الهی است، وقت تحقّق قریب‌الوقوع رؤیای دیرینهٔ بشر برای صلح و آرامش اکنون فرا رسیده است. لذا آنچه با شما در میان می‌گذاریم تنها رؤیایی در قالب الفاظ نیست: ما قدرت اَعمالِ منبعث از ایمان و فداکاری را فرا می‌خوانیم؛ ما تمنّای مشتاقانهٔ هم‌کیشان خویش در سراسر جهان برای حصول صلح و اتّحاد را بیان می‌داریم؛ ما به همهٔ مظلومانی می‌پیوندیم که قربانی تعدّی و تجاوزند، به همهٔ کسانی که در آرزوی خاتمهٔ دشمنی و نزاعند، به تمامی نفوسی که تعلّق‌شان به اصول صلح و نظم جهانی سبب ترویج مقاصد عالیه‌ای می‌شود که خالق مهربان، نوع انسان را برای آن خلق فرموده است.

به منظور ابراز اطمینان عمیق خود از استقرار صلح، این وعدهٔ محکم و مؤکّد حضرت بهاءالله را حسن ختام این نوشتار می‌نماییم که می‌فرماید: "این منازعات بی‌ثمر و جنگ‌های مهلک از میان برخیزد و صلح اکبر تحقّق یابد." (ترجمه)

[امضا: بیت العدل اعظم]

The Promise of World Peace

Portuguese

Outubro de 1985

Aos Povos do Mundo:

A Grande Paz - para a qual as pessoas de boa vontade orientaram os seus corações através dos séculos, acerca da qual inúmeras gerações de profetas e poetas expressaram as suas visões, e cuja promessa foi continuamente reafirmada ao longo das eras nas escrituras sagradas da humanidade - encontra-se agora, finalmente, ao alcance das nações. Pela primeira vez na História, é agora possível ver o planeta em sua totalidade, com os seus mil e um povos diversificados, a partir da mesma perspectiva. A paz mundial não é somente possível, mas inevitável. É o próximo estágio na evolução deste planeta - ou, conforme disse um grande pensador, "a planetização da humanidade".

Se essa paz será alcançada somente depois de horrores inimagináveis, precipitados pelo apego obstinado da humanidade a velhos padrões de comportamento, ou se será concretizada agora através de um ato de vontade coletiva - eis a escolha que se oferece a todos os que habitam a Terra. Nesta conjuntura crítica, em que os problemas de difícil tratamento que confrontam as nações foram fundidos numa preocupação comum pelo bem-estar do mundo todo, a nossa inércia face à maré de conflitos e de desordem seria por demais irresponsável.

Entre os sinais favoráveis que podemos discernir contam-se a força crescente de medidas tomadas em prol da ordem mundial, a partir do primeiro quartel deste século, através da constituição da Liga das Nações, sucedida pela ainda mais ampla Organização das Nações Unidas; a independência obtida pela maioria das nações da terra após a II Guerra Mundial, fato que aponta para a conclusão do processo de construção de nações, e a participação dessas nações mais jovens, juntamente com as mais antigas, na abordagem de questões de interesse mútuo; o grande aumento consequentemente verificado na cooperação, entre povos e grupos antes isolados e antagônicos, em empreendimentos internacionais nos domínios científicos, educativo, jurídico, econômico e cultural; o aparecimento durante as últimas décadas de um número sem precedentes de organizações humanitárias internacionais; a expansão de movimentos femininos e juvenis com o propósito de pôr fim às guerras; e a constituição espontânea de grupos cada vez maiores de pessoas comuns em busca de maior compreensão através da comunicação pessoal.

Os avanços científicos e técnicos que têm ocorrido durante este século invulgarmente abençoado, pressagiam um grande impulso para o progresso na evolução social do planeta, e apontam os meios através dos quais se poderão resolver os problemas práticos da humanidade. Esses avanços materiais oferecem, na verdade, os próximos meios para a administração da vida complexa de um mundo unido. Não obstante, as barreiras persistem. As dúvidas, os equívocos, os preconceitos, as suspeitas e os interesses mesquinhos dominam as nações e os povos em suas relações uns com os outros.

É por isso que, guiados por um profundo sentido de dever moral e espiritual, nos sentimos impelidos a chamar a vossa atenção, neste momento tão oportuno, para as percepções aguçadas que, há mais de um século, foram pela primeira vez comunicadas aos governantes da humanidade por Bahá'u'lláh, Fundador da Fé Bahá'í, da qual somos fideicomissários.

"Os ventos de desespero", escreveu Bahá'u'lláh, "sopram de todas as direções, e a contenda que divide e aflige a raça humana aumenta dia a dia. Os sinais de caos e convulsões iminentes podem agora ser discernidos, na medida em que, lastimavelmente, a ordem predominante demonstra se defeituosa". Este juízo profético tem sido amplamente corroborado pela experiência comum da humanidade. Os defeitos existentes na ordem prevalecente estão patentes na incapacidade manifestada pelos Estados soberanos, organizados nas Nações Unidas, em exorcizar o espectro da guerra, a ameaça de um colapso da ordem econômica internacional, o alastramento da anarquia e do terrorismo, e o sofrimento intenso que estas e outras aflições estão causando a um número crescente de seres humanos. De fato, as agressões e os conflitos têm de tal maneira caracterizado os nossos sistemas sociais, econômicos e religiosos, que muitos já se entregaram à noção de que tal comportamento é intrínseco à natureza humana e, consequentemente, é inextirpável.

Com a consolidação desse ponto de vista, assistimos ao desenvolvimento de uma contradição paralisante nos afazeres humanos. Por um lado, as pessoas de todas as nações proclamam não só o seu anseio de paz e harmonia, mas também a sua disposição de estabelecê-las e de pôr termo às apreensões devastadoras que atormentam as suas vidas diárias. Por outro lado, concede-se aceitação indiscriminada à noção de que os seres humanos são incorrigivelmente egoístas e agressivos, e, portanto, incapazes de erigir um sistema social simultaneamente progressivo e pacífico, dinâmico e harmonioso - um sistema que dê liberdade à iniciativa e à criatividade individuais, mas baseadas na cooperação e na reciprocidade.

À medida que a necessidade de paz se afigura mais urgente, esta contradição fundamental, que impede a sua concretização, exige uma reavaliação das suposições em que se fundamenta a conclusão comumente aceita quanto à triste condição histórica da humanidade. Quando examinadas com imparcialidade, as provas existentes revelam que tal conduta, longe de expressar a verdadeira essência do homem, representa na verdade uma distorção do espírito humano. A aceitação desta conclusão permitirá a todos os povos mobilizar forças sociais construtivas, que, por serem congruentes com a natureza humana, encorajarão a harmonia e a cooperação em vez da guerra e do conflito.

A escolha de tal curso não implica a negação do passado da humanidade, mas sim a sua compreensão. A Fé Bahá'í encara a atual confusão que reina no mundo e o estado calamitoso em que se encontram os afazeres humanos como uma fase natural num processo orgânico que conduzirá, final e irresistivelmente, à unificação do gênero humano sob uma ordem social única, cujos únicos limites serão os do planeta. A humanidade, vista como um todo distinto e orgânico, passou por estágios evolucionários análogos aos estágios de infância e adolescência que ocorrem nas vidas dos seus membros individuais. E, agora, está atravessando o período culminante em que a sua adolescência turbulenta se abeira da tão longamente aguardada maioridade.

O mero reconhecimento de que os preconceitos, as guerras e a exploração têm sido as expressões de estágios imaturos num vasto processo histórico, e de que a humanidade está presentemente experimentando o tumulto inevitável que prenuncia a sua maioridade coletiva, não deve constituir motivo de desespero, mas antes ser encarado como condição prévia para o empreendimento da estupenda tarefa da construção de um mundo pacífico. O tema cujo exame propomos é o de que tal empreendimento é possível, de que as necessárias forças construtivas existem, e de que podem ser erguidas estruturas sociais unificadoras.

Sejam quais forem os sofrimentos e as convulsões que os próximos anos possam encerrar, e por mais sombrias que sejam as circunstâncias imediatas, a Comunidade Bahá'í crê que a humanidade pode enfrentar essa prova suprema com confiança em seu resultado final. Longe de assinalarem o fim da civilização, as transformações convulsivas, em cuja direção a humanidade está sendo cada vez mais rapidamente

impelida, servirão para liberar "as potencialidades inerentes à condição do homem" e revelar "a plena medida do seu
destino sobre a terra, e a excelência inata de sua realidade".

I

Os dons naturais que distinguem o gênero humano
de todas as outras formas de vida encontram-se resumidos
naquilo a que se chama espírito humano; o intelecto é a sua
qualidade essencial. Esses dons permitiram à humanidade
construir civilizações e prosperar materialmente. Mas tais
realizações, por si só, nunca saciaram o espírito humano,
cuja natureza misteriosa o predispõe para a transcendência,
para estender-se em direção a um domínio invisível, à realidade suprema, àquela essência das essências incognoscível
chamada Deus. As religiões, trazidas à humanidade por
uma série de luminares espirituais, têm sido os principais
elos de ligação entre a humanidade e essa realidade suprema, e têm galvanizado e refinado a capacidade da humanidade para alcançar o sucesso espiritual juntamente com o
progresso social.

Nenhuma tentativa séria de endireitar os afazeres humanos e de alcançar a paz mundial pode ignorar a religião.
A sua percepção e prática pelo homem são assuntos amplamente cobertos pela História. Um eminente historiador de-
screveu a religião como "uma faculdade da natureza humana". Que a perversão desta faculdade tenha contribuído em
grande parte à confusão que atualmente reina no mundo, e
os conflitos existentes entre os indivíduos e no seu íntimo,
dificilmente pode ser negado. Ao mesmo tempo, nenhum
observador imparcial pode menosprezar a influência preponderante exercida pela religião sobre as expressões vitais
da civilização. Mais ainda, a sua indispensabilidade à ordem
social tem sido repetidamente demonstrada pelo seu efeito
direto sobre as leis da moralidade.

Falando da religião como força social, Bahá'u'lláh disse: "A religião é o maior de todos os meios para o estabelecimento da ordem no mundo para o contentamento pacífico de todos os que nele habitam". Referindo-se ao eclipse ou à corrupção da religião, ele escreveu: "Se a lâmpada da religião for obscurecida, reinarão o caos e a confusão, e as luzes da equidade, da justiça, da tranquilidade e da paz deixarão de brilhar". Enumerando as consequências disso, as Escrituras Bahá'ís destacam o fato de que, "nestas circunstâncias, a perversão da natureza humana, a degradação do comportamento humano, a corrupção e a dissolução das suas instituições revelam-se em seus aspectos mais repugnantes e revoltantes. O caráter humano é aviltado, a confiança é abalada, os nervos da disciplina são relaxados, a voz da consciência humana é silenciada, o sentido da decência e da vergonha é velado, os conceitos do dever, da solidariedade, da reciprocidade e da lealdade são distorcidos, e os próprios sentimentos de paz, alegria e esperança extinguem-se gradualmente".

Se, por conseguinte, a humanidade chegou a uma situação de conflitos paralisantes, precisa então olhar para si mesma, para a sua própria negligência, para os cantos de sereia a que tem dado ouvidos, para a fonte dos mal-entendidos e da confusão perpetrada em nome da religião. Àqueles que se têm agarrado cega e egoisticamente às suas ortodoxias particulares, e que impuseram aos seus devotos interpretações errôneas e contraditórias dos pronunciamentos dos Profetas de Deus, a esses cabe uma pesada responsabilidade por toda esta confusão - uma confusão agravada pelas barreiras artificiais erguidas entre a fé e a razão, a ciência e a religião. Isto porque, partindo-se de um exame imparcial dos pronunciamentos feitos efetivamente pelos Fundadores das grandes religiões, e levando-se em conta os meios sociais em que tiveram de cumprir as suas missões, não se vislumbram fundamentos para as alegações e os preconceitos que transformam as comunidades religiosas do mundo, e, consequentemente, todos os afazeres humanos.

O ensinamento de que deveríamos tratar os outros tal como gostaríamos de ser tratados, uma ética repetida de várias maneiras em todas as grandes religiões, apoia esta última observação em dois aspectos particulares: resume a atitude moral, o aspecto promotor da paz que emana dessas religiões, independentemente do lugar ou da época em que tiveram a sua origem; e implica também um aspecto de unidade que é a sua virtude essencial, uma virtude que a humanidade, com a sua visão fragmentada da História, não tem podido apreciar.

Se a humanidade tivesse visto os Educadores da sua infância coletiva em seu verdadeiro caráter, como agentes de um processo civilizatório, teria indubitavelmente colhido benefícios incalculavelmente maiores dos efeitos cumulativos das suas sucessivas missões. Desafortunadamente, não o fez.

O ressurgimento da religiosidade fanática, que atualmente se observa em muitas terras, não pode ser visto senão como um derradeiro espasmo antes da sua extinção. A própria natureza dos fenômenos violentos e destrutivos a ele associados é atestado eloquente da falência espiritual que representa. Efetivamente, uma das características mais estranhas e mais tristes de irrupção atual do fanatismo religioso é o modo como, em cada caso, está minando não só os valores espirituais conducentes à unidade da humanidade, mas também aquelas vitórias morais únicas ganhas pela religião particular a que pretende servir.

Por mais vital que tenha sido a sua força ao longo da História da humanidade, e por mais dramático que seja o atual ressurgimento do fanatismo religioso militante, a religião e as instituições religiosas, no decorrer das últimas décadas, estão sendo considerados por um número crescente de pessoas como irrelevantes em relação às principais preocupações do mundo moderno. Em seu lugar, as pessoas voltaramse ou para a procura hedonística da satisfação material, ou para a devoção a ideologias fabricadas pelos homens com o objetivo de salvar a sociedade dos males evidentes de que padece. Lamentavelmente, muitas dessas ideologias, em vez de abraçarem o conceito de unidade da humanidade e promoverem o aumento da concórdia entre os diversos povos, manifestaram tendência a deificar o Estado, a sujeitar o resto da humanidade ao domínio de uma nação, raça ou classe, a procurar suprimir toda a discussão e o intercâmbio de ideias, ou a abandonar friamente milhões de seres humanos à sorte de um sistema de mercado que, de forma mais que patente, está agravando as agruras em que se encontra a maioria da humanidade, ao mesmo tempo que permite que pequenas parcelas vivam em condições de riqueza, com que nossos antepassados dificilmente poderiam sonhar.

Como são trágicos os resultados das fés substitutas que os sábios mundanos da nossa era criaram! Na desilusão maciça de populações inteiras que foram ensinadas a venerar em seus altares, pode ler-se o veredicto irreversível da História acerca do seu valor. Os frutos que essas doutrinas produziram, após décadas de um éxercício cada vez mais irrestrito do poder por aqueles que lhes devem a sua ascensão no mundo dos homens, são as enfermidades sociais e econômicas que invadem todas as regiões do mundo nos anos finais deste século XX. Na base de todas essas aflições exteriores estão os danos espirituais, refletidos na apatia que se apossou da massa dos povos de todas as nações e na extinção da esperança nos corações de milhões de destituídos e angustiados.

Chegou o momento em que aqueles que pregam os dogmas do materialismo, quer do Leste ou do Oeste, tanto o capitalismo quanto o socialismo, terão de apresentar contas da tutela moral que têm presumido exercer. Onde está o "novo mundo" prometido por essas ideologias? Onde está a paz internacional a cujos ideais proclamaram a sua devoção?

Onde estão os avanços para novos domínios de progresso cultural, produzidos pelo enaltecimento desta raça, daquela nação ou de determinada classe? Por que é que a vasta maioria dos povos do mundo está se afundando cada vez mais na fome e na miséria, quando os árbitros atuais dos afazeres humanos têm a sua disposição riquezas incalculáveis, a uma escala jamais concebida pelos Faraós e pelos Césares, e nem mesmo pelas potências imperialistas do século passado?

Muito em especial, é na glorificação das conquistas materiais - simultaneamente origem e característica comum de todas essas ideologias - que encontramos as raízes da falsa crença de que seres humanos são incorrigivelmente egoístas e agressivos. E é aqui que o terreno tem que ser desobstruído para a edificação de um novo mundo digno dos nossos descendentes.

A conclusão de que os ideais materialistas falharam, quando examinados à luz da experiência, evoca um reconhecimento honesto de que tem de ser feito agora um novo esforço para encontrar soluções para os problemas angustiosos do planeta. As condições intoleráveis que predominam na sociedade falam de fracasso comum de todos eles, circunstâncias que tende a reforçar, em vez de aliviar, o entrincheiramento de parte a parte. Claramente, há necessidade urgente de um esforço em comum para remediar tal estado de coisas. O que é preciso, acima de tudo, é uma mudança de atitude. Irá a humanidade continuar com a sua obstinação, apegada a conceitos superados e suposições impraticáveis? Ou irão os seus dirigentes, independentemente das suas ideologias, dar um passo à frente e, animados por uma vontade inabalável, conferenciar uns com os outros, numa procura solidária de soluções apropriadas?

Aqueles que se interessam pelo futuro do gênero humano bem podem ponderar este conselho: "Se os ideais há muito nutridos, se as instituições honradas pelo tempo, se certas suposições sociais ou fórmulas religiosas já não promovem o bem-estar geral da humanidade, se deixaram de corresponder às necessidades de uma humanidade em constante evolução, que sejam, então, repelidos e relegados ao limbo das doutrinas obsoletas e esquecidas. Por que razão, num mundo sujeito à lei imutável da transformação e da decadência, deveriam ficar isentos da deterioração que há necessariamente de alcançar todas as instituições humanas? Afinal, a única finalidade das normas jurídicas, das teorias políticas e econômicas, é a salvaguarda dos interesses da humanidade em seu todo - e não é a humanidade que deve ser crucificada para a preservação da integridade de qualquer lei ou doutrina particular".

II

A proscrição das armas nucleares, a proibição do uso de gases venenosos ou a interdição da guerra bacteriológica não eliminarão as causas básicas das guerras. Por mais importantes que tais medidas práticas obviamente sejam, como elementos do processo de apaziguamento, por si só elas são demasiado superficiais para poderem ter um efeito duradouro. Os povos são suficientemente engenhosos para inventar novos instrumentos de guerra, e para utilizar meios como os alimentos, as matérias-primas, as finanças, o poderio industrial, a ideologia e o terrorismo na subversão uns dos outros, numa procura incessante de supremacia e domínio. Da mesma maneira, não é possível resolver a desarticulação que atualmente reina nos afazeres da humanidade mediante a resolução de conflitos ou dissídios específicos entre as nações. Há que adotar uma estrutura universal genuína.

Decerto que não há falta no reconhecimento pelos líderes nacionais do caráter mundial do problema, que está evidente no volume crescente de questões que os confrontam diariamente. E há também uma acumulação constante de estudos e propostas de soluções apresentadas por muitos grupos interessados e esclarecidos, bem como pelas agências das Nações Unidas, de forma a dissipar qualquer possibilidade de ignorância quanto aos difíceis problemas que é preciso enfrentar. Existe, contudo uma paralisia da vontade; e é isso que tem de ser cuidadosamente examinado e abordado com firmeza. Essa paralisia tem a sua origem, com já afirmamos, numa convicção profundamente entranhada acerca da inevitável belicosidade da humanidade, o que por sua vez produziu uma relutância em considerar a possibilidade de subordinar os interesses apenas nacionais aos requisitos da ordem do estabelecimento de uma autoridade mundial unida. Isso remonta também à incapacidade das massas, em grande parte ignorantes e subjugadas, de articular o seu desejo de uma nova ordem na qual possam viver em paz, harmonia e prosperidade com toda a humanidade.

Os passos hesitantes dados em direção à ordem mundial, especialmente desde a II Guerra Mundial, oferece-nos sinais de esperança. A tendência crescente exibida por grupos de nações, no sentido de formalizarem relações que lhes permitam cooperar em questões de interesse mútuo, sugere que, eventualmente, todas as nações poderão vencer esta paralisia. A Associação das Nações do Sudeste Asiático, a Comunidade e o Mercado Comum das Caraíbas, o Mercado Comum da América Central, o Conselho de Assistência Econômica Mútua, a Comunidade Econômica Europeia, a Liga Árabe, a Organização da Unidade Africana, a Organização dos Estados Americanos, o Fórum do Pacífico Sul - todos os empreendimentos conjuntos representados por organizações como estas preparam o caminho para a ordem mundial.

A atenção crescente que está sendo dedicada a alguns problemas mais enraizados do planeta constitui mais um sinal de esperança. Apesar das deficiências óbvias da ONU, as mais de quarenta declarações e convenções adotadas por esta organização, mesmo quando vários de seus membros não mostraram muito zelo na aplicação de seus compromissos, deram as pessoas comuns uma nova sensação de esperança. A Declaração Universal dos Direitos Humanos, a Convenção sobre a Prevenção e a Punição dos Crimes de Genocídio, e outros instrumentos semelhantes relacionados com a eliminação de todas as formas de discriminação baseadas na raça, no sexo ou na crença religiosa; a afirmação dos direitos da criança; a proteção de todas as pessoas contra a sujeição à tortura; a utilização do progresso científico e tecnológico em prol da paz e em benefício da humanidade - todas estas medidas, caso corajosamente postas em práticas e ampliadas, adiantarão a chegada do dia em que o espectro da guerra terá perdido a sua capacidade de dominar as relações internacionais. É desnecessário realçar aqui os significados dos temas abordados por estas declarações e convenções. Alguns deles, porém, dada a sua relevância imediata para o estabelecimento da paz mundial, merecem alguns comentários adicionais.

O racismo, um dos males mais funestos e persistentes, constitui um obstáculo importante no caminho da paz. A prática perpetra uma violação demasiado ultrajante da dignidade dos seres humanos para poderem ser tolerada sob qualquer pretexto. O racismo retarda o desenvolvimento das potencialidades ilimitadas das suas vítimas, corrompe os seus perpetradores e desvirtua o progresso humano. O reconhecimento da unidade da humanidade, implementando através de disposições jurídicas apropriadas tende de ser universalmente sustentado para que este problema possa ser superado.

A disparidade desmesurada entre ricos e pobres, uma fonte de intenso sofrimento mantém o mundo num estado de instabilidade, virtualmente a beira da guerra. Poucas sociedades têm retratado eficazmente desta questão. A sua solução requer a aplicação combinada de meios espirituais, morais e táticos. É necessário uma nova abordagem do prob-

lema, abrangendo a consulta de especialistas de uma ampla gama de disciplinas, num ambiente isento de polêmicas
econômicas e ideológicas, e envolvendo pessoas diretamente
afetadas pelas decisões que urgentemente terão de ser tomadas. Trata-se de uma questão que está intimamente ligada
não apenas à necessidade de eliminar os extremos de riqueza
e de pobreza, mas também àquelas verdades espirituais cuja
compreensão pode engendrar uma nova atitude universal. A
promoção de tal atitude é, em si mesma, uma parte importante da solução.

O nacionalismo desenfreado, distinto de um patriotismo são e legítimo, deve ceder o lugar de uma lealdade mais
ampla - ao amor à humanidade como um todo. A esse respei-
to, Bahá'u'lláh afirmou que "a terra é um só país, e os seres
humanos seus cidadãos." O conceito da cidadania mundial
é uma consequência direta da contração do mundo através
dos avanços tecnológicos e da incontestável interdependência das nações. O amor a todos os povos do mundo não ex-
clui o amor de cada pessoa ao seu país. E as vantagens das
partes, numa sociedade mundial, são melhor servidas pela
promoção das vantagens do todo. As atividades internacionais atuais, em vários campos que nutrem a afeição mútua
e um sentido de solidariedade entre os povos, precisam ser
substancialmente incrementadas.

Ao longo da História, as lutas religiosas têm sido
a causa de inúmeras guerras e conflitos, uma praga para o
progresso, e são hoje cada vez mais repugnantes - tanto às
pessoas de diferentes fés como àquelas que não professam
nenhum credo. Os adeptos de todas as religiões devem se
dispor a encarar as questões básicas suscitadas por tais dis-
putas, a chegar a conclusões claras. Como deverão ser resolv-
idas as diferenças entre elas, tanto em teoria como na prática?
O problema que enfrentam os líderes religiosos da humanidade é o de contemplarem, com os corações cheios de compaixão e ânsia de verdade, a triste situação atual da humani-

dade, e de perguntarem humildemente a si mesmos, perante o seu Criador Todo Poderoso, se não podem conciliar as suas diferenças teológicas num grande espírito de indulgência mútua, que lhes permita trabalhar conjuntamente em prol da compreensão humana e da paz.

A emancipação da mulher - a concretização da plena igualdade entre os sexos - é um dos pré-requisitos mais importantes, embora dos menos reconhecidos, para o estabelecimento da paz. A negação dessa igualdade perpetra uma injustiça contra metade da população do mundo, e promove entre os homens atitudes e hábitos nocivos que são transportados do ambiente familiar para o local de trabalho, para a vida política, e, em última análise, para a esfera das relações internacionais. Não existem quaisquer fundamentos morais, práticos ou biológicos que justifiquem essa privação. Só quando as mulheres forem bem recebidas em todos os campos de atividade humana, em condições de igualdade, é que se criará o clima moral e psicológico do qual poderá emergir a paz internacional.

A causa da educação universal, que já alistou ao seu serviço um exército de gente dedicada de todas as fés e nações, merece o maior apoio que os governos do mundo lhe possam dispensar. Afinal, a ignorância é indiscutivelmente a principal razão para o declínio e a queda dos povos, e para a perpetuação dos preconceitos. Nenhuma nação pode ter pleno êxito e se considerar realizada enquanto não facultar meios de ensino a todos os seus cidadãos. A escassez de recursos com que se debatem muitos países limita a sua capacidade de satisfazer essa necessidade, o que impõe uma certa ordenação de prioridades. Os órgãos e entidades decisórias envolvidas fariam bem em atribuir prioridades à educação das mulheres e das jovens, dado que é por intermédio de mães educadas que os benefícios do conhecimento podem ser mais rápida e eficazmente difundidos através das sociedades. Atendendo aos imperativos dos nossos dias, deveria também ser dada atenção ao ensino do conceito de cidadania mundial, como elemento integral da educação normal de cada criança.

Uma falta básica de comunicação entre os povos debilita sensivelmente os esforços para o estabelecimento da paz no mundo. A adoção de uma língua auxiliar internacional poderia contribuir muito para a solução desse problema e é um assunto que merece a mais urgente consideração.

Há duas observações que devem ser feitas em relação a todos estes tópicos. Em primeiro lugar, que a abolição da guerra não depende só de assinatura de tratados e protocolos; isso é uma tarefa assaz complexa que requer uma nova dimensão de comprometimento para a solução de questões que não costumam ser associadas à busca da paz. Quando baseada exclusivamente em acordos políticos, a ideia da segurança coletiva não é senão uma quimera. O outro ponto que merece ser destacado é que o principal problema inerente ao tratamento de questões relacionadas com a paz está na elevação do seu contexto ao plano dos princípios, um plano distinto do pragmatismo puro. Porque, essencialmente, a paz advém de um estado interior apoiado por uma atitude espiritual ou moral, e é principalmente através da evocação dessa atitude que se pode chegar à possibilidade de soluções duradouras.

Existem princípios espirituais, ou aquilo a que algumas pessoas chamam valores humanos, por meio dos quais se podem encontrar soluções para todos os problemas sociais. Qualquer grupo bem-intencionado pode, num sentido geral, formular soluções práticas para os seus problemas, mas as boas intenções e os conhecimentos práticos geralmente não são suficientes. O mérito essencial de um princípio espiritual reside no fato de não somente apresentar uma perspectiva que se harmoniza com aquilo que é imanente à natureza humana, mas também de incutir uma atitude, uma dinâmica, uma vontade e uma aspiração que facilitam a identificação e a implementação de medidas práticas. Os dirigentes governamentais e todos aqueles que ocupam postos de autoridade fariam bem se, em seus esforços para resolver problemas, procurassem primeiro identificar os princípios envolvidos e, depois, se deixassem guiar por eles.

III

A primeira questão a resolver é como o mundo presente, com o seu padrão enraizado de conflitos, pode transformar-se em um mundo onde prevaleçam a harmonia e a cooperação.

A ordem mundial só pode ser fundada sobre uma consciência inabalável da unidade da humanidade, uma verdade espiritual que todas as ciências humanas confirmam. A Antropologia, a Fisiologia e a Psicologia reconhecem uma só espécie humana, ainda que infinitamente variada no que se refere aos aspectos secundários da vida. O reconhecimento desta verdade requer o abandono dos preconceitos - de todos os tipos de preconceitos - relacionados com a raça, a classe social, a cor da pele, a crença religiosa, a nacionalidade, o sexo e o grau de civilização material; em suma, de tudo aquilo que faz com que as pessoas se considerem superiores umas às outras.

A aceitação da unidade da humanidade é o pré-requisito fundamental para a reorganização e a administração do mundo como um só país - como o lar da humanidade. A aceitação universal deste princípio espiritual é essencial para o êxito de qualquer tentativa de estabelecer a paz mundial. Deveria, portanto, ser universalmente proclamado, ensinado nas escolas, e constantemente reafirmado em todas as nações como preparação para a transformação orgânica da estrutura da sociedade que isso implica.

Do ponto de vista bahá'í, o reconhecimento da unidade "exige nada menos que a reconstrução e a desmilitarização de todo o mundo civilizado - um mundo organicamente unificado em todos os aspectos essenciais da sua vida, do seu mecanismo político, da sua aspiração espiritual, do seu comércio e das suas finanças, da sua escrita e do seu idioma, e, não obstante tudo isso, infinitamente variado quanto às características nacionais das suas unidades federadas."

Ao expor as implicações deste princípio cardeal, Shoghi Effendi, o Guardião da Fé Bahá'í, comentou em 1931 que: "Longe de se fundamentar na subversão dos alicerces da sociedade existente, ele procura alargar a sua base e remodelar as suas instituições de maneira consoante com as necessidades de um mundo sempre em transição. Não pode estar em conflito com nenhuma obrigação legítima, nem minar qualquer lealdade essencial. O seu fim não é abafar a chama de um patriotismo são e inteligente nos corações dos homens, nem abolir o sistema de autonomia nacional que é tão indispensável como freio dos males da descentralização excessiva. Não desconsidera, tampouco tenta suprimir, a diversidade da origem étnica, do clima, da história, do idioma e da tradição, do pensamento e dos costumes, que diferenciam os povos e as nações do mundo. Ele exige uma lealdade mais ampla, uma aspiração maior que qualquer outra que jamais animou a raça humana. Insiste em que os impulsos e os interesses nacionais sejam subordinados às necessidades de um mundo unificado. Repudia a centralização excessiva por um lado, e, ao mesmo tempo, nega qualquer tentativa de uniformidade. O seu lema é a unidade na diversidade."

O alcance de tais fins requer diversos estágios para o ajustamento das atitudes políticas nacionais, que agora se encontram à beira da anarquia, na ausência de leis claramente definidas ou de princípios universalmente aceitos e aplicáveis no trato das relações entre as nações. A Liga das Nações, a Organização das Nações Unidas, e os diversos organismos e acordos por elas produzidos, têm sido indubitavelmente úteis na atenuação de alguns dos efeitos negativos dos conflitos internacionais, mas têm-se revelado incapazes de evitar a guerra. Na verdade, têm havido dezenas de guerras desde o fim da II Guerra Mundial - e muitas delas continuam ainda a grassar.

Os aspectos dominantes deste problema já tinham emergido no século XIX, quando Bahá'u'lláh apresentou pela primeira vez as suas propostas para o estabelecimento da paz mundial. O princípio da segurança coletiva foi por ele exposto em declarações dirigidas aos governantes do mundo. Conforme Shoghi Effendi observou acerca do seu significado: "O que podem significar essas palavras poderosas", escreveu ele, "senão a limitação inevitável da soberania nacional irrestrita, como prólogo indispensável à formação da futura união de todas as nações do mundo? Alguma forma de superestado mundial há de evoluir, a cuja autoridade todas as nações do mundo cederão de boa vontade todo e qualquer direito de fazer guerra, certos direitos de cobrar impostos, e todos os direitos de possuir armamentos, além do necessário para a manutenção da ordem interna nos seus respectivos domínios. Tal estado incluiria dentro de sua órbita um Executivo Internacional capaz de exercer autoridade suprema e indiscutível sobre qualquer membro recalcitrante da comunidade; um Parlamento Mundial, cujos membros seriam eleitos pelo povo nos seus respectivos países e cuja eleição seria confirmada pelos respectivos governos; e um Supremo Tribunal, cujas decisões teriam efeito compulsório, mesmo no caso das partes envolvidas não concordarem em submeter voluntariamente as questões à sua consideração."

"Uma comunidade mundial em que todas as barreiras econômicas seriam permanentemente demolidas, e definitivamente reconhecida a interdependência do Capital e do Trabalho; em que o clamor do fanatismo religioso e das lutas religiosas teria sido silenciado para todo o sempre; em que a chama da animosidade racial teria sido finalmente extinta; em que um código único de direito internacional - produto do juízo ponderado dos representantes federados do mundo - teria como sua sanção a intervenção imediata e coercitiva das forças combinadas das unidades federadas; e, finalmente, uma comunidade mundial em que a fúria de um nacionalismo caprichoso e militante teria sido transmutada numa consciência permanente da cidadania mundial - assim é, em seus traços mais largos, a Ordem prevista por Bahá'u'lláh, uma Ordem que virá a ser considerada como o mais belo fruto de uma era em lenta maturação".

A implementação destas medidas de longo alcance foi indicada por Bahá'u'lláh: "Haverá de chegar o tempo em que a necessidade imperiosa da convocação de uma vasta e ampla assembleia de homens será universalmente percebida. Os governantes e os reis da terra terão de tomar parte dela, e, participando nas suas deliberações, deverão considerar métodos e meios capazes de assentar os fundamentos para a Paz Maior, mundial, entre os homens".

A coragem, a determinação, a pureza de motivos e o amor desinteressado de um povo por outro - todas as qualidades espirituais e morais necessárias para a efetivação desse passo supremamente importante em direção à paz - estão concentradas sobre a vontade de agir. E é no sentido de despertar a vontade necessária que é preciso proceder a um exame sério da realidade do homem, isto é, do seu pensar. Compreender a relevância desta potente realidade é também apreciar a necessidade social de atualizar o seu valor singular através de consultas francas, serenas e cordiais, e de agir a partir dos resultados desse processo. Bahá'u'lláh chamou insistentemente a atenção para as virtudes e a indispensabilidade da consulta como meio para a ordenação dos afazeres humanos. Ele disse: "A consulta confere maior consciência e transforma as conjecturas em certezas. É uma luz brilhante que, num mundo escuro, ilumina o caminho e guia. Para tudo existe e continuará a existir um estágio de perfeição e maturidade. A maturidade do dom do entendimento é manifestada através da consulta". A própria tentativa de alcançar a paz mediante a ação consultiva por ele proposta pode produzir um espírito tão salutar entre os povos da Terra, que nenhum poder se oporia a um resultado final triunfante.

Acerca dos procedimentos para essa assembleia mundial, 'Abdu'l-Bahá, filho de Bahá'u'lláh e intérprete autorizado dos seus ensinamentos, ofereceu as seguintes explicações: "Terão de fazer da Causa da Paz um objeto de consultas gerais e procurar por todos os meios ao seu alcance o estabelecimento de uma União de nações do mundo. Terão de celebrar um tratado vinculativo e estabelecer um convênio cujas disposições sejam sãs, invioláveis e bem definidas. Terão de proclamá-lo ao mundo inteiro e obter o seu endosso por toda a humanidade. Esse empreendimento nobre e supremo - verdadeira fonte de paz e bem-estar para todo o mundo - deveria ser considerado sagrado por todos os habitantes da Terra. Todas as forças da humanidade têm de ser mobilizadas para assegurar a estabilidade e a permanência deste Grande Convênio. Nesse Pacto todo abrangente deveriam ser claramente fixados os limites e as fronteiras de todas as nações, seriam definitivamente articulados os princípios em que se estabeleceriam as relações entre os governos, e determinadas todas as convenções e obrigações internacionais. Da mesma maneira, os armamentos de cada governo seriam estritamente limitados, pois que, caso se permitisse o aumento das forças militares e dos preparativos bélicos por parte de qualquer deles, isso suscitaria a suspeita dos outros. As bases desse Pacto solene seriam fixadas de modo que, se qualquer governo posteriormente violasse qualquer das suas obrigações, todos os governos da Terra se deveriam erguer e reduzi-lo à submissão total, ou, dito melhor, a humanidade como um todo resolveria empregar todos os meios à sua disposição para destruir tal governo. Se este remédio máximo for aplicado ao seu corpo enfermo, o mundo seguramente se recuperará de todos os seus males e permanecerá eternamente são e salvo".

A realização desta poderosa convocação já deveria ter ocorrido há muito tempo.

Com todo o ardor dos nossos corações, apelamos aos dirigentes de todas as nações para que aproveitem este momento oportuno e deem passos irreversíveis no sentido da convocação dessa conferência mundial. Todas as forças da História impelem a humanidade para este ato, que assinalará para todo o sempre o alvorecer da sua tão longamente aguardada maturidade.

Não irão as Nações Unidas, com pleno apoio dos seus membros, erguer-se à altura dos desígnios desse acontecimento culminante?

Que os homens e as mulheres, os jovens e as crianças em toda parte reconheçam o mérito eterno desta ação imperiosa em prol de todos os povos, e ergam as suas vozes em assentimento voluntário. Melhor ainda, que seja esta a geração a inaugurar este estágio glorioso na evolução da vida social do planeta.

IV

A fonte do otimismo que sentimos é uma visão que transcende o cessar da guerra e a criação de organismos de cooperação internacional. A paz permanente entre as nações é um estágio essencial, mas não, afirma Bahá'u'lláh, a meta final do desenvolvimento social da humanidade. Além do armistício inicial imposto ao mundo pelo medo do holocausto nuclear, além da paz política relutantemente celebrada por nações rivais e desconfiadas, além dos arranjos pragmáticos para a segurança e a coexistência, além das numerosas experiências no domínio da cooperação que estas medidas tornarão possíveis, encontra-se a meta final: a unificação de todos os povos do mundo em uma família universal.

A falta de unidade é um risco que as nações e os povos da Terra já não podem mais suportar; as consequências são demasiado terríveis para poderem ser contempladas, demasiado óbvias para requererem qualquer demonstração. "O bem-estar da humanidade", escreveu Bahá'u'lláh há mais de um século, "a sua paz e segurança, são inatingíveis a não ser que, e até que, a sua unidade seja firmemente estabelecida". Ao observar que "toda a humanidade está gemendo e ansiando por ser conduzida à unificação, e assim terminar o seu martírio secular", Shoghi Effendi acrescentou ainda que "a unificação da humanidade inteira é a etapa distintiva da qual a sociedade humana atualmente se aproxima. A unidade da família, da tribo, da cidade estado e da nação foram sucessivamente tentadas e completamente estabelecidas. A unidade do mundo é agora a meta em direção à qual a humanidade aflita se encaminha. O processo de formar nações já chegou ao fim. A anarquia inerente à soberania estatal aproxima-se de um clímax. Um mundo em amadurecimento deve abandonar esse fetiche, reconhecer a unidade e a universalidade das relações humanas, e estabelecer de uma vez por todas o mecanismo que melhor possa concretizar este princípio fundamental da sua vida".

Todas as forças de transformação contemporânea confirmam este ponto de vista. As provas podem ser discernidas nos numerosos exemplos já mencionados acerca dos sinais favoráveis à paz mundial que se observam nos movimentos e nos acontecimentos internacionais correntes. O exército de homens e mulheres, que serve os diversos órgãos da Organização das Nações Unidas, recrutado virtualmente de todas as culturas, raças e nações da Terra, representa um "funcionalismo civil" planetário, cujas realizações impressionantes são indicativas do grau de cooperação que pode ser conseguido, mesmo sob condições desanimadoras. Um impulso para a unidade, tal como uma primavera espiritual, luta por se expressar através dos inúmeros congressos internacionais que atraem pessoas de uma vasta gama de atividades. Motiva apelos para projetos internacionais envolvendo as crianças e a juventude. Na realidade, constitui a verdadeira fonte do notável movimento para o ecumenismo, através do qual os membros de religiões e seitas historicamente antagônicas parecem irresistivelmente atraídos uns pelos outros. Juntamente com a tendência oposta para a guerra e o auto engrandecimento, contra os quais luta incessantemente, o impulso para a unidade mundial é uma das características dominantes e generalizadas da vida no planeta durante estes anos finais do século XX.

A experiência da Comunidade Bahá'í pode ser vista como exemplo desta unidade crescente. É uma comunidade de cerca de três a quatro milhões de pessoas, originárias de muitas nações, culturas, classes e credos, empenhadas em uma ampla área de atividades ao serviço das necessidades espirituais, sociais e econômicas dos povos de inúmeras regiões. É um organismo social único, representativo da diversidade da família humana, que conduz os seus afazeres através de um sistema de princípios consultivos comumente aceitos, e que preza todas as grandes expressões de orientação divina da História da humanidade. A sua existência é mais uma prova convincente da praticabilidade da visão de um mundo unido exposta pelo seu Fundador, mais uma evidência de que a humanidade pode viver como uma sociedade global, à altura de quaisquer desafios que a sua maioridade possa suscitar. Se a experiência bahá'í puder contribuir em qualquer medida para reforçar a esperança na unidade da humanidade, será com grande satisfação que a oferecemos como modelo de estudo.

Ao contemplarmos a suprema importância da tarefa que agora confronta o mundo inteiro, curvamos humildemente as nossas cabeças perante a majestade infinita do Criador divino, que do Seu amor infinito gerou da mesma matéria toda a humanidade; que exaltou a preciosa realidade do homem; que o honrou com intelecto e sabedoria, nobreza e imortalidade; e que conferiu ao homem "a distinção e capacidade únicas de conhecê-Lo e amá-Lo", uma capacidade que "tem de ser encarada como o ímpeto gerador e o propósito primordial subjacente em toda a criação".

Possuímos a firme convicção de que todos os seres humanos foram criados "para levar avante uma civilização em constante evolução"; de que "agir como os animais do campo é indigno dos homens"; de que as virtudes dignas da condição humana são a honestidade, a indulgência, a misericórdia, a compaixão, a bondade e o amor para com todos os povos. Reafirmamos a crença de que as potencialidades inerentes à condição do homem, a plena medida do seu destino sobre a terra, a excelência inata da sua realidade, têm todas de ser manifestadas neste prometido Dia de Deus. São estes os motivos da nossa fé inabalável de que a unidade e paz são a meta alcançável em direção à qual a humanidade se esforça.

No momento em que se escrevem estas palavras, podem ouvir-se as vozes esperançosas dos bahá'ís, apesar da perseguição que continuam a sofrer na terra onde a sua Fé nasceu. Através do exemplo da sua esperança irredutível, são testemunho da crença de que a realização iminente deste antigo sonho de paz é agora, em virtude dos efeitos transformadores da revelação de Bahá'u'lláh, investida com a força da autoridade divina. Assim, comunicamo-vos não apenas uma visão composta de palavras: invocamos o poder de atos de fé e sacrifício; comunicamos o apelo ansioso de paz e de unidade de todos os nossos companheiros de Fé em todo o mundo. Solidarizamo-nos com todos os que são vítimas de agressão, todos os que anseiam pelo fim dos conflitos e das discórdias, todos aqueles cuja devoção a princípios de paz e de ordem mundial promove os fins enobrecedores para os quais a humanidade foi chamada à existência por um Criador que é todo amor.

Na seriedade do nosso desejo de vos transmitir o fervor da nossa esperança e a profundidade da nossa confiança, citamos a promessa enfática de Bahá'u'lláh: "Estas lutas infrutíferas e estas guerras ruinosas hão de passar, e a Paz Máxima há de chegar".

A CASA UNIVERSAL DE JUSTIÇA

The Promise of World Peace

Russian

Октябрь 1985

К НАРОДАМ МИРА!

Великий Мир, к которому на протяжении столетий склоняют свои сердца люди доброй воли, образ которого создают бесчисленные поколения пророков и поэтов, и который испокон веков постоянно предвещают священные писания к человечеству, наконец-то находится в пределах досягаемости народов. Впервые в истории каждый из нас получил возможность обозреть в единой перспективе всю планету с миллиардами населяющих ее, столь отличающихся друг от друга людей. Мир во всем мире не только возможен, но и неизбежен. Это - следующая стадия эволюции планеты, названная одним из великих мыслителей "планетизацией человечества".

Перед всеми обитателями Земли стоит выбор: будет ли мир достигнут лишь после немыслимых ужасов, низвергнутых на человечество из-за его упрямой приверженности старым стереотипам поведения, или он воцарится сегодня как следствие акта взаимного согласия. В этот критический момент, когда трудноразрешимые проблемы, стоящие перед человечеством, сливаются в общую заботу о судьбах мира, было бы слишком безответственным не остановить волну конфликтов и беспорядков.

К благоприятным факторам следует отнести непрерывно нарастающую мощь движения к мировому порядку, начатого на заре нашего века созданием Лиги Наций и продолженного более всеобъемлющей Организацией Объединенных Наций; свидетельствующее о завершении процесса государственного строительства достижение независимости большинства народов на Земле после II мировой войны и участие этих молодых государств наряду со старшими их собратьями в решении вопросов, представляющих взаимный интерес; последовавшее за этим резкое увеличение масштабов сотрудничества ранее изолированных и антагонистических народов и групп в международных начинаниях, направленных на развитие науки, образования, права, экономики и культуры; появление за последние десятилетия беспрецедентного количества международных гуманитарных организаций; расцвет женских и молодежных движений, участники которых призывают покончить с войной; и все более распространяющаяся стихийная сеть простых людей добивающихся взаимопонимания посредством личных контактов.

Научно-технический прогресс, ознаменовавший на воистину благословенный век, предвещает крупный скачок в социальной эволюции планеты и указывает пути возможного решения практических проблем, стоящих перед человечеством. По существу, он предоставляет средства для управления сложной жизнью объединенного мира. И все же барьеры продолжают существовать. Сомнения, неверные представления, предрассудки, подозрительность и заскорузлое своекорыстие мешают установлению нормальных взаимоотношений между народами и государствами.

Глубокое чувство духовного и морального долга побуждает нас в этот подходящий момент привлечь Ваше внимание к проницательным мыслям, которые более столетия назад впервые высказал правителям мира Бахаулла, основатель Бахаистской религии, доверенными лицами которой мы являемся.

Бахаулла писал: "Увы, ветер отчаяния дует отовсюду и раздоры, разделяющие и поражающие род человеческий, усиливаются с каждым днем. Уже можно различить признаки надвигающейся катастрофы, ибо существующий порядок из рук вон плох". Опыт человечества в полной мере подтвердил это пророческое суждение. Несовершенство господствующего в мире порядка проявляется в неспособности суверенных государств, входящих в Организацию Объединенных Наций, изгнать призрак войны, предотвратить угрозу крушения мировой экономики, распространение анархии и терроризма, жестокие страдания, причиняемые этими и другими бедами миллионам и миллионам людей. Воистину, агрессия и конфликты стали настолько характерны для наших социальных, экономических и религиозных систем, что многие считают такое поведение присущим человеческой природе и, следовательно, неискоренимым.

Укоренение этой точки зрения приводит к противоречию, парализующему человеческие отношения. С одной стороны, люди всех стран мира провозглашают не только готовность, но и стремление к миру гармонии, стремление покончить со страхами, терзающими их в повседневной жизни. С другой стороны, они, не подумав, соглашаются с мнением, что человеческие существа неисправимо эгоистичны и агрессивны и, следовательно, неспособны создать социальную систему, которая одновременно была бы прогрессивной и миролюбивой, динамичной и гармоничной, систему, которая предоставляла бы полную свободу для индивидуального творчества и инициативы, но была бы основана на сотрудничестве и взаимопомощи.

По мере того, как потребность в мире становится все более настоятельной, это коренное противоречие, мешающее достижению мира, делает все более необходимой переоценку предпосылок, лежащих в основе широко распространенных представлений о трудной исторической судьбе человечества. Беспристрастный анализ фактов показывает, что такое поведение вовсе не отражает подлинную сущность человека, а является следствием извращения человеческого духа. Приняв это положение, все люди смогут привести в действие конструктивные социальные силы, которые, находясь в полном согласии с человеческой природой, будут способствовать гармонии и сотрудничеству, а не войне и конфликтам.

Выбор такого пути означает не отрицание, а осознание истории человечества. Бахаистская религия рассматривает смятение в современном мире и бедственное положение дел человеческих, как естественную стадию органичного процесса, который в конечном счете ведет к неотвратимому объединению человеческого рода в социальную систему, границами которой станут границы планеты. Род человеческий, как организм особого склада, прошел через революционные стадии, подобные младенчеству и детству в жизни человека, и находится сейчас в кульминационной стадии мятежной юности, приближаясь к долгожданной поре зрелости.

Искреннее признание того факта, что предрассудки, война и эксплуатация отражают незрелые стадии обширного исторического процесса и, что человеческий род испытывает ныне неизбежное смятение, отражающее его коллективное возмужание, является не поводом для отчаяния, а необходимым условием начала колоссальной работы, направленной на построение миролюбивого мира. Основные мотивы темы, которую мы предлагаем Вашему вниманию, состоят в том, что такая работа возможна, что необходимые для этого конструктивные силы существуют, что объединяющие человечество социальные структуры могут быть построены.

Несмотря на то, что грядущие годы могут принести новые страдания и беды, а ближайшие перспективы неблагоприятны, Бахаистская община убеждена, что человечество встретит это высшее испытание с верой в благополучный исход. Конвульсивные перемены, к которым все быстрее и быстрее движется человечество, отнюдь не знаменуют конец цивилизации. Напротив, они послужат высвобождению "скрытых возможностей человека", выявлению "полной меры его назначения на Земле, внутренней красоты е
ю сущности".

I

Дарования, отличающие род человеческий от всех других форм жизни, складываются в нечто, известное под названием человеческого духа, существенной частью которого является разум. Эти дарования позволили человечеству построить цивилизации и добиться материального процветания. Однако, сами по себе такие достижения никогда не удовлетворяли человеческий дух, таинственная природа которого склоняется к возвышенному, устремляется к невидимому миру, к высшей действительности, к тому непознаваемому существу сути, которое мы называем Богом. Религии, подаренные человечеству плеядой духовных светил, установили первичную связь между людьми и высшей реальностью, вызвали к жизни и усовершенствовали способность человечества добиваться - наряду с социальным прогрессом - духовных побед.

Никакая серьезная попытка поправить дела человеческие, достигнуть мира во всем мире не может игнорировать роль религии. Восприятие и исповедование религии человеком составляет суть истории. Один выдающийся историк определил религию как "дарование человеческой натуры". Трудно отрицать, что извращение этого дарования в значительной степени способствовало смятению в обществе и конфликтам между людьми и в них самих. Но объективный наблюдатель не может сбрасывать со счетов и доминирующее влияние религии на жизненно важные проявления цивилизации. Больше того, незаменимость религии как фактора социального порядка, многократно продемонстрирована ее прямым воздействием на право и мораль.

Размышляя о религии, как о социальной силе, Бахаулла говорил: "Религия является величайшим из всех средств установления порядка в мире и мирного удовлетворения всех его обитателей". В отношении упадка и искажения религии, он писал: "Если погаснет светильник религии, настанет хаос и смятение, перестанет сиять свет честности, справедливости, покоя и мира". Суммируя такого рода последствия, Бахаистские писания подчеркивает, что "извращение человеческой натуры, разрушение норм человеческого поведения, искажение и ликвидация человеческих установлений проявляются в этих условиях с наихудших и отвратительнейших сторон. Человеческий характер портится, доверие подрывается, тетива дисциплины слабеет, голос человеческой совести умолкает, чувства приличия и стыда притупляются, понятия долга, солидарности, взаимопомощи и верности искажаются и самое ощущение покоя, радости и надежды постепенно угасает".

Раз уж человечество докатилось до парализующего конфликта, оно должно оглянуться на себя, на собственную нерадивость, на голоса сирен, к которым оно прислушивалось, на источник смятения и ошибок, совершенных во имя религии. Те, кто слепо и эгоистично придерживались своих ортодоксальных догм, навязывали следовавшим за ними противоречивые и неверные толкования слов Пророков Господа, несут тяжкую ответственность за это смятение, созданное искусственными барьерами, воздвигнутыми между верой и разумом, между наукой и религией. Ибо объективное изучение подлинных высказываний Основателей великих религий и социальных сред, в которых они вынуждены были выполнять СВОЮ) миссию, не дает никаких оснований для предрассудков и раздоров, раздирающих религиозные общины человечества п, следовательно, причиняющих ущерб делам человеческим.

Учение о том, что мы должны относиться к людям так, как нам хотелось бы, чтобы они относились к нам, в разных варианта-- повторяется во всех великих религиях. Этот закон этики подтверждает вышесказанное в двух отношениях. Во-первых, он обобщает моральные и миролюбивые принципы этих религий независимо от места и времени их зарождения. Во-вторых, он олицетворяет единство религий - достоинство, которое человечество с его разобщенными взглядами на историю не сумело оценить.

Если бы человечество распознало подлинную сущность Воспитателей своего коллективного детства, как деятелей цивылизирующего процесса, оно несомненно извлекло бы гораздо больше пользы из суммарных итогов их последовательных миссий. Этого, увы, человечество не сумело.

Возрождение во многих странах фанатического религиозного рвения нельзя рассматривать иначе как предсмертные конвульсии. Сама природа насильственных и разрушительных явлений, связанных с таким рвением, свидетельствует о представляемом им духовном банкротстве. Действительно, одна из наиболее странных и печальных особенностей нынешней вспышки религиозного фанатизма заключается в том, что она существенно подрывает не только духовные ценности, способствующие объединению человечества, но и неповторимые моральные победы той религии, которой, якобы, служат фанатики.

Несмотря на жизненно важную роль религии в истории человечества и драматизм нынешнего возрождения воинствующего религиозного фанатизма, возрастающее количество людей на протяжении ряда десятилетий считало, что религия ее установления не имеют прямого отношения к главным проблемам современного мира. Вместо религии они обратились к гедонистической погоне за материальными благами или надуманным идеологиям, созданным для спасения общества от мучащих его очевидных зол. К сожалению, большинство таких идеологий, вместо того, чтобы воспринять принцип единства человечества и способствовать согласию между народами, стремилось обожествить государство, подчинить одной нации, расе или классу остальное человечество, подавить свободную дискуссию и обмен идеями или предоставить миллионы голодающих на произвол рыночной системы, которая усугубляет плачевное состояние большинства человечества, позволяя небольшой его части жить в роскоши, о которой едва ли могли мечтать каши предки.

Сколь трагичны плоды суррогатов веры, сотворенных "мудрецами" нашего века! В массовом разочаровании целых народов, приученных молиться у их алтарей, можно прочесть бесповоротный приговор истории проповедуемым ими ценностям. Эти доктрины после десятилетий неограниченной власти тех, кто был обязан им своим восхождением на вершины дел человеческих, породили социальные и экономические недуги, которые в завершающие годы XX века поразили все регионы нашего мира. В основе всех этих внешних бедствий лежит духовный ущерб, который нашел отражение в апатии, охватившей массы людей во всех странах, и в угасании надежды в сердцах миллионов обездоленных и страждущих.

Настало время, когда проповедники догм материализма на Востоке и на Западе, в странах капитализма и социализма должны дать отчет о моральном руководстве, которое они, якобы, осуществляют. Где "новый мир", обещанный их идеологиями? Где международный мир, верности идеалам которого они клялись? Где прорывы к новым культурам свершениям, обусловленными возвышением той или иной расы, того или иного народа, того или иного класса? Почему подавляющее большинство человечества все глубже погружается в пучину голода и нищеты, в то время как нынешние вершители дел человеческих владеют богатствами, которые и не снились фараонам. Римским императорам и даже империалистическим магнатам XIX века?

Именно в прославлении погони за материальными благами, являющимися одновременно источником и общей чертой всех таких идеологий, мы находим корни, питающие ложное утверждение о том, что человеческие существа неисправимо своекорыстны и агрессивны. Именно здесь необходимо расчистить место для строительства нового мира, достойного наших потомков.

Опыт показал, что материалистические идеалы не удовлетворяют потребностям человечества. В свете этого следует признать необходимость новой попытки найти ответы на мучительные вопросы, стоящие перед людьми планеты. Невыносимые условия жизни, сложившиеся в обществе, красноречиво свидетельствуют о всеобщем поражении. Тем не менее, каждая из противостоящих сторон укрепляется в своем мировоззрении вместо того, чтобы отказаться от него. Совершенно очевидно, что должна быть предпринята попытка найти универсальное лекарство. Это, прежде всего, вопрос позиции. Будет ли человечество, упорствуя в своих заблуждениях, придерживаться изживших себя принципов и недееспособных гипотез? Или его лидеры, независимо от идеологии, решатся наконец объединить свои усилия в совместном поиске приемлемых решений?

Тем, кому дорого будущее рода человеческого, стоит поразмыслить над этим советом: "Если почитаемые с давних пор идеалы и освященные временем установления, некоторые социальные гипотезы и религиозные формулы перестали содействовать благоденствию всего населения планеты, если они больше не служат потребностям непрерывно развивающегося человечества, их следует отвергнуть и отправить в архив устаревших и забытых доктрин. Почему в мире, подчиненном непреложному закону изменения и разложения, не подлежат они износу, которому неизбежно подвергаются все человеческие установления? Ибо правовые нормы, политические и экономические теории предназначены лишь для охраны интересов всего человечества, и не следует приносить его в жертву ради сохранения неприкосновенности тех или иных законов или доктрин".

II

Запрещение ядерного, химического и бактериологического оружия не устранит коренные причины войны. Разумеется, эти практические меры чрезвычайно важны, но сами по себе они слишком поверхностны для достижения прочного мира. Люди достаточно изобретательны для того, чтобы создать новые виды вооружения и использовать продовольствие, сырье, финансы, индустриальную мощь, идеологию и терроризм как средства нескончаемой борьбы за власть и превосходство. Равным образом, невозможно навести порядок между нациями в нынешнем хаосе дел человеческих простым улаживанием отдельных разногласий и конфликтов. Необходим подлинно универсальный план.

Безусловно, руководители отдельных стран признают всемирный характер проблемы, ибо без универсального подхода им не удастся решить множество вопросов, возникающих в ходе их повседневной деятельности. К тому же, имеются многочисленные исследования и предложения озабоченных состоянием дел и хорошо осведомленных групп, а также учреждений ООН, исключающие элемент неведения относительно настоятельных нужд и потребностей человечества. Наблюдается, однако, какой-то паралич воли. Именно это требует внимательного изучения и решительных действий. Как мы уже указывали выше, этот паралич проистекает из глубоко укоренившейся убежденности в неизбывной агрессивности человечества, что приводит к нежеланию рассматривать возможности подчинения своекорыстных национальных интересов требованиям мирового порядка и мужественно встречать все далеко идущие последствия установления единого всемирного правительства. Он связан также с неспособностью угнетенных и необразованных масс выразить свое стремление к новому порядку, при котором они могли бы жить в мире, гармонии и благоденствии вместе со всем человечеством.

Некоторую надежду вселяют предварительные шаги в направлении мирового порядка, особенно те из них, которые были предприняты после Второй мировой войны. Группы отдельных стран официально оформляют свои взаимоотношения, что позволяет им налаживать сотрудничество по вопросам, представляющим взаимный интерес. Это неизменно усиливающаяся тенденция свидетельствует о том, что, в конечном счете, все страны сумеют преодолеть сковывающий их паралич. Ассоциация Стран Юго-Восточной Азии, Сообщество и Общий Рынок Стран Карибского Бассейна, Общий Рынок Стран Центральной Америки, Совет экономической Взаимопомощи, Европейское Сообщество, Лига Арабских Стран, Организация Африканского Единства, Организация Американских Государств, Форум Стран Южной Части Тихого Океана - все эти организации представляют совместные усилия, прокладывающие путь к мировому порядку.

Обнадеживает также усиливающееся внимание к некоторым из самых закоренелых проблем планеты. Несмотря на очевидные несовершенства ООН, более сорока принятых ею деклараций и конвенций вселили новые надежды в сердца простых людей даже в тех случаях, когда правительства встретили их без особого энтузиазма. Всеобщая декларация прав человека, Конвенция о предотвращении преступлений геноцида и наказании виновных в их совершении, а также другие мероприятия, направленные на ликвидацию всех форм дискриминации по расовым, половым и религиозным признакам, защиту прав ребенка, всеобщее запрещение пыток, борьбу с голодом и недоеданием, использование научно-технического прогресса в интересах мира и на пользу всему человечеству, если они будут осуществлении расширены с необходимой для этого решимостью и отвагой, приблизят тот день, когда призрак войны перестанет вершить международные дела. Нет нужды особо останавливаться на важности вопросов, затронутых в этих декларациях конвенциях. Однако, некоторые из них требуют пояснения в связи с их непосредственным значением для достижения мира во всем мире.

Расизм, одно из самых ядовитых и отвратительных зол. является серьезнейшей преградой на пути к миру.

Ни под каким предлогом расистские убеждения, столь глубоко оскорбляющие достоинство человека, не должны поощряться. Расизм тормозит развитие безграничных возможностей своих жертв, морально разлагает самих расистов и сдерживает прогресс человечества. Чтобы покончить - этим злом, необходимо универсально признать единство мира и узаконить его соответствующими правовыми мерами.

Колоссальный разрыв между богатыми и бедным причиняет людям жестокие страдания и держит мир в состоянии крайней неустойчивости, фактически на грани войны. Немногие общества сумели сократить такой разрыв. Чтобы решить эту проблему, требуется комбинированный подход, учитывающий духовные, моральные и практические ее аспекты. Необходим свежий взгляд на проблему, предусматривающий консультации с широким кругом специалистов без экономической или идеологической полемики и участие людей, непосредственно заинтересованных в срочном решении ряда назревших вопросов. Речь идет не только о необходимости устранения эксцессов богатства и нищеты, но и о духовных истинах, понимание которых способствовало бы новому универсальному подходу к делам планеты. Создание такого подхода, само по себе, составило бы существенную часть решения.

Необузданный национализм, не имеющий ничего общего со здоровым и вполне закономерным патриотизмом, должен уступить дорогу лояльности и любви ко всему человечеству. Бахаулла утверждает: "Земля - единая страна, а все люди - ее граждане". Концепция мирового гражданства непосредственно вытекает из слияния мира в единое сообщество вследствие научных достижений и неоспоримой взаимозависимости стран. Любовь ко всем народам мира вовсе не исключает любовь к собственной стране.

Наибольшую пользу отдельной части всемирного общества можно принести, содействуя благоденствию всего человечества в целом. Необходимо существенно активизировать международное сотрудничество в самых различных областях, ибо оно воспитывает в людях чувства взаимного уважения и солидарности.

На всем протяжении истории человечества религиозные распри служили причиной бесчисленных войн и конфликтов, сдерживали прогресс и теперь все больше вызывают отвращение как среди людей различных вероисповеданий, так и среди неверующих. Приверженцы всех религий должны поставить перед собой основные вопросы, возникающие в связи с такими распрями. и найти на них четкие ответы. Как в теории и на практике разрешить разногласия между различными религиозными учениями? Задача религиозных лидеров состоит в том, чтобы, преисполнив свои сердца чувством милосердия и желанием найти истину, поразмыслить над состоянием человечества и, смирив гордыню перед Всемогущим Творцом, спросить себя: нельзя ли поступиться теологическими разногласиями во имя великого духа взаимной терпимости, которая позволила бы им вместе трудиться на благо мира и взаимопонимания между людьми.

Эмансипация женщины, уравнение ее во всех отношениях с мужчиной, является одним из важнейших, хотя и не общепризнанных, условий достижения мира. Отрицание такого равенства означает несправедливость, совершаемую по отношению к половине человечества и культивирует в мужчинах вредные привычки и обычаи, которые переносятся из семьи в сферу профессиональной деятельности, политическую жизнь и, наконец, в международные отношения. Такое отрицание равенства не имеет под собой никаких моральных, практических или биологических оснований. Только полноправное участие женщин во всех сферах человеческой деятельности создаст моральный и психологический климат, благоприятный для воцарения мира во всем мире.

Всеобщее образование, которому уже служит целая армия преданных делу людей всех вероисповеданий и национальностей, заслуживает максимально возможной поддержки со стороны правительства мира, ибо невежество, вне всякого сомнения, является главной причиной упадка и падения народов и увековечивания предрассудков. Ни одна страна не может добиться успехов, не предоставив благ просвещения всем своим гражданам. Отсутствие ресурсов ограничивает возможности многих стран в этом отношении и вынуждает их проводить образовательные программы в несколько стадий. Органам, принимающим решения по очередности таких стадий, следовало бы начать с предоставления образования женщинам и девочкам, ибо блага знаний наиболее эффективно и быстро распространяются в обществе через просвещенных матерей. В соответствии с велением времени, в программу общего образования каждого ребенка следует включить преподавание учения о всемирном гражданстве.

Отсутствие универсальных средств общения людей существенно ослабляет действенность усилий, направленных на достижение мира во всем мире. Принятие вспомогательного международного языка в значительной степени способствовало бы решению этой проблемы, и это мероприятие требует неотложного внимания.

Подводя итог вышесказанному, следует особо подчеркнуть два момента. Во-первых, невозможно покончить с войной простым подписанием договоров и протоколов. Это - сложная задача, требующая нового подхода к решению вопросов, обычно не связываемых с делом мира. Идея коллективной безопасности, основанной только на политических соглашениях, навсегда останется химерой. Во-вторых, дело мира следует перевести из сферы чистого прагматизма в разряд принципов и идей, ибо, по существу, мир рождается из внутреннего состояния, поддерживаемого духовной или моральной позицией. В создании такой позиции находится возможность прочного решения вопросов, связанных с достижением мира во всем мире.

Существуют духовные принципы (некоторые называют их человеческими ценностями), при помощи которых можно найти решение любой социальной проблемы. Руководствуясь добрыми намерениями, любая группа может разработать общую схему решений стоящих перед нею проблем, но обычно добрых намерений и практических знаний для этого недостаточно. Важное достоинство духовного принципа состоит в том, что он не только дает перспективу, гармонирующую с существом человеческой природы, но и создает отношение, динамику, волю, устремления, помогающие разработать и осуществить практические мероприятия. Главам правительств и всем административным властям, прежде чем предпринимать что-либо для решения той или иной проблемы, следовало бы выявить связанные с нею принципы и затем руководствоваться ими.

III

В первую очередь необходимо решить вопрос, каким путем современный мир, образец глубоко укоренившихся конфликтов, превратится в мир, в котором будут царить гармония и сотрудничество.

Мировой порядок может быть установлен только на основе непоколебимой уверенности в единстве человечества - духовной истине, подтверждаемой всеми гуманитарными науками. Антропология, физиология, психология признают только один род человеческий при всем бесконечном разнообразии второстепенных аспектов жизни. Чтобы признать эту истину, необходимо отречься от всех предрассудков, различающих людей по расовой и классовой принадлежности, цвету кожи, вероисповеданию, национальности, полу, степени развития материальной культуры, отречься от всего, что позволяет людям считать себя выше других.

Признание единства человечества является первой основополагающей предпосылкой реорганизации мира и управления им как одной страной - домом человечества. Всеобщее признание этого принципа необходимо для успеха любой попытки добиться мира во всем мире. Поэтому его следует повсеместно распространять, преподавать в школах и постоянно отстаивать во всех странах в порядке подготовки к предполагаемому им органичному изменению структуры общества.

Согласно учению Бахауллы, принцип единства человечества "требует полной перестройки и демилитаризации всего цивилизованного мира, требует мира, органически объединенного во всех существенных аспектах его жизни, политического устройства, духовных устремлений, торговли и финансов, письменности и языка, но сохраняющего при этом все бесконечное разнообразие национальных особенностей составляющих его частей".

Размышляя о смысле этого основополагающего принципа, Шоги Эффенди, Хранитель Бахаистской религии писал в 1931 году: "Далекий от стремления подорвать существующие устои общества, Всемирный Закон Бахауллы стремится расширить его базу, преобразовать его установления в соответствии с нуждами постоянно изменяющегося мира. Этот принцип не противоречит законным чувствам верности и лояльности. Он не ставит целью ни заглушение пламени здорового и разумного патриотизма в сердцах людей, ни уничтожение системы национальной автономии, столь необходимой для предотвращения бед чрезмерной централизации. Он не игнорирует и не пытается подавить разнообразие этнических корней, климата, истории, языка, традиций, мышления и обычаев, которые отличают народы и страны мира. Он призывает к более широкой лояльности, к более высоким устремлениям, чем те, которые когда-либо вдохновляли человеческий род. Он требует подчинения национальных побуждений и интересов властным требованиям объединенного мира. С одной стороны он отвергает чрезмерную централизацию, а с другой - отрицает всякие попытки к установлению единообразия. Его лозунг - единство в разнообразии".

Для достижения этих целей потребуется несколько стадий преобразования политических позиций стран, позиций, которые сегодня, в виду отсутствия четко сформулированных законов или общепринятых и повсеместно осуществляемых принципов, регулирующих отношения между странами, находятся на грани анархии. Лига Наций. ООН, многие другие организации выработанные ими соглашения, безусловно, способствуют смягчению отрицательных последствий международных конфликтов, но они не были способны предотвратить войну. Ведь после Второй мировой войны мир пережил множество войн; многие из них свирепствуют до сих пор.

Главные аспекты этой проблемы и начали выявляться еще в XIX веке, когда Бахаулла впервые выдвинул свои предложения, касающиеся достижения мира во всем мире. Принцип коллективной безопасности был провозглашен им в обращениях к правителям мира. Шоги Эффенди комментирует смысл этого принципа следующим образом: "Что еще могли означать эти весомые слова, как не указание на неизбежное ограничение безмерного национального суверенитета в рамках необходимой подготовки к формированию будущего Содружества всех народов мира? должна развиться какая-то форма мирового Сверх государства, в пользу которого все страны мира добровольно откажутся от прав вести войны, взимать некоторые налоги и содержать вооруженные силы, кроме сил, необходимых для поддержания внутреннего порядка в своих владениях. Такое государство должно будет включать в себя: Международный Исполнительный Орган, способный применять верховную и неоспоримую власть к любому непокорному члену содружества; Мировой Парламент, члены которого будут избираться народами всех стран и утверждаться их правительствами; Верховный Трибунал, чьи решения будут иметь обязательную силу даже в тех случаях, когда заинтересованные стороны не согласны добровольно представить свое дело на его рассмотрение".

"Мировое сообщество, в котором будут навсегда уничтожены все экономические преграды и со всей определенностью признаны узы взаимной зависимости труда и капитала; в котором навсегда утихнут религиозные распри и исчезнут все проявления религиозного фанатизма; в котором, наконец, будет погашено пламя расовой вражды, в котором единый комплекс международного права - плод обдуманного решения представителей мировой федерации - будет предусматривать ввод немедленных и принудительных санкций объединенных сил членов федерации; в котором ярость своенравного, воинствующего национализма сменится прочным осознанием принадлежности ко всему человечеству, - таким, в самых общих чертах, представляется Порядок, предсказанный Бахауллой,

Порядок, который будет считаться прекраснейшим плодом постепенно созревающей эпохи".

Бахаулла указал, как провести в жизнь эти далеко идущие планы: "Настанет время, когда будет повсеместно признана настоятельная необходимость созвать широкое, всеобъемлющее собрание людей. Цари и правители мира должны будут присутствовать на этом собрании. Участвуя в дискуссиях, они будут обязаны рассмотреть пути и средства, которые заложат основы Великого Мира между людьми во всем мире".

Мужество, решимость, чистота помыслов, бескорыстная любовь ко всему народу, все духовные и моральные качества, необходимые для совершения этого важного шага, концентрируются на воле к действию. А чтобы развить достаточную силу воли, следует серьезнейшим образом рассмотреть подлинную сущность человека, его мышление. Понимание колоссального значения этой сущности одновременно означает осознание социальной потребности в практическом использовании ее уникальной ценности посредством искреннего, непредубежденного и задушевного обмена мнениями и последующих действиях в соответствии с его результатами. Бахаулла настойчиво обращает наше внимание на благотворность обмена мнениями и необходимость этого процесса для упорядочения дел человеческих. Он говорил: "Обмен мнениями дарует глубокую осведомленность, превращает предположение в уверенность. Это сияющий свет, который показывает дорогу и выводит нас из царства тьмы. Все в мире имеет и всегда будет иметь свою меру зрелости и совершенства. Зрелость дара понимания проявляется через обмен мнениями". Сама по себе. попытка достичь мира посредством предложенных им совещаний может высвободить благотворную энергию людей Земли в таких масштабах, что никакая сила не сможет помешать окончательному триумфу дела мира.

Размышляя о проведении такого всемирного собрания, Абдул-Баха, сын Бахауллы и авторитетный толкователь его учений, приходит к следующему заключению: "Они должны сделать Дело Мира предметом всеобщего обсуждения и использовать все имеющиеся в их распоряжении средства, чтобы основать Союз народов мира. Они должны подписать обязательный для всех договор и заключить соглашение на твердых, нерушимых и четко сформулированных условиях. Они должны объявить об этом всему миру и получить санкцию всего человеческого рода. Это величайшее и благородное начинание - подлинный источник мира и благоденствия всего человечества должно стать священным для всех живущих на Земле. Все силы человечества должны быть мобилизованы на обеспечение нерушимости и вечности этого Величайшего Соглашения. В этом всеобъемлющем Договоре должны быть четко указаны рубежи и границы каждой страны, твердо установлены принципы, лежащие в основе взаимоотношений между правительствами, и точно определены все международные соглашения м обязательства. Точно также следует строго ограничить военный потенциал каждого государства, ибо, если одной стране будет дозволено усиление подготовки к войне и наращивание вооружений, это вызовет недоверие у других стран. Основной принцип этого торжественного Договора должен быть сформулирован таким образом, что, если какое-либо правительство нарушит любую из его статей, все государства мира поднимутся, чтобы заставить его подчиниться. Нет, весь человеческий род должен будет решиться использовать все свои силы, чтобы уничтожить такое правительство. Если это сильнейшее лекарство будет применено, больной мир несомненно исцелится от своих недугов и навсегда останется здоровым и невредимым".

Время для созыва такого колоссального совещания давно назрело.

Со всем пылом наших сердец мы призываем лидеров всех стран воспользоваться нынешним благоприятным моментом и предпринять бесповоротные шаги к проведению такого всемирного собрания. Все силы истории побуждают человеческий род к этому акту, который на все времена ознаменует зарю долгожданной зрелости человечества.

Сможет ли Организация Объединенных Наций при полной поддержке ее членов подняться до уровня возвышенных трелей этого венчающего дело событиями?

Пусть же мужчины и женщины, юноши и дети всего мира признают непреходящее значение этого неотложного акта для всего человечества и в полном согласии отдадут ему свои голоса! Воистину, пусть наше поколение откроет эту славную стадию эволюции общественной жизни планеты!

IV

Источником нашего оптимизма является видение будущего, которое наступит после прекращения войн и создания органов международного сотрудничества. Бахаулла утверждает, что вечный мир между народами является важной стадией, но не конечной целью общественного развития человечества. За первоначальным перемирием, на которое мир вынужден будет пойти под страхом ядерной катастрофы, за политическим миром, неохотно поддержанным недоверяющими друг другу соперничающими странами, за прагматическими соглашениями о безопасности и сосуществовании, за многочисленными экспериментами в области сотрудничества, которые станут возможными вследствие перечисленных выше шагов, лежит заветная конечная цель - объединение всех народов мира в единую семью.

Разобщенность представляет собой опасность, с которой больше не могут мириться народы и государства. Последствия ее настолько ужасны, что их невозможно себе и представить, и настолько очевидны, что не требуют каких-либо доказательств. Более столетия тому назад Бахаулла писал:"Благоденствие человечества, его мир и безопасность недостижимы, если и пока не будет установлено прочное единство". Отметив, что "человечество стонет и жаждет, чтобы его вели к единству и покончили с его вековыми мучениями", Шоги Эффенди поясняет: "Объединение человечества является характернейшим признаком той ступени развития, к которой приближается сегодня человеческое общество. Успешные попытки привели к полному объединению семьи, рода, города-государства, нации. Мировое единство является целью, к которой стремится смятенное человечество. Процесс формирования национальных государств завершен. Анархизм, присущий национальному суверенитету, приближается к кульминационной точке. Мир, приближающийся к зрелости, должен отказаться от этого фетиша, признать единство и целостность человеческих отношений и установить раз и навсегда порядок, наиболее полно воплощающий этот основополагающий принцип жизни человечества".

Все силы современности, способствующие переменам, подтверждают правильность этой точки зрения. Доказательством тому служат многочисленные, упоминавшиеся ранее международные движения и события, способствующие достижению мира во всем мире. Целая армия мужчин и женщин, представляющих практически все культуры, расы и народы Земли, составляет в рамках разнообразных учреждений ООН всемирный "служебный корпус", впечатляющие успехи которого показывают, какой высокий уровень сотрудничества может быть достигнут даже при неблагоприятных условиях. Стремление к единству, подобно духовной весне, проявляется на бессчетных международных конгрессах, собирающих людей самых разных профессий. Оно стимулирует развитие международных детских и молодежных мероприятий. По существу, оно является источником мощного выдающегося движения, неудержимо сближающего приверженцев некогда враждовавших между собой религий и сект. Наряду с противоположной тенденцией к войне и самовозвеличиванию, с которой оно непрестанно противоборствует, стремление к всемирному единству господствует и проникает во все уголки жизни планеты в эти последние годы XX века.

Опыт Бахаистской общины можно рассматривать как пример такого увеличивающегося единства. Это - сообщество трех-четырех миллионов людей, принадлежащих ко многим народам, культурам, классам и вероисповеданиям и занимающихся самой разнообразной деятельностью для удовлетворения духовных, социальных и экономических потребностей людей во многих странах. Это - единый социальный организм, представляющий все многообразие семьи человечества, осуществляющий свою деятельность через систему общепризнанных принципов обмена мнениями и в равной степени почитающий все великие проявления божественного руководства в истории. Его существование является еще одним убедительным доказательством осуществимости мечты Основателя Учения, мечты оп едином мире, еще одним убедительным доказательством того, что человечество может жить как всемирное общество, которому будут по плечу любые задачи поры возмужания. Если бахаистский опыт сможет в какой-то мере укрепить надежд. на единение человеческого рода, мы будем счастливы предоставить его людям в качестве модели для изучения.

Размышляя об исключительной важности задачи, стоящей ныне перед всем миром, мы смиренно склоняем головы перед величием Божественного Создателя, который в своей беспредельной милости сотворил все человечество одним племенем. возвеличил драгоценную сущность человека, наградил его разумом и мудростью, благородством и бессмертием, наделил людей "уникальной способностью познать Его и возлюбить Его" способностью, которую "следует считать начальным импульсом и первичной целью всего творения".

Мы твердо придерживаемся убеждения, что все человеческие существа были созданы "нести эстафету вечно развивающейся цивилизации", что "уподобляться диким зверям недостойно человека", что добродетелями, достойными человека, являются верность, терпимость, милосердие, сострадание и добрая воля ко всем людям. Мы утверждаем веру в то, что "срытые возможности человека, полная мера его назначения на Земле, внутренняя красота его сущности должны проявиться в обетованный День Господа". Таковы основания нашей непоколебимой уверенности в том, что единство и мир являются достижимыми целями, к которым стремится человечество.

В этот момент, когда пишется наше послание, голос надежды бахаистов звучит вопреки гонениям, которым они подвергаются в стране, где родилась их Вера. Их непоколебимая надежда свидетельствует о том, что вера в неминуемое осуществление вековой мечты о мире, под действием преобразующего влияния откровений Бахауллы, наделена ныне силой божественного авторитета. Итак, мы не только передаем вам словесный образ, но и взываем к силе деяний веры и самопожертвования, посылаем всем страстный призыв наших собратьев по религии к миру и единству. Мы солидарны со всеми жертвами агрессии, с теми, кто жаждет покончить с враждой и раздорами, с теми, чья преданность принципам мира и мирового порядка способствует достижению благородных целей, ради которых Всемилостивый Создатель и сотворил человечество.

От всей души, желая передать вам весь жар нашей надежды и всю глубину нашей веры, мы приводим твердое обещание Бахауллы: "Эти бесплодные раздоры и разрушительные войны минуют и наступит "Величайший Мир".

Всемирный Дом Справедливости

The Promise of World Peace

Spanish

Octubre 1985

A los Pueblos del Mundo:

La Gran Paz hacia la que las gentes de buena voluntad han inclinado sus corazones a lo largo de los siglos, esa paz que los videntes y los poetas han vaticinado generación tras generación y que han prometido constantemente las sagradas escrituras de la humanidad, está, por fin, al alcance de todas las naciones. Por primera vez en la historia puede contemplarse el planeta entero, con toda su gran variedad de pueblos, en una sola perspectiva. La paz del mundo no sólo es posible, sino también inevitable. La próxima etapa en la evolución de este planeta es, en palabras de un gran pensador, «la planetización de la humanidad».

Que la paz haya de alcanzarse sólo después de inimaginables horrores provocados por el empecinado apego de la humanidad a viejas normas de conducta, o que haya de abrazarse ahora, por medio de un acto voluntario resultado de una gran consulta, es lo que tienen que decidir todos los habitantes de la tierra. En esta encrucijada decisiva, cuando los arduos problemas que enfrentan a las naciones han sido fundidos en una sola preocupación para todo el mundo, el no frenar la corriente de conflicto y desorden sería un acto inconscientemente irresponsable.

Entre las señales favorables están el creciente fortalecimiento de las medidas destinadas a establecer un nuevo orden mundial que se tomaron inicialmente, casi al comienzo de este siglo, con la creación de la Liga de las Naciones, seguida por la Organización de las Naciones Unidas, de más amplio alcance; el hecho de que, después de la Segunda Guerra Mundial, la mayor parte de las naciones de la tierra lograra su independencia -prueba de madurez del proceso de formación nacional de los pueblos-, así como la cooperación de estas naciones incipientes con las naciones más antiguas en la búsqueda de soluciones a problemas comunes; el aumento consiguiente de la cooperación entre pueblos y grupos, hasta entonces aislados y antagonistas, en los campos de la ciencia, la educación, el derecho, la economía y la cultura; el surgimiento, durante los últimos decenios, de un número sin precedentes de organizaciones humanitarias internacionales; la proliferación de movimientos femeninos y juveniles que trabajan para que se ponga fin a las guerras, y la generación espontánea de crecientes asociaciones de gente común en busca de la comprensión mediante la comunicación personal.

Los adelantos científicos y tecnológicos logrados en este siglo extraordinario presagian un gran salto hacia adelante en la evolución social del planeta e indican los medios para resolver los problemas materiales de la humanidad. En realidad, estos adelantos constituyen los medios mismos para la administración de la compleja vida de un mundo unido. Pero los obstáculos todavía existen. Las dudas, los conceptos erróneos, los prejuicios, las sospechas y las mezquindades acosan a los pueblos y naciones en sus relaciones mutuas.

Como resultado de un profundo sentimiento del deber espiritual y moral, nos vemos obligados, en este momento oportuno, a llamar la atención de ustedes sobre las penetrantes ideas -de las cuales nosotros somos depositarios- que Bahá'u'lláh, el fundador de la Fe bahá'í, comunicó en primicia a los gobernantes de la humanidad hace más de un siglo.

Escribió Bahá'u'lláh: «Los vientos de la desesperación, lamentablemente, soplan desde todas direcciones, y la disensión que divide y aflige a la raza humana aumenta día a día. Ya se perciben los signos de convulsiones y caos inminentes, por cuanto el orden prevaleciente demuestra ser deplorablemente defectuoso». Este juicio profético ha sido ampliamente confirmado por la experiencia general de la humanidad. Las deficiencias del orden establecido se reflejan en la incapacidad de los estados soberanos que forman las Naciones Unidas para exorcizar el espectro de la guerra, el amenazante fracaso del orden económico internacional, la expansión de la anarquía y el terrorismo, y el atroz sufrimiento que éstos y otros males causan cada vez a más millones de seres humanos. En verdad, tanta agresión y conflicto han llegado a caracterizar de tal forma nuestros sistemas sociales, económicos y religiosos que muchas personas han sucumbido a la creencia de que dicha conducta es intrínseca a la naturaleza humana y que, por lo tanto, no se puede erradicar.

Con el afianzamiento de este punto de vista, se ha desarrollado una contradicción paralizante en los acontecimientos humanos. Por una parte, gentes de todas las naciones proclaman no sólo su buena disposición, sino también su anhelo de paz y concordia para que desaparezcan los acuciantes temores que atormentan su vida diaria. Por otra parte, se acepta con conformidad la tesis de que los seres humanos son incorregiblemente egoístas y agresivos y, por lo tanto, incapaces de construir un sistema social que sea a la vez progresista y pacífico, dinámico y armónico, un sistema que permita el libre juego de la creatividad e iniciativa individuales, pero basado en la cooperación y la reciprocidad.

A medida que la necesidad de la paz se vuelve más apremiante, esta contradicción fundamental, que impide su realización, exige una nueva evaluación de las suposiciones sobre las que se basa el punto de vista común del destino histórico de la humanidad. Examinándola desapasionadamente, la evidencia revela que dicha conducta, lejos de reflejar la genuina naturaleza del hombre, representa una tergiversación de su espíritu. La rectificación de este punto de vista permitirá a todos poner en marcha las fuerzas sociales constructivas que, por ser acordes con la naturaleza humana, producirán concordia y cooperación en vez de guerras y conflictos.

El seguir tal camino no es negar el pasado de la humanidad, sino comprenderlo. La Fe bahá'í contempla la confusión actual del mundo y el lastimoso estado de los acontecimientos humanos como una etapa natural de un proceso orgánico que llevará, final e inevitablemente, a la unificación de la humanidad dentro de un orden social único, cuyos límites serán los del planeta. La humanidad, como unidad orgánica característica, ha pasado por etapas evolutivas análogas a las etapas de la infancia y la adolescencia de los individuos y se encuentra ahora en el período de culminación de su turbulenta adolescencia, llegando a su tan esperada mayoría de edad.

Un reconocimiento sincero de que el prejuicio, la guerra y la explotación han sido la expresión de etapas de inmadurez de un vasto proceso histórico, y que la humanidad experimenta hoy el inevitable tumulto que indica la llegada colectiva a su mayoría de edad, no es razón para desesperarse, sino un requisito previo para emprender la formidable tarea de construir un mundo pacífico. Que semejante empresa es posible, que existen las fuerzas constructivas que se necesitan para tal fin, que es posible levantar estructuras sociales unificadoras, es el tema que les exhortamos a examinar.

Sea cual fuere el sufrimiento y la confusión que nos deparen los próximos años, así como la oscuridad de las circunstancias inmediatas, la comunidad bahá'í cree que la humanidad puede enfrentarse a esta prueba suprema con confianza en el resultado final. Lejos de ser indicios del fin de la civilización, los cambios convulsivos hacia los cuales la humanidad se precipita cada vez más rápidamente servirán para desencadenar las «potencialidades inherentes a la posición del hombre» y para revelar «la medida plena de su destino en el mundo y la excelencia innata de su realidad».

I

Los dones que distinguen al ser humano de todas las demás formas de vida se resumen en lo que se conoce como el espíritu humano; la mente es su característica fundamental. Estos dones han hecho posible que la humanidad construyera civilizaciones y disfrutara de prosperidad material. Pero tales triunfos por sí solos no han satisfecho nunca al espíritu humano, cuya naturaleza misteriosa le inclina hacia lo trascendente, hacia un anhelo de alcanzar un reino invisible, hacia una realidad última, hacia esa desconocida esencia de las esencias que se llama Dios. Las religiones, reveladas a la humanidad por una sucesión de luminarias espirituales, han sido el vínculo fundamental entre el ser humano y esa realidad última y han galvanizado y refinado la capacidad de la humanidad para alcanzar el éxito espiritual junto con el progreso social.

Ningún intento serio para corregir los asuntos humanos, para alcanzar la paz mundial, puede prescindir de la religión. El concepto y práctica de la misma por el hombre son, de manera determinante, el material de la historia. Un eminente historiador describió la religión como una «facultad de la naturaleza humana». Ahora bien, no se puede negar que la perversión de esta facultad ha contribuido a crear confusión en la sociedad y conflictos entre los individuos. Pero tampoco puede ningún observador sensato descartar la influencia preponderante que ha ejercido la religión sobre las expresiones vitales de la civilización. Más aún, su carácter indispensable para el orden social ha sido demostrado repetidamente por su efecto directo sobre la ley y la moral.

Al referirse a la religión como una fuerza social, Bahá'u'lláh escribió: «La religión es el mayor de todos los medios para el establecimiento del orden en el mundo y para la pacífica satisfacción de todos los que lo habitan». Respecto al eclipse o corrupción de la religión, escribió: «Si la lámpara de la religión se apagara, el caos y la confusión sobrevendrían, y las luces de la equidad, de la justicia, de la tranquilidad y de la paz dejarían de brillar». En una enumeración de dichas consecuencias, las escrituras bahá'ís señalan que la «perversión de la naturaleza humana, la degradación de la conducta humana, la corrupción y la disolución de las instituciones humanas, se revelan ellas mismas, bajo tales circunstancias, en sus peores y más repugnantes aspectos. Se envilece el carácter humano, la confianza vacila, los nervios de la disciplina se relajan, la decencia y la vergüenza se oscurecen, las concepciones del deber, de la solidaridad, de la reciprocidad y de la lealtad se distorsionan, y hasta el sentimiento de paz, de alegría y de esperanza se extingue gradualmente».

En consecuencia, si la humanidad ha llegado a un punto de conflicto paralizante, debe buscar dentro de sí misma, dentro de su propia negligencia en los cantos de sirena que ha escuchado, hasta encontrar la fuente de la incomprensión y la confusión perpetradas en nombre de la religión. Aquellos que se han aferrado ciega y egoístamente a sus propias ortodoxias, quienes han impuesto sobre sus fervientes devotos interpretaciones erróneas y conflictivas de las declaraciones de los Profetas de Dios, tienen una gran responsabilidad por esta confusión que se complica por las barreras artificiales que se levantan entre la fe y la razón, la religión y la ciencia. Pues si se hace un sereno examen de las verdaderas aseveraciones de los Fundadores de las grandes religiones, y de los medios sociales en que se vieron obligados a realizar sus misiones, no hay nada que apoye las contiendas y prejuicios que trastornan a las comunidades religiosas de la humanidad y, por lo tanto, a todos los asuntos humanos.

La máxima de que deberíamos tratar a los demás como quisiéramos que se nos tratara a nosotros mismos, un principio de ética que se repite constantemente en las enseñanzas de todas las grandes religiones, fortalece esta última observación en dos aspectos particulares: resume la actividad moral, el aspecto pacificador que caracteriza a estas religiones, independientemente de su lugar o época de origen; también revela un aspecto de unidad que es su virtud fundamental, una virtud que la humanidad en su visión disociada de la historia no ha sabido apreciar.

Si la humanidad hubiera visto a los Educadores de su infancia colectiva en su verdadera dimensión, como agentes de un proceso civilizador, no hay duda que hubiera cosechado beneficios mucho mayores por el efecto acumulado de las misiones sucesivas de tales Educadores. Esto, lamentablemente, no ha sucedido así.

El resurgimiento del fervor fanático religioso que se observa en muchos países no puede calificarse más que de convulsión agonizante. La naturaleza propia de los fenómenos violentos y disociadores, que se relacionan con dicho resurgimiento, da testimonio de la bancarrota espiritual que representa. Realmente, una de las características más extrañas y tristes del fanatismo religioso es el extremo hasta el que está socavando, en cada caso particular, no sólo los valores espirituales que conducen a la unidad de la humanidad, sino también aquellas singulares victorias morales ganadas por la religión determinada a la que pretende servir.

Pese a que la religión haya sido una gran fuerza vital en la historia de la humanidad, y por dramático que sea el actual resurgimiento del fanatismo religioso militante, desde hace décadas, un número cada vez mayor de personas considera que la religión y las instituciones religiosas están desconectadas de las principales inquietudes del mundo moderno. En lugar suyo, la gente se ha entregado a la búsqueda hedonista de la satisfacción material, o a ideologías del origen humano, diseñadas para rescatar a la sociedad de los males evidentes bajo los cuales sufre. Lamentablemente, muchas de estas ideologías, en vez de abrazar el concepto de la unidad de la humanidad y de promover una creciente concordia entre los diferentes pueblos, han tendido a deificar el Estado, a subordinar al resto de la humanidad a los dictados de una nación, raza o clase, a intentar suprimir toda discusión e intercambio de ideas, o a abandonar despiadadamente a merced de la economía de mercado a millones de seres hambrientos; todo lo cual agrava claramente la situación de la mayoría de la humanidad, mientras permite que pequeños sectores vivan en una prosperidad que difícilmente hubieran imaginado nuestros antepasados.

Cuán trágico es el historial de las falsas religiones creadas por los sabios mundanos de nuestra época. En la desilusión masiva de poblaciones enteras a quienes se les ha enseñado a adorar en los altares de dichas religiones, puede leerse el veredicto irrevocable de la historia sobre los valores de las mismas. Los frutos que han producido estas doctrinas, después de decenios de un creciente y desenfrenado ejercicio de poder por parte de aquellos que les deben su ascendencia en los asuntos humanos, son los males sociales y económicos que afligen a cada región de nuestro mundo en los años finales del siglo XX. Fundamentando todas estas aflicciones exteriores está el daño espiritual, reflejado en la apatía que ha atrapado a las masas de los pueblos de todas las naciones, y la desaparición de la esperanza en los corazones de millones de seres despojados y angustiados.

Ha llegado la hora de que aquellos que predican los dogmas del materialismo, ya sean de Oriente o de Occidente, ya sean los del capitalismo o los del socialismo, rindan cuenta del liderazgo moral que presumen haber ejercido. ¿Dónde está el «nuevo mundo» prometido por estas ideologías? ¿Dónde está la paz internacional a cuyos ideales proclaman su devoción? ¿Dónde están los adelantos en nuevos campos de realizaciones culturales producidos por el engrandecimiento de tal raza, de tal nación o de tal clase en particular? ¿Por qué la inmensa mayoría de los pueblos del mundo se está hundiendo cada vez más en el hambre y la miseria, mientras la riqueza, en una escala que nunca soñaron los faraones, los césares o aun las potencias imperialistas del siglo XIX, está a disposición de los actuales árbitros de los asuntos humanos?

Muy especialmente, en la glorificación de los fines materiales, a la vez origen y característica común de todas esas ideologías, es donde se encuentran las raíces con las que se nutre el sofisma de que los seres humanos son incorregiblemente egoístas y agresivos. Es aquí, precisamente, donde debe limpiarse el terreno para construir un nuevo mundo digno de nuestros descendientes.

El hecho de que los ideales materialistas, a la luz de la experiencia, hayan fracasado en satisfacer las necesidades de la humanidad, reclama a un reconocimiento sincero de que hay que hacer un nuevo esfuerzo para encontrar las soluciones a los angustiosos problemas del planeta. Las condiciones intolerables que prevalecen en la sociedad reflejan un fracaso común de todos ellos, circunstancia que incrementa, en vez de aliviarlas, las tensiones que predominan en todos los bandos. Está claro que se requiere un esfuerzo común para remediarlo. Es primordialmente una cuestión de actitud. ¿Continuará la humanidad a la deriva, aferrándose a conceptos obsoletos y a creencias impracticables? ¿O darán sus líderes un paso adelante con voluntad decidida, prescindiendo de ideologías, para unirse en la búsqueda conjunta de soluciones adecuadas?

Quienes se preocupan por el porvenir de la humanidad bien debieran reflexionar sobre este consejo: «Si los ideales por tanto tiempo apreciados y las instituciones por tanto tiempo veneradas; si ciertas suposiciones sociales y fórmulas religiosas han dejado de fomentar el bienestar de la mayoría de la humanidad; si ya no satisfacen las necesidades de una humanidad en continua evolución, que se descarten y releguen al limbo de las doctrinas obsoletas y olvidadas.

¿Por qué éstas, en un mundo sujeto a la inmutable ley del cambio y la decadencia, han de quedar exentas del deterioro que necesariamente se apodera de toda institución humana? Porque las normas legales, las teorías políticas y económicas han sido diseñadas únicamente para defender los intereses de toda la humanidad y no para que ésta sea crucificada por la conservación de la integridad de alguna ley o doctrina determinada».

II

Prohibir las armas nucleares, el uso de gases venenosos o declarar ilegal la guerra bacteriológica no eliminará de raíz las causas de las guerras. Por muy importantes que sean dichas medidas prácticas como parte del proceso de paz, son en sí demasiado superficiales como para ejercer alguna influencia duradera. Los hombres son lo suficientemente ingeniosos como para inventar otras formas de guerra y usar los alimentos, las materias primas, las finanzas, el poder industrial, la ideología y el terrorismo como instrumentos de subversión de unos contra otros en una interminable pugna por la supremacía y el dominio. Tampoco es posible resolver el trastorno masivo de los asuntos de la humanidad arreglando problemas o conflictos específicos entre las naciones. Debe adoptarse un auténtico sistema universal.

Ciertamente, los líderes de las naciones son conscientes de la naturaleza mundial del problema, les es evidente dados los conflictos con que se enfrentan cada día. Y se han propuesto y acumulado estudios y soluciones por muchos grupos cultos y concienciados, así como por los organismos de las Naciones Unidas, para eliminar cualquier posible ignorancia en cuanto a los desafiantes requerimientos que se deben satisfacer. Existe, sin embargo, una parálisis de voluntad, y es esto precisamente lo que hay que analizar y tratar resueltamente. Esta parálisis radica, como hemos dicho, en una convicción profunda sobre la naturaleza inevitablemente belicosa de la humanidad; esto ha llevado a no querer considerar la posible subordinación del interés nacional a las exigencias del orden mundial y a una falta de voluntad para encarar valientemente las inmensas implicaciones que se derivarían del establecimiento de una autoridad en un mundo unido. Se puede atribuir también a la incapacidad de las masas ignorantes y subyugadas para expresar su deseo de un nuevo orden en el que puedan vivir en paz, concordia y prosperidad con toda la humanidad.

Los pasos y tentativas hacia un orden mundial, especialmente desde la Segunda Guerra Mundial, dan señales de esperanza. La creciente tendencia de grupos de naciones a formalizar relaciones que les permitan cooperar en asuntos de interés mutuo indica que, a la postre, todas las naciones podrían superar esta parálisis. La Asociación de Naciones del Sudeste de Asia, la Comunidad y el Mercado Común del Caribe, el Mercado Común Centroamericano, el Consejo para Asistencia Económica Mutua, las Comunidades Europeas, la Liga de Estados Árabes, la Organización para la Unidad Africana, la Organización de Estados Americanos, el Foro del Pacífico Sur..., todos los esfuerzos conjuntos representados por dichas organizaciones preparan el camino hacia un orden mundial.

La creciente atención que se presta a algunos de los problemas más serios del planeta es otra señal de esperanza. A pesar de las claras deficiencias de las Naciones Unidas, la multitud de declaraciones y convenciones adoptadas por dicha organización, aun aquellas en las que los Gobiernos no se han comprometido con entusiasmo, le han dado a la gente común una nueva esperanza en la vida. La Declaración Universal de los Derechos Humanos, la Convención para la Prevención y Castigo del Delito de Genocidio, así como las medidas similares relativas a la eliminación de toda forma de discriminación basada en la raza, el sexo o las creencias religiosas; la defensa de los derechos de los niños; las medidas de protección contra la tortura de los seres humanos; la erradicación del hambre y la desnutrición; el uso del progreso científico y tecnológico para fines pacíficos y en beneficio de la humanidad, todas estas medidas, si se aplican y se extienden con valentía, adelantarán la llegada del día en que el espectro de la guerra pierda su fuerza para dominar las relaciones internacionales. No es preciso subrayar la importancia de los asuntos que tratan dichas declaraciones y convenciones, pero algunos en concreto, debido a su repercusión inmediata en el establecimiento de la paz mundial, merecen mayores comentarios.

El racismo, uno de los males más funestos y persistentes, es un gran obstáculo para la paz. Su práctica perpetra una violación tan ultrajante de la dignidad de los seres humanos que no debe fomentarse bajo ningún pretexto. El racismo retrasa el desarrollo de las potencialidades ilimitadas de sus víctimas, corrompe a los que lo cometen y malogra el progreso humano. El reconocimiento de la unidad de la humanidad, llevado a cabo por medidas legales adecuadas, debe ser universalmente defendido para poder superar este problema.

La excesiva desigualdad entre ricos y pobres, fuente de grandes sufrimientos, mantiene al mundo en estado de constante inestabilidad, virtualmente al borde de la guerra. Pocas sociedades han encarado de forma efectiva esta situación. La solución exige la aplicación conjunta de enfoques espirituales, morales y prácticos. Hay que observar el problema con una mirada nueva, libre de polémicas económicas e ideológicas, lo cual implica consultar con expertos en una amplia gama de disciplinas y lograr la participación de las gentes que resultarían directamente afectadas por las decisiones que deben tomarse con urgencia. Es un asunto que está ligado no sólo con la necesidad de eliminar los extremos de riqueza y pobreza, sino también con aquellas realidades espirituales cuya comprensión puede producir una nueva actitud universal. El promover tal actitud es ya, en sí mismo, una parte importante de la solución.

El nacionalismo desenfrenado, que es diferente de un patriotismo sano y legítimo, debe ceder ante una lealtad más amplia: el amor a toda la humanidad. La declaración de Bahá'u'lláh es la siguiente: «La tierra es un solo país, y la humanidad, sus ciudadanos». El concepto de la ciudadanía mundial es el resultado directo de la contracción del mundo en una sola vecindad por medio de los adelantos científicos y de la indiscutible dependencia entre las naciones. El amor a todos los pueblos del mundo no excluye el amor al propio país. Se beneficia más una parte determinada de la sociedad mundial cuando se fomenta el beneficio de la totalidad. Las actividades internacionales actuales en diversos campos, que estimulan el afecto mutuo y el sentido de la solidaridad entre los pueblos, deben ser ampliamente multiplicadas.

El conflicto religioso a lo largo de la historia ha sido causa de innumerables guerras y contiendas, un gran obstáculo para el progreso y algo cada vez más aborrecible para creyentes e incrédulos. Los creyentes de todas las religiones deben estar dispuestos a afrontar las preguntas fundamentales que plantean estos conflictos y llegar a respuestas claras. ¿Cómo deben resolverse las diferencias entre ellos tanto en la teoría como en la práctica? El desafío con el que se enfrentan los líderes religiosos de la humanidad consiste en contemplar la situación de la misma, con sus corazones llenos de espíritu de compasión y de anhelo por la verdad, y preguntarse a sí mismos si no pueden, humildemente ante su Creador Todopoderoso, disolver sus diferencias teológicas en un gran espíritu de tolerancia mutua que les permita trabajar juntos por el progreso de la comprensión y la paz humanas.

La emancipación de las mujeres, el logro de la igualdad total entre ambos sexos, es uno de los más importantes requisitos previos para la paz, aunque sea uno de los menos reconocidos. La negación de dicha igualdad perpetra una injusticia contra la mitad de la población del mundo y provoca en los hombres actitudes y costumbres nocivas que se llevan de la familia al trabajo, a la vida política y, por último, a las relaciones internacionales. No existen bases morales, prácticas ni biológicas para justificar tal negación. Sólo en la medida en que las mujeres sean aceptadas con plena igualdad en todos los campos del quehacer humano, se creará el clima moral y psicológico del que puede surgir la paz internacional.

La causa de la educación universal, en la que ya presta sus servicios todo un ejército de personas abnegadas de todos los credos y países, merece el mayor apoyo que le puedan dar los Gobiernos del mundo, pues, indiscutiblemente, la ignorancia es la razón principal de la decadencia y caída de los pueblos y de la perpetuación de los prejuicios. Ninguna nación podrá alcanzar el éxito si no pone la educación al alcance de todos los ciudadanos. La falta de recursos limita la capacidad de muchas naciones para cumplir con esta necesidad, lo que impone un cierto orden de prioridades. Los estamentos responsables deberían considerar la necesidad de dar prioridad a la educación de las mujeres y niñas, puesto que es a través de madres formadas como se pueden transmitir, más efectiva y rápidamente a la sociedad, los beneficios del conocimiento. Para cumplir con los requisitos de nuestro tiempo, debe prestarse atención también a la enseñanza del concepto de ciudadanía mundial como parte del programa educativo de cada niño.

Una carencia fundamental de comunicación entre los pueblos perjudica seriamente los esfuerzos que se hacen para alcanzar la paz mundial. La adopción de un idioma auxiliar internacional contribuiría mucho a resolver este problema, por lo que urge prestarle la máxima atención.

De todos estos asuntos hay dos que merecen destacarse. El primero es que la abolición de la guerra no es simplemente cuestión de firmar tratados y protocolos; es una tarea compleja que exige un nuevo nivel de compromiso para resolver los problemas que habitualmente no se relacionan con la búsqueda de la paz. Al basarse solamente en convenios políticos, la idea de la seguridad colectiva resulta ser una quimera. El otro es que el desafío primordial al tratar de los asuntos de la paz consiste en elevar el contexto al nivel de los principios para diferenciarlo de un mero pragmatismo. Porque, en esencia, la paz proviene de un estado interior apoyado por una actitud espiritual o moral, y es precisamente en la evocación de esta actitud donde puede encontrarse la posibilidad de soluciones duraderas.

Hay principios espirituales, o lo que algunos llaman valores humanos, con los que es posible encontrar soluciones para todo problema social. Cualquier grupo bienintencionado puede elaborar soluciones prácticas para sus problemas en un sentido general, pero las buenas intenciones y los conocimientos prácticos no suelen ser suficientes. El mérito esencial del principio espiritual consiste no sólo en que presenta una perspectiva acorde con lo que es inherente a la naturaleza humana, sino que también induce a una actitud, una dinámica, una voluntad, una aspiración que facilitan el descubrimiento y la aplicación de medidas prácticas. Los gobernantes y todos los que ostentan alguna autoridad tendrían más éxito en sus esfuerzos por resolver los problemas si primero intentaran identificar los principios en cuestión y luego se guiaran por ellos.

III

El dilema primordial que hay que resolver es cómo el mundo actual, con su intrínseca pauta de conflicto, puede cambiarse por un mundo en el que prevalezcan la armonía y la cooperación.

El orden mundial sólo puede fundarse sobre una imperturbable conciencia de la unidad de la humanidad, verdad espiritual que confirman todas las ciencias humanas. La antropología, la fisiología y la psicología reconocen sólo una especie humana, aunque con infinitas variantes en los aspectos biológicos secundarios. Para admitir esta verdad hay que abandonar los prejuicios, toda clase de prejuicios: de raza, clase, color, credo, nación, sexo, grado de civilización material; todo lo que hace que la gente se considere superior a los demás.

La aceptación de la unidad de la humanidad es el requisito previo fundamental para la reorganización y administración del mundo como un solo país: el hogar de la raza humana. La aceptación universal de este principio espiritual es indispensable para tener éxito en cualquier intento de establecer la paz mundial. Por lo tanto, debe proclamarse universalmente, debe enseñarse en las escuelas y afirmarse constantemente en todas las naciones como preparación para el cambio orgánico en la estructura social que esta aceptación implica.

Desde el punto de vista bahá'í, el reconocimiento de la unidad de la humanidad «requiere nada menos que la reconstrucción y la desmilitarización de todo el mundo civilizado como un mundo orgánicamente unificado en todos los aspectos esenciales de su vida, de su maquinaria política, de su anhelo espiritual, de su comercio y de sus finanzas, de su escritura e idioma, y, aun así, infinito en la diversidad de las características nacionales de sus unidades federadas».

Al considerar las implicaciones de este principio cardinal, Shoghi Effendi, el Guardián de la Fe bahá'í, comentaba en 1931: «Lejos de pretender la subversión de los fundamentos actuales de la sociedad, trata de ampliar su base, de amoldar sus instituciones en consonancia con las necesidades de un mundo en constante cambio. No está en conflicto con alianzas legítimas ni socava lealtades esenciales. Su propósito no es sofocar la llama de un sano e inteligente patriotismo en el corazón del hombre, ni abolir el sistema de autonomía nacional, tan esencial para evitar los males de un exagerado centralismo. No ignora ni intenta suprimir la diversidad de orígenes étnicos, de climas, de historia, de idioma y tradición, de pensamiento y costumbres que distinguen a los pueblos y naciones del mundo. Reclama una lealtad más amplia, una aspiración mayor que cualquiera de las que ha sentido la humanidad. Insiste en la subordinación de impulsos e intereses nacionales a las exigencias imperativas de un mundo unificado. Repudia, por una parte, el centralismo excesivo, y, por otra, rechaza todo intento de uniformidad. Su consigna es la unidad en la diversidad».

El logro de tales fines exige varias etapas en el ajuste de las actitudes políticas nacionales, que ahora lindan con la anarquía, a falta de leyes claramente definidas o de principios universalmente aceptados y obligatorios que regulen las relaciones entre las naciones. La Liga de las Naciones, las Naciones Unidas y las muchas organizaciones y acuerdos producidos por ellas, han sido indudablemente provechosos, al atenuar ciertos efectos negativos de los conflictos internacionales, pero se han mostrado incapaces de prevenir la guerra. De hecho, ha habido una gran cantidad de guerras desde que terminó la Segunda Guerra Mundial. Muchas están ardiendo todavía.

Los aspectos predominantes de este problema ya habían aparecido en el siglo XIX cuando Bahá'u'lláh hizo públicas por primera vez sus propuestas para el establecimiento de la paz mundial. El principio de seguridad colectiva fue propuesto por Él en las declaraciones que dirigió a los gobernantes del mundo. Comentando su significado, escribió Shoghi Effendi: «¿Qué otra cosa podrían significar estas importantes palabras sino una referencia a la inevitable reducción de las ilimitadas soberanías nacionales como requisito indispensable para la formación de la futura mancomunidad de todas las naciones del mundo? Es necesario desarrollar cierta forma de superestado mundial, a favor del cual todas las naciones del mundo habrán de abandonar voluntariamente toda pretensión de hacer la guerra, ciertos derechos de gravar con impuestos, y todos los derechos de poseer armamentos, salvo con el propósito de mantener el orden interno dentro de sus respectivos dominios. Dicho Estado habrá de incluir en su órbita un poder ejecutivo internacional con capacidad para hacer valer su autoridad suprema e indiscutible sobre todo miembro recalcitrante de la mancomunidad; un Parlamento mundial cuyos miembros serán elegidos por los habitantes de sus respectivos países y cuya elección será confirmada por sus respectivos Gobiernos; y un tribunal supremo cuyos dictámenes tendrán carácter obligatorio aun en los casos en que las partes interesadas no hayan acordado voluntariamente someter el litigio a su consideración».

«Una comunidad mundial en la que todas las barreras económicas habrán quedado totalmente derribadas y en la que se reconocerá definitivamente la interdependencia del capital y el trabajo; en la que el clamor del fanatismo y del conflicto religioso habrá sido acallado para siempre; en la que estará definitivamente extinguida la llama de la animosidad racial; en la que un código único de derecho internacional -producto de un juicioso análisis de los representantes federados del mundo- será sancionado por la intervención instantánea y coercitiva de las fuerzas combinadas de las unidades federadas; y, finalmente, una comunidad mundial en la que el furor de un nacionalismo caprichoso y militante será trocado por una perdurable conciencia de ciudadanía mundial; así es como se presenta, a grandes rasgos, el Orden anunciado por Bahá'u'lláh, un Orden que habrá de ser considerado el más hermoso fruto de una época que madura lentamente».

La puesta en práctica de estas medidas de largo alcance fue indicada por Bahá'u'lláh: «Debe llegar el tiempo en que se reconozca universalmente la imperativa necesidad de celebrar una reunión vasta y omnímoda de personas. Los gobernantes y reyes de la tierra deben necesariamente concurrir a ella y, participando en sus deliberaciones, deben considerar los medios y arbitrios para echar los cimientos de la Gran Paz mundial entre los hombres».

El valor, la resolución, la motivación pura, el amor desinteresado de un pueblo a otro -todas las cualidades espirituales y morales necesarias para efectuar este trascendente paso hacia la paz- se concentran en la voluntad de actuar. Y es para provocar la voluntad necesaria por lo que se debe meditar seriamente sobre la realidad del hombre, esto es, su pensamiento. Comprender la importancia de esta poderosa realidad es también apreciar la necesidad social de poner en práctica su valor único por medio de un proceso de consultas sinceras, desapasionadas y cordiales, y actuar en consecuencia con los resultados de este proceso. Bahá'u'lláh recalcó insistentemente las virtudes de la consulta y lo indispensable que es para poner en orden los asuntos humanos. Dijo: «La consulta confiere un mejor conocimiento y convierte la conjetura en certeza. Es una luz brillante que, en un mundo oscuro, muestra el camino y sirve de guía. Para cada cosa hay y seguirá habiendo un estado de perfección y madurez. La madurez del don del entendimiento se manifiesta a través de la consulta». El intento mismo de alcanzar la paz por medio de la consulta, como Él propuso, puede desencadenar ese espíritu saludable entre los pueblos de la tierra, de tal forma que ningún poder podría resistir su resultado triunfal definitivo.

En cuanto a los procedimientos para esta asamblea mundial, 'Abdu'l-Bahá, el hijo de Bahá'u'lláh e intérprete autorizado de Sus enseñanzas, ofreció esta profunda explicación: «Deben hacer de la causa de la paz el objeto de la consulta general e intentar, por todos los medios a su alcance, establecer una unión de las naciones del mundo. Deben concertar un tratado de obligado cumplimiento y establecer un convenio cuyas disposiciones sean sólidas, inviolables y definitivas. Deben proclamarlo a todo el mundo y obtener para él la sanción de toda la raza humana. Esta suprema y noble empresa -la verdadera fuente de paz y bienestar de todo el mundo- ha de considerarse como sagrada por todos los moradores de la tierra. Todas las fuerzas de la humanidad deben ser movilizadas para asegurar la estabilidad y permanencia de este Supremo Convenio. En este pacto universal se deben fijar claramente los límites y fronteras de cada una de las naciones, establecer definitivamente los principios fundamentales de las relaciones entre los Gobiernos y determinar todos los acuerdos y obligaciones internacionales. De la misma manera, se debe limitar estrictamente la cantidad de armamentos de cada Gobierno, pues si se permitiera incrementar los preparativos para la guerra y las fuerzas militares de cualquier nación, se provocaría la desconfianza de las otras. El principio fundamental de este pacto solemne se debe fijar de tal manera que si algún Gobierno, más adelante, violara alguna de sus disposiciones, todos los Gobiernos de la tierra deberán levantarse para reducirlo a completa sumisión; incluso la raza humana entera debería tomar la resolución de destruir este Gobierno con todos los poderes a su alcance. Si se aplica este, el mayor de los remedios al cuerpo enfermo del mundo, con seguridad se recobrará de sus enfermedades y permanecerá a salvo y seguro».

La realización de esta magna convocatoria se retrasa ya demasiado.

Con todo el fervor de nuestros corazones, pedimos a los líderes de todas las naciones que aprovechen esta oportunidad y den pasos irreversibles para convocar esta asamblea mundial. Todas las fuerzas de la historia impulsan a la humanidad hacia este acto que señalará definitivamente la aurora de su tan esperada madurez.

¿No se levantarán las Naciones Unidas, con el pleno apoyo de sus miembros, para alcanzar los elevados propósitos de tan magno acontecimiento?

Que los hombres y las mujeres, los jóvenes y los niños de todo el mundo reconozcan el eterno mérito de esta acción imperativa para todos los pueblos y eleven sus voces de aprobación decidida. ¡Que esta generación sea la que inaugure esta gloriosa etapa en la evolución de la vida social del planeta!

IV

La fuente del optimismo que sentimos es una visión que trasciende el cese de la guerra y la creación de organismos de cooperación internacional. La paz permanente entre las naciones es una etapa esencial, pero no es -según proclama Bahá'u'lláh- la meta final del desarrollo social de la humanidad. Más allá del armisticio inicial impuesto al mundo por el temor a un holocausto nuclear, más allá de la paz política introducida a la fuerza por naciones rivales y desconfiadas, más allá de acuerdos pragmáticos para la seguridad y la coexistencia, incluso más allá de los muchos experimentos de cooperación que tales pasos harán posibles, se halla la meta final: la unificación de todos los pueblos del mundo en una familia universal.

La falta de unidad es un peligro que las naciones y los pueblos de la tierra ya no pueden soportar; sus consecuencias son demasiado terribles para contemplarlas, demasiado obvias para que exijan alguna demostración. Hace más de un siglo escribió Bahá'u'lláh: «El bienestar de la humanidad, su paz y seguridad son inalcanzables, a menos y hasta que su unidad sea firmemente establecida». Al observar que «toda la humanidad está gimiendo, ansiando ser conducida a la unidad y terminar con su largo martirio», Shoghi Effendi comentó, además: «La unificación de toda la humanidad es el distintivo de la etapa a la cual la sociedad está llegando ahora. La unidad de la familia, de la tribu, de la ciudad-estado y de la nación han sido intentadas sucesivamente y alcanzadas por completo. La unidad del mundo es la meta por la que lucha una humanidad hostigada. La formación de naciones ha llegado a su fin. La anarquía inherente a la soberanía del Estado va hacia su punto culminante. Un mundo cercano a la madurez debe abandonar este fetichismo, reconocer la unidad y la integridad de las relaciones humanas y establecer, de una vez por todas, el mecanismo que mejor pueda encarnar este principio fundamental para su existencia».

Todas las fuerzas contemporáneas que propician los cambios corroboran este punto de vista. Las pruebas pueden discernirse en los muchos ejemplos que se han citado de presagios favorables para la paz mundial en los actuales movimientos y sucesos internacionales. El ejército de hombres y mujeres, reclutados prácticamente de entre toda cultura, raza y nación de la tierra, que presta servicio en los diversos organismos de las Naciones Unidas, representa un «servicio civil» planetario cuyos impresionantes éxitos son indicios del grado de cooperación que se puede lograr hasta en las condiciones más desalentadoras. Un impulso hacia la unidad, como una primavera espiritual, lucha por expresarse mediante los incontables congresos internacionales que reúnen a personas de una amplia gama de disciplinas. Motiva proyectos internacionales que implican a niños y jóvenes. En verdad, es la auténtica fuente del notable movimiento hacia el ecumenismo por el que los miembros de las religiones y sectas históricamente antagonistas se sienten recíproca e irresistiblemente atraídos. Junto a la tendencia contraria a favor de la guerra y el engrandecimiento propio, contra la cual lucha incesantemente, el impulso hacia la unidad mundial es una de las características más dominantes y extendidas en la vida del planeta durante los últimos años del siglo veinte.

La experiencia de la comunidad bahá'í puede verse como un ejemplo de esta creciente unidad. Es una comunidad de unos tres o cuatro millones de personas provenientes de muchas naciones, culturas, clases y credos, que se dedican a múltiples actividades al servicio de las necesidades espirituales, sociales y económicas de los pueblos de muchas tierras. Es un solo organismo social que representa la diversidad de la familia humana, que dirige sus asuntos por medio de un sistema de principios consultivos comúnmente aceptados y que aprecia igualmente a todas las grandes corrientes de guía divina a lo largo de la historia. Su existencia es otra prueba convincente de que la visión de su Fundador de un mundo unido es practicable, otra prueba de que la humanidad puede convivir como una sociedad global dispuesta a afrontar los desafíos que pueda implicar la llegada a su mayoría de edad. Si la experiencia bahá'í puede contribuir en cualquier medida a fortalecer la esperanza en la unidad de la humanidad, nos sentimos felices de ofrecerla como modelo para su estudio.

Al contemplar la suprema importancia de la tarea que ahora se presenta como un desafío ante todo el mundo, nos inclinamos humildemente ante la sublime majestad del divino Creador, Quien por su infinito amor ha creado a toda la humanidad de la misma materia, ha exaltado la valiosa realidad del hombre, le ha honrado con intelecto y sabiduría, nobleza e inmortalidad, y le ha dotado de «la distinción y capacidad únicas de conocerle y amarle», capacidad «que debe considerarse como el impulso generador y el objetivo primordial que sostiene a la creación entera».

Mantenemos la firme convicción de que «todos los hombres han sido creados para llevar adelante una civilización en continuo progreso», que «actuar como las bestias salvajes no es digno del hombre», que las virtudes que benefician a la dignidad humana son la honradez, la indulgencia, la misericordia, la compasión y la generosidad amorosa hacia todas las gentes. Reafirmamos la creencia de que «las potencialidades inherentes a la posición del hombre, la medida plena de su destino en el mundo y la excelencia innata de su realidad, deben todas manifestarse en este prometido Día de Dios». Éstas son las motivaciones de nuestra fe inalterable en que la unidad y la paz son la meta asequible por la que la humanidad está esforzándose.

Al escribirse esto, pueden oírse las voces esperanzadas de los bahá'ís, a pesar de la persecución de la que son víctimas en el país donde nació su Fe. Con su ejemplo de esperanza irreductible, dan testimonio de la creencia de que la realización inminente de este antiguo sueño de paz está ahora, en virtud de los transformadores efectos de la revelación de Bahá'u'lláh, investida con la fuerza de la autoridad divina. Por lo que les transmitimos a ustedes no sólo una visión en palabras; convocamos el poder de las hazañas de fe y sacrificio; transmitimos la ansiosa defensa de la paz y la unidad en nombre de nuestros correligionarios de todas partes. Nos unimos a todos los que son víctimas de la agresión, a todos los que anhelan el fin de los conflictos y la violencia, a todos aquellos que por su devoción a los principios de la paz y del orden mundial promueven los nobles propósitos para los que fue llamada a la existencia la humanidad por un Creador Todoamoroso.

Con nuestro sincero deseo de impartirles a ustedes el fervor de nuestra esperanza y nuestra confianza más profunda, citamos la promesa categórica de Bahá'u'lláh: «Estas luchas estériles, estas guerras desastrosas pasarán y la 'Paz Mayor' reinará».

LA CASA UNIVERSAL DE JUSTICIA

The Promise of World Peace

Swahili

Oktoba 1985

Kwa Watu wa Ulimwengu:

Amani Kuu ambayo kwake watu wa nia njema katika karne zote wamekuwa wakielekeza mioyo yao, ambayo kwayo manabii na washairi kwa vizazi visivyohesabika wameeleza njozi yao, na kwayo toka wakati hadi wakati maandishi matakatifu ya binadamu wakati wote yamekuwa yakiahidi, hivi sasa baada ya muda mrefu iko karibu ya mataifa. Kwa mara ya kwanza katika historia inawezekana kwa kila mtu kuiona dunia nzima, pamoja na watu wake mbalimbali, katika mtazamo mmoja. Amani ya ulimwengu sio tu kwamba inawezekana lakini haiepukiki. Ni hatua ifuatayo katika ukuaji uendeleao wa dunia hii – katika maneno ya mtafakari mmoja mkuu, "usayarishaji wa binadamu."

Ama amani itafikiwa tu baada ya maafa yasiyowazika yakiharakishwa na ung'ang'aniaji wa ukaidi wa binadamu kwenye jinsi za zamani za mwenendo, au itakubaliwa hivi sasa kwa kitendo cha hiari cha kushauriana, ni uchaguzi ulio mbele ya wakazi wote wa dunia. Katika wakati huu wa hatari wakati matatizo magumu yanayoyakabili mataifa yamechanganishwa katika jambo moja la pamoja (lihusulo watu wote) kwa ulimwengu mzima, kushindwa kuzuia wimbi la mapambano na machafuko itakuwa ni utovu wa wajibu bila kufahamu.

Kati ya dalili zifaazo ni nguvu zikuazo kwa taratibu za hatua kuelekea utaratibu wa ulimwengu zilizochukuliwa kwanza karibu na mwanzoni mwa karne hii, kama mwanzo katika uundaji wa Ushirika wa Mataifa, ikifuatiwa na shirika lililo na msingi mpana zaidi la Umoja wa Mataifa; upataji uhuru tangu Vita ya Pili ya Ulimwengu wa wingi wa mataifa ya dunia, ikiashiria mwisho wa mchakato wa ujengaji taifa, na kujiingiza kwa mataifa haya machanga pamoja na mengine ya zamani zaidi katika mambo ya uwiano wa pamoja;

ongezeko kubwa hatimaye katika ushirikiano kati ya watu mmoja mmoja na vikundi ambavyo hapo kabla walikuwa maadui na wametengana katika shughuli za kimataifa katika fani za sayansi, elimu, sheria, nyanja za kiuchumi na kiutamaduni; ongezeko katika miongo ya hivi karibuni kwa idadi isiyo na kifani ya mashirika ya ufadhili kwa binadamu ya kimataifa; ueneaji wa harakati za wanawake na vijana zikitaka ukomeshwaji vita; na uibukaji wakati huo huo wa mtandao unaopanuka wa shughuli za watu wa kawaida wakitafuta uelewano kwa njia za mawasiliano ya kibinafsi.

Maendeleo ya kisayansi na kiteknolojia yatokeayo katika hii karne isiyo ya kawaida huashiria muumuko mkuu katika ukuaji uendeleao wa kijamii wa dunia, na huashiria nyenzo ambazo kwazo matatizo yawezekanayo ya binadamu yaweza kutatuliwa. Hutoa, kwa kweli, nyenzo hasa kwa ajili ya usimamiaji wa maisha changamani ya ulimwengu uliounganika. Walakini vipingamizi bado vipo. Mashaka, kutoelewa, chuki, kutoaminiana na ubinafsi finyu, huyasonga mataifa na watu katika uhusiano wao mmoja kwa mwingine.

Ni kutokana na ufahamu wa ndani wa wajibu wa kiroho na uadilifu kwamba tunahimizwa mioyoni katika wakati huu ufaao kuwaelekeza kwenye busara zinazopenya ambazo zilitolewa kwa mara ya kwanza kwa watawala wa binadamu zaidi ya karne moja iliyopita na Baha'u'llah, Mwanzilishi wa Imani ya Kibaha'i, ambayo sisi ni Wadhamini wake.

"Pepo za ukataji tamaa," Baha'u'llah aliandika, "ole, zinavuma toka pande zote, na ugomvi ugawanyao na kusumbua jamii ya binadamu siku zote unaongezeka. Dalili za misukosuko ikaribiayo na machafuko sasa yaweza kuonekana, kama vile utaratibu uliotapakaa hivi sasa huonekana wenye dosari ya kuhuzunisha." Hukumu hii ya unabii imethibitishwa vya kutosha na uzoefu wa pamoja wa binadamu. Hitilafu katika utaratibu uliotapakaa hivi sasa huonekana wazi katika kutokuweza kwa mataifa huru yaliyoshikamana kama Umoja wa Mataifa kupunga mzuka wa vita, kuvunjika kunakotishiwa kwa utaratibu wa kiuchumi wa kimataifa, ueneaji wa ombwe la mamlaka na ugaidi, na maumivu makali ambayo mateso haya na mengineyo yanafanya kwa mamilioni yaongezekayo. Kwa kweli, ni kwa kiwango kikubwa mno uchokozi na ugomvi vimefikia kuainisha taratibu zetu za kijamii, kiuchumi na kidini, kwamba wengi wamefikia kukubali maoni kwamba tabia kama hiyo ni asili kwa hulka ya binadamu na kwa hiyo isiyoweza kufutika.

Kwa kuingiwa ndani na maoni haya, ukinzani unaofadhaisha umekuwa katika shughuli za binadamu. Kwa upande mmoja, watu wa mataifa yote hutangaza sio tu utayari wao lakini pia hamu (shauku) yao kwa kutaka amani na upatano, kumalizwa kwa hofu zinazohuzunisha zinazoumiza maisha yao ya kila siku. Kwa upande mwingine, ukubali usio na udadisi unatolewa kwa shauri kwamba binadamu ni wenye ubinafsi usiorudika na wachokozi na hivyo wasioweza kusimamisha utaratibu wa kijamii ambao mara moja utakuwa wa kuendelea na uliojaa amani, wenye nguvu na wa upatano, utaratibu uruhusuo uvumbuzi na uanzishaji wa mambo wa mtu mmoja mmoja lakini vikiwa kwenye msingi wa ushirikiano na uwiano.

Kama haja ya amani iwavyo muhimu zaidi, ukinzani huu wa kimsingi, ambao huzuia kupatikana kwake, huhitaji upimaji tena wa mawazo ambayo juu yake maoni yashikiliwayo na watu wote ya hatari ya kihistoria ya binadamu yamewekewa msingi. Ikichunguzwa kwa uadilifu, ushuhuda hudhihirisha kwamba mwenendo kama huo, mbali na kuonyesha uhalisi hasa wa nafsi ya mtu, huonyesha tu badala yake uumbuaji wa roho ya binadamu. Ridhaa juu ya jambo hili itawezesha watu wote kuanzisha mwendo wa nguvu za ujengaji za kijamii, ambazo kwa kuwa hulingana na asili ya binadamu, zitatia moyo upatano na ushirikiano badala ya vita na ugomvi.

Kuchagua njia kama hiyo sio kukanusha wakati ulio-pita wa binadamu lakini ni kuuelewa. Imani ya Kibaha'i hu-fikiria ghasia za hivi sasa za ulimwengu na hali ya kimsiba katika mambo ya binadamu kama sehemu ya kikanuni kati-ka jinsi ya mafuatano ikiongozea hatimaye na bila kuzuilika kwenye uunganishaji wa jamii ya binadamu katika utaratibu mmoja wa kijamii ambao mipaka yake ni ile ya dunia. Jamii ya binadamu, kama kiumbe hai na kilicho tofauti kabisa, imepitia katika hatua za ukuaji zinazo fanana na hatua za uchanga na utoto katika maisha ya watu wake mmoja mmo-ja, na sasa imo katika kipindi chake cha mwisho cha ujana wenye msukosuko ikikaribia utu-uzima wake uliotazamiwa kwa muda mrefu sana.

Ukiri wa ukweli kwamba chuki, vita na unyonyaji (utumiaji nguvu za wengine kwa maisha ya mtu) vimekuwa uonyesho wa hatua za uchanga (kutopevuka) katika mafua-tano makubwa mno ya mambo ya kihistoria na kwamba jamii ya binadamu hivi leo inapatwa na msukosuko usioepukika ambao huainisha utu-uzima wake wa pamoja sio sababu ya kufa moyo lakini ni uelewa wa hitaji la mbele kwa kujifunga kwa kazi kubwa mno ya ujengaji wa ulimwengu wa am-ani. Kwamba kazi kama hiyo inawezekana, kwamba nguvu za ujengaji zihitajiwazo zipo, kwamba miundo ya kijamii ya uunganishaji inaweza kusimamishwa, ni jambo ambalo tunawasihi kulichunguza.

Iwe ya taabu na misukosuko ya jinsi gani miaka ya hivi karibuni, yawe ya giza jinsi gani mambo ya hivi sasa, jamii ya Kibaha'i huamini kwamba jamii ya binadamu in-aweza kulikabili jaribu hili kuu kwa imani katika matokeo yake ya hatimaye. Mbali na kuashiria mwisho wa ustaarabu, haya mabadiliko ya misukosuko ambayo kuelekea kwake jamii ya binadamu zaidi na zaidi kwa haraka inasukumizwa yatasaidia kufungulia zile "nguvu zisizodhihirika za kiasili katika daraja la mtu" na kudhihirisha "kipimo kizima cha

214

hali ya maisha yake duniani, ubora wa kiasili (kimaumbile) wa uhalisi wake."

I

Majaliwa haya ambayo hutofautisha jamii ya binadamu toka aina zote nyingine za uhai hujumlika katika kile kijulikanacho kama roho ya binadamu; akili ikiwa ni sifa (tabia) yake ya lazima. Majaliwa haya yameiwezesha jamii ya binadamu kujenga ustaarabu mbali mbali na kufanikiwa kimwili. Lakini mafanikio kama hayo pekee hayajairidhisha kamwe roho ya binadamu, ambayo asili yake isiyofahamika huielekeza kwenye ubora mkuu kabisa (uungu), ufikiaji kuelekea milki isiyoonekana, kuelekea uhalisi wa mwisho, ile asili isiyojulikana ya asili zote iitwayo Mungu. Dini zilizoletwa kwa binadamu na mifuatano ya miangaza ya kiroho zimekuwa ndio kiungo cha msingi kati ya binadamu na ule uhalisi wa mwisho, na zimeamsha na kutakasa uwezo wa binadamu kupata mafanikio ya kiroho pamoja na maendeleo ya kijamii.

Hakuna jitihada ya kweli kuweka mambo ya binadamu sawa sawa, kupata amani ya dunia, inaweza kupuuza dini. Ufahamivu wa watu na uzoefu wake zaidi ni jambo la historia. Mtaalamu wa historia mashuhuri aliieleza dini kama "nguvu ya asili ya binadamu." Kwamba upotofu wa nguvu hii umechangia kwenye wingi wa ghasia katika jamii na mapambano ndani na kati ya watu mmoja mmoja ni vigumu kuweza kukanushwa. Lakini pia hakuna mchunguzi yeyote wa haki awezaye kudharau nguvu kubwa mno zilizofanywa na dini juu ya madhihirisho ya maana sana ya ustaarabu. Zaidi ya hayo, kutokuepukika kwake katika utaratibu wa kijamii kumeoneshwa kila mara na matokeo yake juu ya sheria na uadilifu.

Akiandika juu ya dini kama nguvu ya kijamii, Baha'u'llah alisema: "Dini ni njia kuu kabisa katika zote kwa usimamishaji wa utaratibu katika ulimwengu na kwa ridhaa ya amani ya wote wale waishio humo." Akitaja juu ya kutiwa giza au uchafuzi wa dini, yeye aliandika: "Kama taa ya dini ikitiwa giza, machafuko na ghasia vitafuata, na miangaza ya usawa, ya haki, ya utulivu na amani itakoma kuwaka." Katika kuhesabu matokeo kama hayo maandishi ya Kibaha'i huonyesha kwamba ule "upotofu wa asili ya binadamu, udhilifu wa tabia ya binadamu, uchafuzi na uvunjaji wa desturi (sheria au mila) za kibinadamu, hujidhihirisha vyenyewe, katika hali kama hiyo, katika jinsi zao mbaya kabisa na zichukizazo mno. Tabia ya kibinadamu imedhalilishwa, imani imetikiswa, mishipa ya adabu imelegezwa, sauti ya moyo wa binadamu imenyamazishwa, ile fahamu ya ustahifu na aibu imetiwa giza, mawazo juu ya wajibu, juu ya uwiano na uaminifu yamepotoshwa, na maono yenyewe ya amani, ya furaha na tumaini yanazimishwa taratibu."

Kama, kwa hiyo, jamii ya binadamu imefikia kilele cha ugomvi unaopoozesha ni lazima ijiangalie yenyewe, iangalie kwenye kutojali kwake yenyewe, iangalie kwenye sauti za maonyo ambazo imezisikia, kwa ajili ya chanzo cha kutoelewa kule na machafuko vilivyofanywa katika jina la dini. Wale ambao wameshikilia kwa upofu na kwa ubinafsi kwenye imani zao maalum halisi, ambao wamewatwisha wafuasi wao waliojifunga tafsiri zenye makosa na za kupingana za matamshi ya Mitume wa Mungu, wanachukua jukumu zito kwa mkanganyiko huu – mkanganyiko ambao umezidishwa na vile vizuizi vya kubuniwa tu vilivyowekwa kati ya imani na akili, sayansi na dini. Kwa kuwa kutokana na uchunguzi wa haki wa maneno hasa ya Waanzilishi wa dini hizi kuu, na wa mazingira ya kijamii ambamo walilazimika kutimiza ujumbe wao, hakuna chochote kinachounga mkono ugomvi na chuki zinazochafua jamii za kidini za binadamu na hivyo shughuli zote za binadamu.

Fundisho kwamba ni lazima tuwatendee wengine kama sisi wenyewe tungependa tutendewe, kanuni ya

uadilifu iliyokaririwa katika dini zote kuu, huuthibitisha uchunguzi huu wa pili katika jinsi mbili maalum: hujumlisha
mwenendo wa uadilifu, jinsi ile iletayo amani, ieneayo kupitia dini hizi bila kujali mahali pao au wakati zilipoanzia;
pia huwa na maana ya jinsi ya umoja ambao ndio nguvu (ya
wema) yao ya asili, nguvu ambayo binadamu katika mtazamo wao wa historia uliogawanyika wameshindwa kuithami-
ni vyema.

Kama jamii ya binadamu ingewaona Waelimishaji wa
utoto wake wa pamoja katika jinsi yao halisi, kama mawakili
wa kazi moja ya ustaarabishaji, bila shaka ingevuna manufaa
makubwa zaidi yasiyohesabika toka matokeo yaongezekayo
ya kazi zao zinazofuatana. Hili, ole, imeshindwa kufanya.

Muumuko tena wa ushupavu wa kidini ukitokea katika nchi nyingi hauwezi kufikiriwa zaidi ya msukosuko un-
aotulia. Hali yenyewe hasa ya jambo la nguvu na uharibifu
ambavyo uhusiana nao huthibitisha juu ya ufilisikaji wa kiroho ambao inaiwakilisha. Kweli, jambo mojawapo la kustaajabisha mno na kuhuzunisha mno katika tukio la ghafla la
wakati huu la ushupavu wa kidini ni kadiri ambavyo, katika
kila tukio, hudhoofisha sio tu mambo bora sana ya thamani
ya kiroho ambayo husaidia kuleta umoja wa binadamu lakini pia mambo yale ya kipekee ya ushindi wa kiuadilifu
uliopatwa na dini hiyo maalum ambayo hudai kuitumikia.

Ingawaje dini imekuwa nguvu ya maana sana katika
historia ya binadamu, na ingawa ni wa vituko jinsi gani muumuko tena wa hivi sasa wa ushupavu wa kidini wa kivita,
dini na mashirika ya kidini, kwa miongo mingi, vimeonwa
na idadi iongezekayo ya watu kama visivyohusika kabisa
kwenye mambo makubwa ya ulimwengu wa kisasa. Badala yake, wamegeukia ama kwenye ufuatiliaji wa anasa wa
ridhaa za kidunia au kwenye ufuatiliaji wa nadharia zilizo-
tungwa na binadamu zikikusudiwa kuokoa jamii kutokana
na maovu dhahiri ambayo chini yake jamii hiyo hupiga kite.

Nyingi zaidi mno ya nadharia hizi, ole, badala ya kukubali wazo la umoja wa binadamu na kuendeleza uongezekaji wa mapatano kati ya watu wa tabaka mbali mbali, zimeelekea kuabudu serikali, kuwaweka binadamu wote wengine chini ya mamlaka ya taifa moja, jamii au tabaka, kujaribu kunyamazisha mahojiano yote na ubadilishano wa mawazo, au bila huruma kutelekeza mamilioni ya watu wanaokufa njaa kwenye utendaji kazi wa mfumo wa soko ambao kwa udhahiri kabisa huzidisha hali ya taabu ya wengi wa binadamu, na wakati huo huo kuwezesha sehemu ndogo kuishi katika hali ya utajiri ambayo haikuotewa hata kidogo na mababu zetu.

Inahuzunisha kiasi gani kumbukumbu ya imani mbadala ambazo watu wa busara za kidunia wameziunda. Katika hali kubwa ya kukinaikiwa kwa watu wote waliofunzwa kuabudu kwenye madhabahu yao inaweza kusomwa hukumu ya historia isiyotanguka juu ya thamani yao. Matunda ambayo mafundisho haya yametoa, baada ya miongo ya zoezi la mamlaka yasiyozuiwa na yaongezekayo na wale ambao wamepata ukuu katika mambo ya dunia toka kwao, ni maradhi ya kijamii na kiuchumi ambayo hunyausha kila sehemu ya dunia yetu katika miaka ya mwisho ya karne ya ishirini. Chimbuko ya mateso yote haya ya nje ni uharibifu wa kiroho unaoakisiwa katika utepetevu wa moyo ambao umewakamata watu wengi wa mataifa yote na uzimaji wa tumaini katika mioyo ya mamilioni ya watu wanaohitaji na walio na machungu.

Wakati umewadia ambapo wale wahubirio fundisho la kanuni ya mambo ya kidunia (kinyume cha mambo ya kiroho), ikiwa wa mashariki au wa magharibi, ikiwa wa kibepari au kisoshalisti, lazima watoe maelezo juu ya usimamizi wa uadilifu ambao wamethubutu kuufanya. Upo wapi ule "ulimwengu mpya" ulioahidiwa na nadharia hizi? Iko wapi amani ya kimataifa ambayo juu ya fikra zake bora wao hutangaza kujifunga kwao? Yako wapi yale mafanikio

ya maana katika milki mpya za ufanisi wa kiutamaduni ulio-
tolewa na utukuzaji wa jamii hii ya watu, ya taifa lile au wa
tabaka maalum? Kwanini sehemu kubwa mno ya watu wa
dunia inazama chini daima kwenye njaa na udhalili wakati
utajiri katika kiwango kisichootewa na Mafirauni (watawala
wa kale wa Misri), Makaisari (watawala wa zamani wa Uru-
mi), au hata mataifa ya kibeberu ya karne ya kumi na tisa
uko mikononi mwa wakata hukumu wa hivi sasa wa mambo
ya binadamu?

Hususan, ni katika utukuzaji wa ufuataji wa mambo ya kimwili, papo hapo mzazi (asili) na jinsi ya kawaida
ya nadharia zote kama hizo, kwamba tunakuta mizizi ili-
shayo dhana potofu kwamba binadamu ni wenye ubinafsi
na wachokozi vibaya sana kiasi cha kutoweza kujirudi. Ni
hapa kwamba uwanja lazima usafishwe kwa ujengaji wa
ulimwengu mpya ufaao kwa vizazi vyetu.

Kwamba mitazamo hiyo ya kidunia (ya kutaka kujilimb-
ikizia mali), kwa mujibu wa uzoefu uliopatikana, imeshindwa kuridhisha mahitaji ya wanadamu huhitaji kukubali ki-
kamilifu kwamba jitihada mpya sasa zinabidi kufanywa ili
kutafuta masuluhisho kwa matatizo yanayoelemea ya sayari
hii. Hali zisizoweza kuvumilika zilizoenea pote katika jamii
huonyesha kushindwa kwa pamoja kwa wote, jambo ambalo
huelekea zaidi kuamsha kuliko kupunguza ukaribiaji wao
katika kila upande. Ni wazi kwamba jitihada iponyayo ya
wote inahitajika kwa haraka. Kimsingi ni jambo la mwelekeo.
Je, jamii ya binadamu itaendelea katika upotovu wake, iki-
shikilia kwenye fikira zilizochakaa na mawazo yasiyoweza
kutumika? Au viongozi wake, bila kujali nadharia, watakuja
mbele na, wakiwa na nia thabiti watashauriana pamoja katika utafutaji ulioungania kwa majawabu yafaayo?

Wale ambao hujali wakati ujao wa jamii ya binadamu waweza kutafakari vyema ushauri huu. "Kama fikira
zilizotunzwa kwa muda mrefu na kawaida ziheshimiwazo

za wakati huu, kama mawazo fulani ya kijamii na kanuni za kidini vimekoma kuendeleza usitawi wa jamii ya binadamu, kama vimekoma kuhudumia mahitaji ya jamii ya binadamu ambayo wakati wote inakua, acha hivi vifagiliwe kando na kuachwa kwenye ahera la mafundisho chakavu yaliyosahauliwa. Kwanini haya, katika ulimwengu ambao upo chini ya sheria isiyobadilika ya mageuko na uozaji, yasamehewe kutokana na uchakavu ambao lazima upate kila kawaida na binadamu? Kwa ajili ya kanuni za kisheria, mawazo ya kisiasa na kiuchumi yamebuniwa tu kulinda mambo ya manufaa ya jamii ya binadamu kwa ujumla, na sio jamii ya binadamu kusulubiwa kwa ajili ya hifadhi ya usahihi wa sheria yeyote maalum au kanuni."

II

Upigaji marufuku silaha kali, ukatazaji utumiaji wa hewa ya sumu, au kuharamisha vita vya vijidudu havitaondoa vyanzo hasa vya vita. Ingawa hatua za kivitendo kama hizo ni za maana sana bila shaka kama mambo ya kimsingi ya kazi ya amani, pekee yao ni za juu juu kabisa kutoa nguvu ya kudumu juu ya suala hilo. Watu ni stadi vya kutosha kubuni namna nyingine zaidi za vita, na kutumia chakula, mali ghafi, fedha, uwezo wa viwanda, nadharia, udhalimu kupinduana mmoja kwa mwingine katika utafutaji usio na mwisho wa ukuu na enzi. Wala utanguzi huu mkubwa wa hivi sasa katika shughuli za binadamu hauwezi kuondolewa kwa usuluhishi wa tofauti maalum na ugomvi kati ya mataifa. Mfumo halisi ueneao pote lazima uchaguliwe.

Kwa yakini, hakuna ukosefu wa utambuzi wa viongozi wa kitaifa juu ya jinsi tatizo hili lihusuvyo ulimwengu mzima, jambo ambalo ni dhahiri katika mambo yaongezekayo yanayowakabili kila siku. Na kuna uchunguzi ukusanyikao na majawabu washauriwayo na vikundi vingi vinavyojihusisha na vyenye maarifa vile vile na mawakala ya Umoja wa Mataifa, kuondoa uwezekano wowote wa ujinga juu ya mahitaji ya ushindani ya kutimizwa. Upo, la-kini, upoozaji wa nia; na ni jambo hili ambalo ni lazima lic-hunguzwe kwa uangalifu na kwa uthabiti kushughulikiwa. Upoozaji huu umewekwa imara, kama tulivyosema, katika imani ya ndani sana ya asili ya kiugomvi isiyoepukika ya binadamu, imani ambayo imeongozea kwenye kutotaka ku-fikiria uwezekano wa kuweka chini mambo yahusuyo taifa moja pekee kwa ajili ya mahitaji ya utaratibu wa dunia, na katika kutopenda kukabili kwa ujasiri maana halisi ya ma-tukio mengi ya uanzishaji wa mamlaka ya ulimwengu yaliyo-ounganishwa. Huweza kuonekana pia kwenye ukosefu wa uwezo wa watu wengi kabisa ambao ni wajinga na ambao wameshindwa kusema wazi haja yao kwa utaratibu mpya ambamo wataweza kuishi kwa amani, mapatano na ufanisi pamoja na ulimwengu mzima.

Hatua za majaribio kuelekea utaratibu wa dunia, hasa tangu Vita ya Pili ya Dunia, hutoa ishara za matumaini. Maelekeo yaongezekayo ya vikundi vya mataifa kufanya uhusiano rasmi ambao unawawezesha kushirikiana katika mambo yenye faida baina hudokezea kwamba hatimaye mataifa yote yanaweza kushinda upoozaji huu. Ushirikiano wa Mataifa ya Kusini Mashariki, Jumuiya ya Caribbean na Soko la Pamoja, Soko la Pamoja la Amerika ya Kati, Baraza kwa Kusaidiana Kiuchumi, Jumuiya ya Ulaya, Ushirika wa Madola ya Kiarabu, Umoja wa Nchi huru za Afrika, Umoja wa Madola ya Amerika, Baraza la Pacific ya Kusini – jitihada zote za pamoja zilizowakilishwa na mashirika kama hayo huandaa njia kwa utaratibu wa dunia.

Uangalizi uongezekao unaokaziwa kwenye baadhi ya matatizo yenye mizizi ya kina sana ya dunia hii ni ishara ny-ingine zaidi iliyojaa matumaini. Bila kujali kasoro dhahiri za Umoja wa Mataifa, ile zaidi ya korija mbili za maazimio na mikataba iliyokubaliwa na shirika hilo, hata ambapo serikali hazikuwa na shauku katika ahadi yao, yamewapa watu wa kawaida fahamu ya matazamio mapya ya furaha katika maisha. Tangazo la Ulimwengu la Haki za Binadamu, Mkataba juu ya Uzuiaji na Uadhibishaji wa Jinai ya Uangamizaji jamii ya watu, na hatua kama hizi zihusikazo na uondoaji aina zote za ubaguzi ukitegemezwa juu ya jamii ya watu, jinsia au imani ya kidini; uteteaji wa haki za mtoto; kulinda watu wote dhidi ya kutiwa matesoni; uondoaji njaa na utapiamlo; utumiaji wa maendeleo ya kisayansi na kiteknolojia kwa ajili ya amani na manufaa ya binadamu – hatua zote kama hizo, kama zikitiliwa nguvu kwa ujasiri na kupanuliwa, zitaleta karibu zaidi siku ambapo mzuka wa vita utakuwa umepoteza uwezo wake kutawala uhusiano wa kimataifa. Hakuna haja ya kusisitiza umuhimu wa mambo yaliyotajwa na maazimio haya na mikataba. Lakini, machache ya mambo haya, kwa sababu ya uhusikaji wao wa papo hapo kwa uanzishaji wa amani ya dunia, hustahili ufafanuzi zaidi.

Ubaguzi wa rangi, mojawapo wa maovu ya madhara mno na ya kudumu, ni kipingamizi kikubwa kwa amani. Uzoefu wake hufanya kitendo kibaya cha uvunjaji wa ujeuri mno wa heshima ya binadamu kikiidhinishwa chini ya visingizio vyovyote. Ubaguzi wa rangi hurudisha udhihirikaji wa nguvu zisizo na mipaka za kiasili na zisizodhihirika za wateswaji wake, hupotosha watendaji wake, na hunyausha maendeleo ya binadamu. Utambuzi wa umoja wa binadamu, ukitimilizwa na hatua za kisheria zifaazo, lazima utetewe na wote kama tatizo hili ni la kushindwa.

Hitilafu iliyokithiri kati ya tajiri na maskini, chanzo cha maumivu makali, huuweka ulimwengu katika hali ya kutokuwa imara, karibu ukingoni mwa vita. Jamii chache za watu zimeshughulika ifaavyo na hali hii. Jawabu huhitaji utumiaji wa pamoja wa njia za kiroho, kimaadili na kivitendo. Mtazamo mpya kwenye tatizo hilo unahitajiwa, ukiandamana na ushauriano na wataalamu toka msafa mpana wa fani, wakiwa hawana mabishano ya kiuchumi na kinadharia, na kuhusisha moja kwa moja watu waathiriwao katika maamuzi ambayo lazima kwa haraka yafanywe.

Ni jambo ambalo limefungamana sio tu na umuhimu kwa uondoaji wingi wa kukithiri wa utajiri na umaskini lakini pia na yale mambo ya kweli ya kiroho ambayo kuyaelewa kwake kunaweza kutoa mwelekeo mpya ueneao pote. Ukuzaji mwelekeo kama huo peke yake ni sehemu kubwa ya jawabu lenyewe.

Utaifa usiozuiwa, ukitofautishwa toka upendo wa akili timamu na halali wa mtu kwa nchi yake, ni lazima upishe njia kwa uaminifu (utii) mpana zaidi, kwa upendo wa jamii ya ulimwengu kwa ujumla. Maneno ya Baha'u'llah ni haya: "Dunia ni nchi moja tu, na binadamu ni raia wake." Wazo la uraia wa dunia ni tokeo la moja kwa moja la unyweaji wa dunia kwenye ujirani mmoja kwa kupitia maendeleo ya kisayansi na la utengamano usiokanika wa mataifa. Upendo wa watu wote wa dunia hauwekei mbali upendo wa mtu kwa nchi yake. Manufaa ya sehemu katika jamii ya ulimwengu huhudumiwa kwa ubora kabisa kwa kuendeleza manufaa ya wote. Shughuli za kimataifa za hivi sasa katika fani mbali mbali zikuzazo upendano na fahamu ya umoja kati ya watu huhitaji kabisa kuongezwa.

Ugomvi wa kidini, wakati wote wa historia, umekuwa chanzo cha vita nyingi na mapambano, maradhi makubwa kwa maendeleo, na unakuwa wa kuchukiza zaidi na zaidi kwa watu wa dini zote na wale wasio na dini. Wafuasi wa dini zote lazima wawe tayari kuyakabili maswali ya kimsingi ambayo ugomvi huu huamsha, na kufikia kwenye majibu wazi. Jinsi gani tofauti zilizopo baina yao zitaondolewa, vyote katika mawazo na katika vitendo? Changamoto inaowakabili viongozi wa kidini wa binadamu ni kutafakari, kwa mioyo iliyojawa na roho ya huruma na hamu kwa ukweli, juu ya hali mbaya mno ya binadamu, na kujiuliza wenyewe kama hawawezi, kwa unyenyekevu mbele ya Mwenyezi Muumba wao, kuzamisha tofauti zao za elimu ya dini katika moyo mkuu wa kuvumiliana ambao utawawezesha kufanya kazi

pamoja kwa ajili ya uendelezaji wa uelewa wa binadamu
na amani.

Uwekaji huru wa wanawake, upataji wa usawa kamili kati ya wanaume na wanawake, ni mojawapo ya mahitaji msingi kabisa la amani, ingawa linakubalika kidogo.
Unyimaji wa usawa kama huo hufanyia udhalimu dhidi ya
nusu moja ya idadi ya watu wa dunia na huendeleza katika
wanaume mwenendo mibaya na tabia ambazo huchukuliwa
toka kwenye familia hadi kwenye sehemu za kazi, kwenye
maisha ya kisiasa, na hatimaye kwenye uhusiano wa kimataifa. Hakuna sababu, kimaadili, kivitendo, au kimaumbile,
ambazo juu yake unyimaji kama huo unaweza kustahilish-
wa. Ni hapo tu wanawake wakaribishwapo kwenye ushirika kamili katika fani zote za jitihada za binadamu hali ya
kimaadili na ya kiakili itaumbwa ambamo amani ya kimataifa
inaweza kutokea.

Hoja ya elimu kwa watu wote, ambayo tayari imekwisha orodhesha katika utumishi wake jeshi la watu waliojifunga kutoka kila imani na taifa, hustahili msaada mkubwa kabisa ambao serikali za dunia zinaweza kuipa. Kwa
kuwa ujinga bila kukanika ni sababu kubwa ya kushuka na
kuanguka kwa watu na udumishaji wa chuki. Hakuna taifa linaloweza kupata ufanisi mpaka elimu imetolewa kwa
raia wake wote. Ukosefu wa mali hukatiza uwezo wa mataifa mengi kutimiza haja hii ya lazima, ukitwisha upangaji maalum wa mambo yastahiliyo umuhimu wa kwanza.
Yale mawakala yahusikayo na ufanyaji uamuzi yangefanya
vyema kufikiria kutoa umuhimu wa kwanza kwenye ueli-
mishaji wa wanawake na wasichana, kwa kuwa ni kwa kupitia mama walioelimika kwamba manufaa ya elimu huweza
kuenezwa ifaavyo kabisa na kwa haraka katika jamii nzima.
Kwa kulingana na mahitaji ya nyakati hizi, uangalifu pia
lazima utolewe kwenye ufundishaji wazo la uraia wa dunia
kama sehemu ya kiwango cha elimu ya kila mtoto.

Ukosefu wa kimsingi wa mawasiliano kati ya watu hudhoofisha sana jitihada kuelekea amani ya ulimwengu. Uchaguaji wa lugha moja ya msaada ya kimataifa ungekwenda mbali katika kuondoa tatizo hili na hulazimisha uangalizi wa haraka kabisa.

Mambo mawili ni ya kusisitizwa katika mambo yote haya. Moja ni kwamba uondoaji vita sio tu jambo rahisi la kutia sahihi mikataba na kumbukumbu za mapatano; ni kazi ngumu inayohitaji kiwango kipya cha ahadi kwa uondoaji wa mambo ambayo kwa kawaida hayahusiki na utafutaji wa amani. Likiwekwa kwenye msingi wa mapatano ya kisiasa pekee, wazo la usalama wa watu wote ni jambo la ndoto tu. Jambo lingine ni kwamba changamoto ya kimsingi katika kushughulikia mambo ya amani ni kuinua maana yake hasa mpaka kwenye kiwango cha kanuni, kama itofautishwavyo na ushughulikaji mtupu na mambo kama yazukavyo. Kwa kuwa, katika kiini, amani hutokana na hali ya ndani ikitegemezwa na mwelekeo wa kiroho au kimaadili, na ni hasa katika uamshaji mwelekeo huu kwamba uwezekano wa majawabu ya kudumu unaweza kupatikana.

Kuna kanuni za kiroho, au baadhi ya watu huyaita mambo ya thamani ya binadamu, ambazo kwazo majibu yanaweza kupatikana, kwa kila tatizo la kijamii. Kikundi chochote chenye nia njema kinaweza kwa ujumla kubuni majawabu ya kivitendo kwa matatizo yake, lakini nia njema na elimu ya kivitendo kwa kawaida havitoshi. Ubora wa kiasili wa kanuni ya kiroho ni kwamba huonyesha sio tu mtazamo ambao hupatana na kile ambacho kimo kiasili katika maumbile ya binadamu, pia hushawishi mwelekeo, nguvu, nia, tamanio, ambavyo husaidia ugunduzi na utimilizaji wa hatua za kivitendo. Viongozi wa serikali na wote walio katika mamlaka watasaidiwa vyema katika jitihada zao kutatua matatizo kama wangetafuta kwanza kutambua kanuni zipasazo na halafu kuongozwa nazo.

III

Swali la msingi kupatiwa jawabu ni jinsi gani ulimwengu wa hivi sasa, na aina zake za ugomvi zilizoimarishwa sana, unaweza kubadilika kuwa ulimwengu ambamo upatano na ushirikiano vitashinda.

Utaratibu wa ulimwengu unaweza kuanzishwa tu katika ufahamu wa akilini usiotikisika wa umoja wa binadamu, ukweli wa kiroho ambao sayansi zote za binadamu huthibitisha. Elimu juu ya asili, utamaduni na maendeleo ya binadamu, elimu juu ya viumbe hai, elimu juu ya akili (roho, moyo, fahamu) ya binadamu, hutambua tu aina moja ya binadamu, ingawa ya jinsi mbali mbali kabisa katika jinsi za umuhimu wa pili za maisha. Utambuzi wa ukweli huu huhitaji uachaji chuki – chuki ya kila aina – jamii ya kijadi, tabaka, rangi, dini, taifa, jinsia, kiwango cha ustaarabu wa kimwili, kila kitu kiwawezeshacho watu kujifikiria wenyewe bora kuliko wengine.

Ukubali wa umoja wa binadamu ni hitaji la kwanza la kimsingi kwa utengenezaji upya na usimamiaji wa ulimwengu kama nchi moja, nyumbani pa binadamu. Ukubali wa watu wote wa kanuni hii ya kiroho ni lazima kwa jaribio lolote la mafanikio kuanzisha amani ya ulimwengu. Kwa hiyo ni lazima itangazwe ulimwengu mzima, ifundishwe mashuleni, na wakati wote kusisitizwa katika kila taifa kama matayarisho kwa mabadiliko ya kimsingi katika mfumo wa jamii ambayo huyaamanisha.

Katika maoni ya Kibaha'i, utambuzi wa umoja wa binadamu "huhitaji siyo kingine zaidi bali ujengaji upya na uondoaji majeshi na hali ya kivita ya ulimwengu mzima uliostaarabika – ulimwengu ambao umeunganika kimsingi katika jinsi zake za kiasili zote za uhai wake, vyombo vyake vya kisiasa, matamanio yake ya kiroho, biashara yake na fedha, mwandiko wake na lugha, na lakini bado ukiwa tofauti sana katika jinsi za kitaifa za sehemu zake zilizounganishwa."

Akielezea maana hasa za kanuni hii ya maana sana Shoghi Effendi, Mlinzi wa Imani ya Kibaha'i, alifafanua katika mwaka 1931 kwamba: "Mbali na kukusudia kwenye mapinduzi ya misingi iliyopo ya jamii, hutafuta kupanua chanzo chake, kuumba upya mashirika yake katika namna ya kulingana na mahitaji ya ulimwengu ubadilikao daima. Haiwezi kupingana na utii (uaminifu) wa halali wowote, wala kudhoofisha uaminifu wa kiasili. Madhumuni yake sio kuzima mwali wa moto wa upendo wa taifa wenye akili timamu na ufahamivu katika mioyo ya watu, wala kuondolea mbali utaratibu wa uhuru wa kitaifa wa kujitawala wenyewe wa lazima sana kama maovu ya ukaziaji uliokithiri wa mamlaka katika sehemu moja ni wa kuepukwa. Haipuuzi, wala haijaribu kuzuia, tofauti za asili za kikabila (kikundi), za hali ya nchi, za historia, za lugha na mila, za mawazo na tabia, ambazo hutofautisha watu na mataifa ya ulimwengu. Hutaka utii (uaminifu) mpana zaidi, matamanio makubwa zaidi kuliko yeyote yale yaliyohuisha jamii ya binadamu. Husisitizia juu ya uwekaji chini wa hamaki za kitaifa na mambo yapasayo taifa kwa ajili ya madai ya muhimu sana ya ulimwengu ulio.unganishwa. Hukatalia mbali ukaziaji mamlaka katika sehemu moja uliokithiri kwa upande mmoja, na hukanusha majaribio yeyote kuelekea ulinganifu kwa upande mwingine. Neno lake la shime ni umoja katika tofauti."

Ufikiaji wa madhumuni kama hayo huhitaji hatua kadhaa katika urekebishaji wa mielekeo ya kisiasa ya kitaifa ambayo hivi sasa hukaribia ukosekano wa mamlaka kwa kutokuwepo kwa sheria zilizoelezwa wazi kabisa au zilizo kubaliwa na wote na kanuni zinazoweza kutiliwa nguvu zitawalazo uhusiano kati ya mataifa. Ushirika wa Mataifa, Umoja wa Mataifa, na yale mashirika mengi na mapatano yaliyotolewa nayo bila shaka vimekuwa vya msaada katika kupunguza baadhi ya matokeo yasiyofaa kabisa ya mapambano ya kimataifa, lakini vimejionyesha vyenyewe kutokuwa na uwezo wa kuzuia vita. Kweli, kumekuwa na korija za vita tangu mwisho wa Vita ya Pili ya Dunia; vingi bado vinavuma.

Jinsi kuu za tatizo hili zilikuwa zimekwishajitokeza katika karne ya kumi na tisa wakati Baha'u'llah kwa mara ya kwanza alipotoa mbele mashauri yake kwa usimamishaji wa amani ya ulimwengu. Kanuni ya usalama wa watu wote iliyotolewa na yeye katika matamko yaliyotolewa kwa watawala wa ulimwengu. Shoghi Effendi alifafanua juu ya maana yake: "Ni kipi kingine maneno haya yenye uzito yangeweza kumaanisha," yeye aliandika, "kama hayakuelekeza kwenye ukatizaji (ufupisho au upunguzaji) wa enzi isiyo zuilika ya kitaifa kama utangulizi usioepukika kwa uundaji wa Jumuiya ya Madola ya mataifa yote ya ulimwengu? Aina fulani ya serikali kuu ya ulimwengu ni lazima itokeze na kuendelezwa, ambayo kwake mataifa yote ya ulimwengu yatakuwa kwa hiari yameacha kila dai kufanya vita, haki fulani kutoza kodi na haki zote kuweka zana za vita, isipokuwa kwa ajili ya kudumisha hali ya amani (utaratibu) ya ndani katika milki zao husika. Serikali kuu kama hiyo lazima iwe na chombo cha Utendaji cha Kimataifa katika mamlaka yake kifaacho kutekeleza mamlaka makuu na yasiyopingwa juu ya kila mshiriki mkaidi wa dola hiyo; Bunge Kuu la Ulimwengu ambalo wajumbe wake watachaguliwa na watu katika nchi zao husika na ambao uchaguzi wao utathibitishwa na serikali zao husika ; na Baraza la Mahakama Kuu ya Ulimwengu ambayo hukumu yake itakuwa na nguvu hata pale ambapo pande husika hazikukubaliana kwa hiari kupeleka shauri lao kwa kufikiriwa nalo.

"Jamii ya ulimwengu ambamo vizuizi vyote vya kiuchumi vitakuwa daima vimeondolewa mbali na kutegemeana kwa Raslimali na Utumishi kutambuliwa kwa uhalisi; ambamo ghasia za ushupavu wa kidini na ugomvi vitakuwa daima vimetulizwa; ambamo mwali wa moto wa chuki ya rangi utakuwa kwa mara ya mwisho umezimwa; ambamo orodha moja ya sheria za kimataifa – matokeo ya hukumu iliyofikiriwa na wawakilishi waliounganika wa ulimwengu – itatoa mamlaka ya papo hapo kwa uingiliaji wa nguvu wa majeshi yaliyounganika ya mataifa; na hatimaye jamii ya ulimwengu ambamo ghadhabu kali ya utaifa wa kigeugeu itakuwa imegeuzwa kuwa ufahamu wa kudumu wa uraia wa ulimwengu – huo kweli, huonekana katika muhtasari wake mpana kabisa, Utaratibu uliotazamiwa na Baha'u'llah, Utaratibu ambao utakuja kuonwa kama tunda bora kabisa la enzi ipevukayo pole pole."

Utimilizaji wa hatua hizi za matokeo makubwa uliashiriwa na Baha'u'llah: "Wakati lazima utafika ambapo sharti la muhimu sana kwa ufanyaji wa mkusanyiko (mkutano) mkubwa, utakaokuwa na watu wote litatambuliwa na watu wote. Watawala na wafalme wa dunia lazima wahudhurie, na, wakishiriki katika majadiliano yake ya uangalifu, lazima wafikirie namna na jinsi za kufanya mambo ambazo zitaweka misingi ya Amani Kuu ya ulimwengu kati ya watu."

Ujasiri, maamuzi, nia safi, upendo usio na nafsi wa watu wa jamii moja kwa nyingine – tabia zote za kiroho na kimaadili zihitajiwazo kwa utimilizaji hatua hii kuu ya maana sana kuelekea amani hukaziwa katika nia ya kutenda. Na ni kuelekea uamshaji wa hiari hii ihitajiwayo kwamba fikra ya juhudi lazima ifanywe juu ya uhalisi wa mtu, yaani, fikra yake. Kufahamu uhusiano wa uhalisi huu wa nguvu pia ni kuthamini haja ya kijamii ya kuyakinisha thamani yake ya kipekee kwa njia ya ushauriano wa kweli, wa uadilifu na mkunjufu, na ya utendaji wa matokeo ya njia hii. Baha'u'llah alivutia kwa kusisitiza uangalifu kwenye njema na kutoweza kuwekwa kando kwa ushauriano kwa upangaji vyema mambo ya binadamu. Yeye alisema: "Ushauriano hujalia ufahamu mkubwa zaidi na hugeuza dhana kuwa uhakika. Ni mwangaza ung'aao ambao katika ulimwengu wa giza, huelekeza njia na kuongoza. Kwa kila jambo ipo na itaendelea kuwepo daraja ya ukamilifu na upevukaji. Upevu wa kipaji cha akili hudhihirishwa kwa kupitia njia ya ushauriano." Jaribio lenyewe kupata amani kwa njia ya kupitia kitendo hiki cha ushauriano ambacho alikishauri linaweza kufungulia moyo mwema kabisa kati ya watu wa dunia kwamba hakuna nguvu ambayo ingeweza kuzuia matokeo ya mwisho, ya ushindi.

Kuhusu mambo ya kujadiliwa kwa ajili ya mkusanyiko huu wa ulimwengu, 'Abdu'l-Baha, mwana wa kiume wa Baha'u'llah na mfafanuzi aliye idhinishwa wa mafundisho yake, alitoa busara hizi: "Lazima wafanye Hoja ya Amani kusudi la ushauriano wa wote, na kutafuta kwa kila njia katika uwezo wao kusimamisha Umoja wa Mataifa ya ulimwengu. Lazima wafanye mkataba wa masharti na kuanzisha mapatano, ambavyo masharti yao yatakuwa imara, yasiyoweza kuvunjwa na halisi. Lazima wautangaze (mkataba huo) kwa ulimwengu wote na kupata kwa ajili yake idhini ya jamii yote ya binadamu. Kazi hii kuu na bora – chanzo hasa cha amani na hali njema ya ulimwengu wote – lazima ionwe kama takatifu kabisa na wote wale waishio duniani. Nguvu zote za binadamu lazima zikusanywe kuhakikisha uimara na uendeleaji wa kudumu wa Mkataba huu Mkuu kabisa. Katika Mkataba huu uchukuao watu wote ukomo na mipaka ya kila taifa lazima kwa uwazi iwekwe, kanuni chini ya misingi ya uhusiano wa serikali moja kwa nyingine kwa uhalisi kuwekwa, na mapatano yote ya kimataifa na wajibu kuhakikishwa. Kadhalika, ukubwa wa zana za vita za kila serikali lazima kwa uhalisi uwekewe mipaka, kwa kuwa kama matayarisho kwa vita na majeshi ya kivita ya taifa lolote vitaruhusiwa kuongezeka, vitaamsha tuhuma ya mengine. Kanuni ya kimsingi iliyo asili ya Mkataba huu mtakatifu kabisa lazima iwekwe kwa namna ambayo kwamba kama serikali yeyote baadaye itavunja yeyote mojawapo ya masharti yake, serikali zote duniani lazima ziinuke kuivunja hadi kujisalimisha kabisa, la hasha, jamii ya binadamu

kwa ujumla lazima iazimie, kwa kila uwezo ilio nao, kuanga-
miza serikali hiyo. Kama dawa hii kubwa kati ya zote ingetu-
miwa kwenye mwili uumwao wa ulimwengu huu, bila shaka utapona kutokana na magonjwa yake na utabaki milele
salama salimini."

Ufanyaji wa mkutano huu wa nguvu umekawia
mno zaidi.

Kwa shauku yote ya mioyo yetu, tunawaomba viongozi wa mataifa yote kutwaa wakati huu ufaao na kuchukua
hatua zisizoweza kurudishwa nyuma kukutanisha mkutano
huu wa ulimwengu. Nguvu zote za historia husukuma jamii
ya binadamu kuelekea kitendo hiki ambacho kitaainisha
kwa wakati wote mapambazuko ya upevukaji wake uliotazamiwa kwa muda mrefu.

Je, Umoja wa Mataifa, ukiwa na msaada wote kamili
wa ushirika wake, hautainuka kwenye madhumuni ya juu
ya tukio la kuvisha taji kama hilo?

Acha waume kwa wake, vijana na watoto kila mahali
watambue ubora wa milele wa kitendo hiki cha lazima kwa
watu wote na kuinua sauti zao katika idhini ya hiari. Kwa
kweli, acha iwe kizazi hiki ambacho huanzisha hatua hii tu-
kufu katika ukuaji uendeleao wa maisha ya kijamii kwenye
dunia hii.

IV

Chanzo cha matumaini yetu kuwa matukio yote
yatakuwa bora kabisa tunaona ni njozi ipitayo kabisa
mwisho wa vita na ufanyizaji wa mawakala ya ushirikiano
wa kimataifa. Amani ya kudumu kati ya mataifa ni hatua
ya lazima, lakini sio, Baha'u'llah hudai, lengo la mwisho la
maendeleo ya kijamii ya binadamu. Mbele kabisa ya amani
ya muda ya mwanzo iliyolazimishwa juu ya ulimwengu na

woga wa maangamizi kutokana na silaha kali, mbele kabisa ya amani ya kisiasa iliyofanywa kwa kutopenda na mataifa yashindanayo yatilianayo mashaka, mbele ya matayarisho yatokanayo na ushughulikiwaji wa matukio kama yazuka-vyo kwa usalama na kuishi pamoja, mbele ya hata majaribio mengi katika ushirikiano ambao hatua hizi zitafanya uweze-kane lipo lengo la uvishaji taji: uunganishaji wa watu wote wa ulimwengu katika ukoo mmoja wa watu wote.

Utengano ni hatari ambao mataifa na watu wa dunia hawawezi zaidi kuuvumilia: matokeo ni ya kuogofya mno kuyatafakari, ni ya udhahiri mno kuhitaji wonyesho wowote, "Hali njema ya binadamu," Baha'u'llah aliandika zaidi ya karne moja iliyopita, "amani yake na usalama, haviwezi ku-patikana ila tu na mpaka umoja wake umewekwa imara." Katika kutanabahi kwamba "jamii ya binadamu inapiga kite, inakufa kuongozwa kwenye umoja, na kumaliza kuua-wa kwake kama shahidi kwa muda mrefu," Shoghi Effendi alifafanua zaidi kwamba: "uunganishaji wa jamii nzima ya binadamu ndio alama ya ubora wa hatua ambayo jamii ya binadamu sasa inakaribia. Umoja wa ukoo, wa kabila, wa serikali ya mji, na taifa vimejaribiwa kwa mafanikio na kusi-mamishwa kwa ukamilifu. Umoja wa ulimwengu ndio lengo ambalo kuelekea kwake ulimwengu usumbuliwao unajitahi-di. Ujengaji-taifa umefikia mwisho. Ukosekano wa mamlaka uliomo kwa asili katika serikali ya nchi unakwenda kuelekea kiwango cha juu kabisa. Ulimwengu, ukuao kuelekea upevu-kaji, lazima uache tambiko hili, utambue umoja na ukamilifu wa uhusiano wa jamii ya binadamu, na kusimamisha mara moja na kwa wakati wote chombo ambacho kinaweza vyema kabisa kuipa umbo kanuni hii ya kimsingi ya maisha yake."

Nguvu zote za wakati huu za mabadiliko huhalalisha maoni haya. Mathibitisho yanaweza kuonekana katika mi-fano mingi ambayo tayari imekwisha tajwa ya ishara zifaazo kuelekea amani ya ulimwengu katika harakati na maendeleo ya kimataifa ya wakati huu. Jeshi la waume kwa wake, kutoka karibu kila utamaduni, jamii ya kijadi na taifa duniani, ambao huhudumia mawakala mengi mbalimbali ya Umoja wa Mataifa, huwakilisha "utumishi wa serikali" wa dunia ambao matimilizo yake ya kustaajabisha huonyesha kipimo cha ushirikiano ambao unaweza kufikiwa hata katika hali za kukatisha tamaa. Ari kuelekea umoja, kama hali ya majira mema ya kiroho, inajibidisha kujieleza yenyewe kwa kupitia mikutano ya watu ya kimataifa isiyohesabika ambayo huwaleta pamoja watu toka mkusanyiko mkubwa wa fani mbalimbali. Huamsha maombi kwa miradi ya kimataifa ihusuyo watoto na vijana. Kwa kweli, ndio chanzo hasa cha harakati ya kustaajabisha kuelekea umoja wa makanisa ya ulimwengu mzima ambao kwao washiriki wa dini na madhehebu ambayo kihistoria yalikuwa maadui hujiona kuvutiwa bila kujizuia kimoja kwa kingine. Pamoja na maelekeo ya upinzani kuelekea vita na utukuzaji wa nafsi ambavyo dhidi yake hushindana bila kukoma, msukumo kuelekea umoja wa ulimwengu ni mojawapo wa jinsi zenye nguvu, za kuenea pote, za maisha katika dunia hii wakati wa miaka ya mwisho wa karne ya ishirini.

Uzoefu wa jamii ya Kibaha'i unaweza kuonwa kama mfano wa umoja huu ukuao mkubwa. Ni jamii ya kama watu milioni tatu hadi nne hivi kutoka mataifa mengi, utamaduni, tabaka na dini, ikijishughulisha katika msafa mpana wa shughuli kuhudumia mahitaji ya kiroho, kijamii na kiuchumi ya watu wa nchi nyingi. Ni kiumbe hai kimoja cha jamii, kikiwakilisha tofauti mbalimbali za jamii ya binadamu, kikiendesha mambo yake kupitia utaratibu wa kanuni za ushauriano zikubaliwazo na wote, na kutunza sana moyoni kwa usawa mimiminiko yote mikuu ya uongozi mtakatifu katika historia ya binadamu. Kuweko kwake ni uthibitisho mwingine tena wa kusadikisha wa uhalisia wa njozi ya Mwanzilishi wake ya ulimwengu ulioungganishwa, ushahidi mwingine kwamba jamii ya binadamu inaweza kuishi kama jamii moja ya dunia, ikiwa tayari kupambana na changamoto zozote ziletwazo na kufikia utu-uzima wake. Kama uzoefu wa Kibaha'i unaweza kuchangia katika kiwango chochote katika kuimarisha tumaini katika umoja wa jamii ya binadamu, tuna furaha kuutoa kama kielelezo kwa kuchunguzwa.

Katika kutafakari umuhimu mkuu kabisa wa kazi hivi sasa inayoukabili ulimwengu mzima, tunainamisha vichwa vyetu katika unyenyekevu mbele ya utukufu wa ajabu wa Muumba mtakatifu, ambaye kutokana na upendo Wake usio na mwisho ameumba jamii ya binadamu yote toka shina moja; akiutukuza uhalisi ulio kama kito cha thamani wa mtu; akauheshimu kwa kuupa akili na hekima, asili bora na uhai wa milele; na kumjalia mtu ile "heshima ya kipekee na uwezo kumjua Yeye na kumpenda Yeye," uwezo ambao "lazima ufikiriwe kama msukumo (nguvu) wa ufanyizaji na kusudi la msingi la muumbo wote."

Tunashikilia imara imani kwamba wanadamu wote wameumbwa "kuendeleza mbele ustaarabu uendeleao mbele daima;" kwamba "kutenda kama wanyama wa pori hamkustahili mtu;" kwamba zile njema zistahilizo heshima ya binadamu ni uaminifu, uvumilivu, rehema, huruma na wema wa upendo kwa watu wote. Tunathibitisha tena imani kwamba zile "nguvu zisizodhihirika zilizo asili katika daraja la mtu, kiwango kamili cha hali ya maisha yake duniani, ubora wa kiasili wa uhalisi wake, vyote lazima vidhihirishwe katika Siku hii ya Mungu iliyoahidiwa." Hii ndiyo misukumo kwa imani yetu isiyotikisika kwamba umoja na amani ni lengo la kufikiwa ambalo kuelekea kwake jamii ya binadamu inajitahidi.

Kwenye kuandika huku, sauti za matazamio za Wa-Baha'i zaweza kusikika bila kujali mateso ambayo bado wanayavumilia katika nchi ambamo Imani yao ilizaliwa. Kwa mfano wao wa tumaini thabiti, hushuhudia kwenye imani kwamba utimilizwaji wa karibu sana wa ndoto hii ya muda mrefu sana ya amani hivi sasa, kwa ajili ya matokeo ya ubadilishaji ya ufunuo wa Baha'u'llah, umevikwa nguvu ya

mamlaka ya Mungu. Hivyo tunawaletea sio tu maono katika maneno; tunaita nguvu ya matendo ya imani na kujitoa
dhabihu; tunawaletea ombi la shauku mno la wafuasi wa
dini wenzetu kila mahali kwa amani na umoja. Tunaungana
na wale wote ambao ni wateswaji wa mashambulio, wote
ambao hutamani sana mwisho wa ugomvi na mashindano,
wote ambao juhudi zao za moyo kwa kanuni za amani na
utaratibu wa ulimwengu kuendeleza madhumuni yafany-
izayo utu ambayo kwayo jamii ya binadamu imeumbwa na
Muumba apendaye wote.

Katika juhudi za shauku yetu kuwapa moyo wa bi-
dii wa tumaini letu na undani wa imani yetu, tunataja ahadi
iliyotiliwa mkazo ya Baha'u'llah: "Huu ugomvi usio na matunda, hivi vita vya uangamizaji vitapita, na ile 'Amani Kuu
Kabisa' itakuja."

MYUMBA YA HAKI YA ULIMWENGU

Made in the USA
Middletown, DE
03 August 2021

45288988R10137